Neil

Warnock's
Wembley
Way

The Manager's inside story of Plymouth Argyle's Promotion Campaign

With Richard Cowdery

Best wish

GW00500060

Little Kingston Books

ACKNOWLEDGEMENTS

DEBTS of gratitude are due to a number of people, without whose patience, efforts, guidance and help the production of this book would not have been possible.

Many thanks to: Margaret, for everything; Neil and Sharon; Chips and Sally Barber at Obelisk Publications; Teresa Whitell, for her hours at the word-processor; *Western Morning News* Editor Barrie Williams and *Evening Herald* Editor Alan Cooper, for their kind permission to use the excellent photographs taken by their staff-photographers, Mike Cox, Wayne Perry, Samantha Pritchard, Al Stewart and Richard Taylor (copies available); freelance photographers Tony Carney – especially for Ronnie's magic moment – Guy Channing and Dave Rowntree; Peter Holdgate; Grizzly Adams; Ian Adams; Bob Day; Jon Harris, Simon Mills; Ross Reid; Mike Sampson; friends and colleagues on the *Western Morning News, Evening Herald, Sunday Independent* and various publications across the country; the officials, staff and players of Plymouth Argyle Football Club; the Green Army; the staff at Wembley; and, last, but not least, the person or people who have almost certainly, and certainly undeservedly, been overlooked in compiling this list.

First published in 1996
Designed and typeset by
Obelisk Publications, Exeter, Devon for
Little Kingston Books
19 Poplar Close, Plympton, Devon, PL7 3GE
Printed in Great Britain by
The Devonshire Press Ltd, Torquay, Devon

CONTENTS

Wembley Celebrations, Saturday, 25 May, 1996

FOREWORD

by Barrie Williams, Editor, Western Morning News

WHEN Neil Warnock was sacked by Notts County, he invited the Press into his office, cracked open a bottle of champagne, and proceeded to celebrate his dismissal.

"What'll I do? Dunno. I could always go back to chiropody," he said.

Not for our Neil the bitter recriminations and moans more common to such occasions. He left, as he had entered, with a laugh, a joke and his head held high. He had, after all, taken Notts County from a relegation position in the old Third Division into the Premiership (or First Division as it was then) in successive seasons. Nobody could take that away from him, even if the fickle fortunes of football meant that his reward for such a phenomenal achievement was to be kicked out after just one run of bad results.

A more vindictive man would have taken pleasure from the fact that, in the successive seasons which followed, Notts County ended up back where he had found them. Neil's not like that but he wouldn't be human if he wasn't relishing the new season's encounters with the club at which he made his name.

Neil's record, in repeating promotion success with Huddersfield and Plymouth Argyle (not to mention taking Scarborough into the Football League before he joined Notts) is one that will arguably never be repeated. Yet, in the West Country, we know he's only just started – and I've stated publicly in the *Western Morning News* that he will take Argyle all the way to the Premiership.

When Neil joined Notts County I was editing the *Nottingham Evening Post* – and we met, for the first time, when I bought him lunch just before the season started. Neil's famous superstition is such that after his successful first season we had to repeat that lunch the next season … and the one after that. When coincidence brought us both to the West Country last year and we were able to renew the friendship we had struck in Nottingham, the pre-season lunch became imperative again … and it worked! We'll keep on doing it – the only trouble being that the superstition apparently also demands that, since I paid on that first occasion and have ever since, I must continue to do so. Or maybe that's just a manifestation of the fabled Yorkshire motto: *Brasso Infisto Intacto*. (As another well-known Nottingham manager would say: "I'm only joking!")

I'm privileged to enjoy Neil Warnock's friendship and honoured to introduce his book with this little bit of nonsense. Good luck to you, mate. Nobody in football works harder to deserve it.

INTRODUCTION

IF Neil Warnock ever considered looking for a bushel under which to hide his light, it is doubtful whether he would be able to find one large enough. The man is a shining example of what can be achieved by the power of self-belief when it is allied to hard work.

Scarborough, Notts County, Huddersfield and Plymouth Argyle have all benefited from the force of his incredible managerial drive and will to win – five promotions in 10 seasons is a record without parallel among his peers in the lower divisions of the Football League.

This book is an in-depth look at his most recent triumph. In 1995/96, he not only won promotion for Plymouth Argyle, taking them from the Endsleigh League Third Division to the Second in his first season, after completely rebuilding the club, but he did it by winning his fourth Wembley play-off final.

It might not have been the easiest way to take a club up, but it was certainly the most exciting – Argyle had never before been to Wembley in their 110-year history and their supporters made the very most of their day out in town.

The book is split into two, intertwined, parts. I deal with the facts and figures of Argyle's ultimately successful campaign, while Neil Warnock provides the background details and compelling insights into the emotions and passions which swept the Pilgrims to Wembley on a tidal-wave of support. Many of these have never before been made public.

Enjoy reliving the Pilgrimage to Wembley.

Richard Cowdery
1996

"YOU ARE GOING TO REMEMBER THIS DAY FOR THE REST OF YOUR LIVES"

SUNDAY, May 26, 1996, was not the brightest late Spring morning that the city of Plymouth had ever seen – rain hung listlessly in the muggy air – but it was certainly one of the loveliest.

The previous day, Plymouth Argyle had won the 1995/96 Endsleigh League Third Division play-off final on their first ever visit to Wembley, beating Darlington 1-0 in a tense match to win promotion to the Second Division, and nothing could dampen the euphoric ardour of the club's fans – the self-styled Green Army.

Several hundred of the Army's foot soldiers were massed at Home Park long before manager Neil Warnock and his triumphant players began arriving at the club's ground in advance of an open-top bus victory parade around the city. Each and every one was afforded a hero's welcome as the crowd of well-wishers, many of who had been celebrating well into the early hours of the morning since returning from London, swelled by the minute.

At shortly before 1.00 p.m., the players and officials, resplendent in their Wembley blazers and club ties, filed out of the ground and made for the bus, cutting a smart swathe through the green and white. Among the happy throng was Beatrice Jago, 83-years-old, blind and wheelchair-bound, who had been waiting in the morning drizzle to greet her favourites. Mrs Jago, an Argyle fan since 1931, had not been at Wembley, but she had lived every minute of the Pilgrims' success, "I was shouting at the radio," she said. "Shouting at the referee to blow his whistle."

Ronnie Maugé, the Pilgrims' 27-year-old midfielder who had scored a glorious 65th-minute winning goal the previous afternoon, stopped en route to the bus, flung his arms around the happy pensioner, and, to great cheers, planted a smacking kiss on her cheek.

Maugé's gesture typified the relationship between Argyle's players and their fans – 30,000 of whom had cheered them to victory in the 110-year-old club's first Wembley appearance – and it set in motion a momentous mutual celebration as the bus embarked on its tour of the city, followed by a convoy of horn-blaring cars.

Thousands of fans lined the route, forsaking their Sunday roast to cheer the victorious homecoming Pilgrims, many waving banners and flying flags that had been joyously brandished at Wembley the previous day. They climbed trees, clambered up walls, shinnied lamp-posts or simply stepped out of their front doors to hail Warnock and his men. At the top of Western Approach, an RAF veteran in full, pristine, uniform stood and saluted, ramrod rigid and eyes front. Young and old, male and female, waged and unwaged – for Plymouth Argyle, read Plymouth united.

"It's fantastic," said 46-year-old Pilgrims' supporter Roger Fitze, of nearby Ivybridge. "People who are 65 are running around like 15-year-olds."

The appreciation was certainly not all one way. The players returned the fans' acclamation with vigorous applause of their own. If they had the time or energy to shake all of the outstretched hands, you felt they would have done it. "They are superb," said Maugé, waving the play-off trophy towards the supporters. "I have never felt anything like this before."

Argyle defender Mark Patterson, who had laid on the cross which Maugé headed home the previous afternoon, spent most of the journey video-taping the crowd scenes, as did Warnock. "This is what it's all about," he said. "This is why you play football."

As the victory parade entered Royal Parade, the city centre's main thoroughfare, traffic slowed to a near standstill. The bus swung left, towards the Civic Centre, where Plymouth City Council had arranged a victory reception, and every single jaw on the top deck of the vehicle dropped. Massed in front of the council chambers were thousands more fans, a glory of green – green hats, green wigs, green shirts, green jackets, green scarves, green banners, green hair, green faces – singing their hearts out for the lads: "Green Army!"

A powerful public address system pumped out Westcountry TV's commentary of the final nerve-wracked minutes at Wembley the day before, the rising crescendo of the taped noise being echoed by the cheers of supporters living the moment again. Then a chorus of Queen's *We Are The Champions*, then Tina Turner's *Simply The Best*, the rock ballad adopted by manager Warnock at the start of the season because "whenever we've played it at my previous clubs, we've always won promotion."

The players left the bus and momentarily disappeared from the supporters' view, but were greeted with ecstatic cheers all over again a few minutes later when they reappeared on the Civic Centre balcony. Plymouth's new mayor, Councillor Sylvia Bellamy, dressed thoughtfully in club colours, led the praise. "You're simply the best! Better than all the rest! And they are the best, aren't they?" she asked. "I think I speak for the whole city when I say 'Thank you for everything.' Don't I? [Loud cheers]. I can't hear you… Don't I? [Deafening cheers].

"This is a fantastic day, not just for the club, but for the city, and even the whole of Devon and Cornwall."

On the balcony of the Guildhall for the civic reception

After Councillor Bellamy and Pilgrims' chairman Dan McCauley duetted on a reprise of *We Are The Champions*, Warnock took the microphone. "You are going to remember this day for the rest of your lives," he told the sea of green and white happiness.

"People ask me why we don't get crowds of 30,000 every week. I tell them 'If I do my job right, we will.' It just shows what can be done when everyone works hard."

Even in his moment of triumph, Warnock took pause to send a message of sympathy to the family of Kelvin Noon, the 24-year-old Argyle supporter whose death outside the national stadium the previous afternoon had cast a shadow across the celebrations. "We have to remember there is one family in Plymouth who will be suffering today and the club's support and thoughts go out to them," he said. His words underlined the family nature of the ongoing celebrations and reiterated the relationship between the club and its followers.

Surveying the jubilant scenes, McCauley said: "These are the people who this is all about. They have been starved of success for a long, long time. This is what makes it all worthwhile. I have had a lot of failures at this club, but this vindicates everything."

The fans, though, respectfully declined to accept the credit for the Pilgrims' progress to Division Two. "The team are getting the support they deserve," said Dave Jane, of Plymstock. "This is the best manager we have ever had, the best chairman we have ever had, and the best blend of players."

The joyous scenes, unbridled admiration, lavish praise and enthusiasm for the future were all a far cry from the depression that had engulfed Home Park little more than 12 months previously.

"ALL WE ARE DOING IS PLAYING RUSSIAN ROULETTE"

THE 1994/95 football season was, without doubt, the worst in Plymouth Argyle's 109-year history. It began, amid high hopes, with an unimaginable 5-1 home defeat by Brentford and ended with relegation to England's lowest professional division for the first time since the north and south sections of the old Third Division were combined to create Divisions Three and Four in 1958.

If Argyle's sudden metamorphosis from a turbo-charged Green Machine that finished one victory short of winning promotion the previous season into a spluttering old banger kangarooing towards the scrapyard of the Endsleigh League Third Division was barely believable, events off the field completely stretched the bounds of credulity.

Between August and May, the club lurched from one crisis to another as Home Park took on the appearance of a set for a soap-opera (for *Coronation Street*, read *Outland Road*), except that if some budding young writer had submitted a synopsis of a script outlining what actually happened in city suburb PL2, he would have had it rejected on the grounds that it was too implausible.

The central characters in the not so everyday tale of West Country folk were the club's volatile chairman Dan McCauley and the manager at the beginning of the turbulent season, Peter Shilton. To suggest the two disliked each other would be akin to saying the Balkans conflict was a minor spat: worse still, neither had an ounce of respect for the other.

The gradual utter breakdown of their relationship was anything but a private affair. Every turn in the downward spiral was charted by the local and national media, who could hardly believe the rich diet of stories which emanated from previously homely Home Park.

The season was less than a month old when McCauley and his fellow directors felt compelled to ask Shilton and assistant John McGovern why the Pilgrims had taken one point from their first four Second Division matches; suffered successive humiliating 5-1 home defeats; and been knocked out of the Coca-Cola Cup by Third Division Walsall, who beat then 4-0 in the first leg of their first-round match.

The demise was particularly galling because memories of the previous season, in which Argyle were the country's leading goalscorers and had been a highly entertaining side to watch, had given cause for the optimism reflected in bookies' odds which had made them 10-1 third favourites to win promotion.

The leaking of goals was of prime concern, given that Shilton's only addition to the squad which had carried almost all before them in the 1993/94 campaign had been Port Vale central defender Peter Swan, for a club-record £300,000.

Swan had six months earlier single-handedly – or, more accurately, single-footedly – defied Argyle automatic promotion with a last-ditch tackle on Pilgrims' midfielder Paul Dalton during the match between Vale and Argyle at Vale Park. Had Swan not intervened and Dalton scored, as he seemed certain to do, Argyle would have drawn and, in the final analysis, the point they would have earned and the two which Vale would have been denied would have resulted in Argyle pipping the Potteries' side for second place. As it was, Vale went up, and Argyle went out in the play-offs, losing to Burnley in the two-leg semi-final.

Shilton had made Swan his captain after apparently falling out with the previous season's leader Steve Castle, who angered his manager by asking for a transfer on the eve of the new season. It turned out to be a disastrous appointment as Swan struggled to cope with a new club, a new system, new responsibilities and new team-mates, some of who reacted to Swan's promotion by insisting on referring to Castle as "skipper."

McCauley, never one to fail to notice which way the wind is blowing, may have known this when, on the eve of the club's September board meeting, he said: "It doesn't seem to be a happy squad. There's something wrong. It's either the management or the players. There could be problems off the pitch. Whether there's a little bit of feeling in the club, I don't know, but if there is, it's best to stamp it out before it festers. You can't turn round from being one of the top goalscoring sides in the country to our current position without something being wrong and we want to find out what it is."

Shilton's position entering the board-meeting was significantly more precarious than when he left it. Despite having agreed a new two-year contract with the club the day after the play-off failure, he had yet to sign it because the board was insisting on linking terms and conditions from his previous contract to the new one.

However, by the time the meeting concluded, Shilton had signed up for another two years at the helm of the good ship Pilgrim, and avoided the dreaded vote of confidence to boot. "Everything went quite amicably," reported McCauley. "There was one matter which had to be resolved but our solicitors and Peter Shilton's [solicitors] spoke to each other to sort it out and there was no problem."

Actually, as events would later prove, in signing the contract, Shilton had also signed his death-warrant. The mysterious, unexplained 'linkage' to which he had agreed would eventually prove his undoing.

An uneasy brief peace descended on Home Park as Shilton apologised publicly for the disastrous start to the season and Castle withdrew his transfer request, but the calm did little to improve Argyle's desperate straits. After Neil Warnock's Huddersfield turned them over 3-0 at Home Park on Saturday, September 10, they were positioned third from bottom of the Endsleigh Second Division with the worst defensive record in the country – 25 goals shipped in eight matches. Nor was it only form which was deserting the Pilgrims: the gate against Huddersfield was 2,500 down on that of the season's opening day.

The peace was shattered the following Monday when John McGovern unexpectedly walked out on the club, having signed a two-year contract worth around £100,000 in the summer. At the time, McGovern would only say that he had resigned "for personal reasons", although McCauley revealed a little more when he said that the resignation was "all to do with money."

All became clear three months later when McGovern, who had teamed up with former Nottingham Forest playing colleague Archie Gemmill to manage Rotherham United two days after leaving Home Park, related his side of the split over three pages of December 11's *Sunday Mirror*, under the lurid headline "World Exclusive – Peter Shilton Betrayed Me."

Despite the brash treatment given to the story by the *Sunday Mirror* (and no-one could deny them their moment, given that they had secured the tale every tabloid newspaper wanted to tell), the article basically consisted of a measured statement by McGovern and a brief interview in which he revealed that his relationship had foundered over an unpaid loan.

McGovern explained he had loaned Shilton £7,000 in July, 1993, which the Argyle manager had agreed to repay in full – with interest – within six months. McGovern said he was aware of his former Forest team-mate's money problems, but wanted to help him because of their long-standing friendship.

"This was the man who had brought me back into football after more than four years out of the game," the former Bolton Wanderers manager told reporter Bob Harris. "I stood shoulder to shoulder with him as we took Plymouth towards the play-offs and when he told me he had a cash-flow problem, I wanted to help him. He told me he only needed the money for a month but I gave him six months and he still let me down. I am not completely stupid. Knowing his financial problems, I made him sign [a] letter acknowledging the debt. He was due to pay me back the amount – just short of £9,000 with interest – by December 1993 but he did not return one penny until I walked out on Plymouth." Half the debt, McGovern said, was still outstanding.

Shilton's immediate, and equally measured, response came the following day through the rather less high-profile Plymouth *Evening Herald*, his favoured local media outlet. In an article which the *Herald* pointedly underlined he had received no payment for, he said he had "already repaid a substantial amount of the money owing, which is nearly the full sum of the original loan" and had "agreed to pay an additional figure on top to cover inconvenience in addition to the interest."

He also said he believed McGovern found it convenient to claim personal problems as the means of ending a recently-signed contract at Home Park to take up the position at Rotherham. "I had had an inkling a few weeks before that he was not entirely happy at the club," he said.

"He left to go to Rotherham with his old friend Archie Gemmill. That did not happen overnight. I feel it was in his interest that there was no compensation involved and it may have helped him to indicate that all was not well personally."

Ironically, on the day that McGovern's resignation was made public, Argyle's on-field fortunes began to take an upturn when they secured their first home league point in an uninspiring 0-0 draw with Cambridge United which was witnessed by the lowest Home Park crowd for nine years – 3,824. Afterwards, Shilton refused to answer Press questions about "non-footballing matters".

Four days later, Steve Castle earned the Pilgrims their first victory of the season with the only goal of the game at Cardiff City; the following weekend they beat Chester City 1-0 through Chris Twiddy's fourth-minute goal; and the subsequent Saturday they went to Brisbane Road and triumphed 2-0 against Leyton Orient, thanks to two Richard Landon goals.

Three successive wins, 360 minutes without conceding a goal: perhaps, as Shilton had glibly promised after the 5-1 stuffing by Brentford, things could only get better.

As it was, the unbeaten sequence flattered to deceive (it was not coincidence that Cambridge, Cardiff, Chester and Orient were all relegated with Argyle at the end of the season) and actually, things had taken a significant turn for the worse – for Shilton personally and the club's well-being in general – hours before the victory at Leyton.

This time it was the *Sun* which put the events on the field in the shade as Argyle's dirty linen was held out to dry over three pages of the country's most widely-read newspaper. "Shilton Begged £100,000 Off Me" screamed the back-page headline which topped Ben Bacon's interview with Dan McCauley.

Cutting through the normal tabloid hyperbole, the extent of McCauley's revelations was that Shilton had asked for £100,000 in advances on his salary during his time at Home Park. The straw that had broken the chairman's silence came during the summer, when he gave Shilton £25,000 after he agreed his new contract. Days later, Shilton had asked for further financial help with "cash-flow" problems.

"I just couldn't believe it," said McCauley. "I felt insulted. Like a mug, I tried to do something to help and he slapped me in the face straight away. I've never felt so insulted in all my life. His situation must be far worse than even I envisaged. He says he hasn't got financial problems, but cash-flow problems. He must have come to me seven times for advances, though, to be fair, I did offer last time. I would estimate they totalled £100,000. It won't happen again."

Far more damning than the embarrassing but not altogether shocking revelation that Argyle's manager had wanted parts of his contract paid up early were other, more personal, remarks made by the chairman which alerted Argyle supporters for the first time to the extent of the bad blood that existed between chairman and manager.

"As a person, I don't like him," said McCauley. "I've had lots of rows with him. I would say he hasn't got a friend on the board"; and "If I'd known I was going to have as many problems with Shilton, we'd have tried a different manager"; and "My relationship with him today is the worst it has been."

McCauley also revealed he would not let Shilton have an assistant to replace McGovern. "Why do you need an assistant when you are only working eight hours a week?" he asked sarcastically.

Shilton did not deign to dignify his chairman's scathing attack with a comment except to say he was "shocked and fed up with Mr McCauley's public attacks ... over the last two years, which are very distressing for my wife and family. It needs sorting out."

The following day, McCauley retorted: "He says he's fed up; well, I'm fed up with fighting for Plymouth Argyle, trying to keep football at the top of the agenda. He wouldn't have any trouble from me if he took his money problems out of the club."

Despite the fact that two parties had so dismally failed to see eye to eye since Ben Turpin's chance encounter with Clarence the Cross-eyed Lion, regular Argyle-watchers were not the least bit surprised that the following Thursday's board-meeting resulted in neither the sacking nor the resignation of Argyle's beleaguered manager.

Equally unsurprising was the revelation that the feuding twosome had discovered a new point of conflict: Shilton emerged from the $1^3/4$-hour meeting demanding an apology from his chairman over his "eight-hour week" remark and another suggestion that Shilton had attempted to sign a player on loan after McCauley had refused him permission so to do.

Board spokesman Ivor Jones, a gentle director who often found himself in the United Nations role between the two warring factions, said there would be no apology. "It's obvious... that they don't get on well together," conceded Jones, "but you don't necessarily have to get on well to have a good working relationship." He did not add: "... but it helps rather a lot."

McCauley's shoot-from-the-lip policy did little to endear himself to the club's supporters, some of whom were agitating for an organised protest against him. His response was unequivocal. "I don't want to leave," he said, "but the fans obviously look at me as the villain in this case and, if that's the case, I don't want to stay around."

However, in another bizarre twist to the equally bizarre relationship between manager and chairman, McCauley received support from an unexpected quarter – Shilton. "I do not agree with demonstrations at football clubs for whatever reason," he said. "At the moment, it is important for all fans to concentrate on getting behind the team." The official Plymouth Argyle Supporters Club also appealed to fans not to force McCauley to resign and issued a statement expressing support for both chairman and manager.

The calls for peace appeared to have their desired effect as fans concentrated on supporting their team rather than taking sides in what was becoming a diminishing internal dispute. Shilton and McCauley gave their versions of recent events in interviews broadcast on consecutive nights on BBC Radio's *Evening Sou' West* programme which cleared the air somewhat. McCauley stated unequivocally that he would not sack Shilton, and the chairman acquiesced to Shilton's request for an apology over the "eight-hour week" slur, which he always insisted was a joke taken out of context.

McCauley, though, had identified another target for hostility – the Plymouth *Evening Herald*. He imposed a two-way ban on the city newspaper, withdrawing Press facilities to its representatives and barring club officials – including Shilton – from talking to the publication.

He took the action, he told the *Herald*, "due to the political stance of your newspaper personnel, which has not been in the best interest of the club." The bland statement failed to spell out the real reason behind McCauley's apparently independently taken stance so it was left to the *Herald* to reveal all in their leader column. "McCauley accuses us of taking sides and of being his manager's mouthpiece," they explained, before adding pointedly: "Surely they are both on the same side?"

Like all good newspapers who find themselves in such a position from time to time, the *Herald* made capital out of the Press bar. "Desperate Dan's silly ban won't stop us," they promised, and neither did it. They upped their coverage, with their veteran Argyle correspondent Graham Hambly reporting on the game from the unfamiliar position of a seat in the Lyndhurst Road stand, and generally milked the situation for all it was worth. It has to be said that the Press box was a much poorer place for the absence of Hambly's larger-than-life character. Thankfully, it was not long before he was back in accustomed surroundings, stopwatch in hand, carrying out his duties for which the Plymouth public had come to know and admire him during 27 seasons of covering the Pilgrims' fortunes.

On the field, Argyle's brief revival stalled. Beset by injuries that had plagued them for most of the season, they went out of the Auto Windscreens Shield when they were easily beaten 3-1 at Home Park by Devon rivals Exeter City, and failed to notch another win until late

October, when they surprisingly beat third-placed Stockport County 4-2 at Edgeley Park.

However, they did avoid the banana-skin of an FA Cup defeat by non-league Kettering Town. Such was Argyle's perceived state, the bookies made them the underdogs for the tricky away tie at the previous season's GM Vauxhall Conference runners-up. The match was covered live on *Sky Sports*, who were hardly at Rockingham Road to see Argyle pop a hatful past the Poppies, but Craig Skinner's 46th-minute goal denied the non-leaguers a shock story.

A 4-1 league victory the following weekend over Wrexham, in which the Welshmen contributed two own goals thus making the signing of veteran striker Mick Quinn on loan from Coventry City an unnecessary luxury, briefly lifted the club out of one of the five relegation positions, before Shilton's financial problems hit the headlines once more.

Firstly, it was revealed that the Argyle manager faced a bankruptcy petition filed in the County Court over an unpaid debt of £3,000 to racehorse trainer Martin Pipe for unpaid stabling fees on two horses, and, although Shilton immediately settled the debt, he and McCauley then clashed over a tax-demand from the Inland Revenue.

The club received an IR request for a sum approaching £50,000 in taxes that should have been paid on Shilton's signing-on fee. McCauley believed Shilton should have paid the money himself, insisting that this had been stipulated when Shilton agreed his new contract, and was furious his manager had left the club to foot the bill. "He has had the money and he hasn't paid the tax-man," said McCauley. "The onus has now come back to us."

Heaping further woe on Shilton's already overfull plate, the board told the manager he had four games within which to improve matters on the field. With visits to Brentford, Swansea City and Shrewsbury Town and home clashes with Bristol Rovers and Crewe Alexandra before Argyle were scheduled to travel to Shilton's former club Nottingham Forest in the FA Cup, and half the squad injured or suspended, the writing appeared to be on the wall.

"It's about time I had a bit of help at this club in what has been a very difficult start to the season," said Shilton in a rare public outburst. "I don't think setting targets is an answer to anything. It's a very negative thing to do."

By 4.45 p.m. the following Saturday – December 17 – the writing was not so much on the wall as scrawled in 10-foot high capitals on Plymouth's historic Barbican: Brentford 7 Plymouth Argyle 0, the club's worst defeat for more than two decades. Not much prospect for a happy Christmas for Shilton or Argyle supporters.

The team did nothing to relieve supporters' Boxing Day hangovers against Swansea City at the Vetch Field, where the Swans crushed Argyle's ugly ducklings 3-0, before Shilton's third match of his board-room ultimatum – at home to Bristol Rovers – was washed out.

The postponement allowed the Argyle directors to hold an emergency board meeting at which Shilton's future was discussed. The board considered sacking him on one of two counts: for bringing the club into disrepute over his various financial problems, or for failing to turn around the club's disastrous on-field form.

They settled on sending Shilton a solicitor's letter threatening him with dismissal if the £50,000 income-tax bill was not paid within a week. Shilton, complaining that "the chairman's continued comments about financial arrangements between myself and the club is a breach of duty and confidence which I think he owes me", did not deny liability for the debt. "I am just asking for a reasonable opportunity to come up with a payment proposal."

He did not get it. The day before he was supposed to repay the £50,000, McCauley admitted to the *Western Morning News*: "It doesn't really matter whether the money is paid before the deadline. The relationship between myself and Mr Shilton is at a such a low ebb, it appears it really is in the club's best interests to change the manager. Even if he should find the money, I don't see that it would solve the underlying financial problems that he has which have caused our relationship to reach rock-bottom. All we are doing is playing Russian Roulette, waiting for the right bullet to come round."

On January 4, 1995, Shilton ceased to be Plymouth Argyle's manager after 1,037 days in charge of the 'Pilgrims' negative progress. Although he had officially been suspended on full pay, it was clear that he would be stepping into the manager's office at Home Park only to clear out his desk. Legal niceties, exemplified by the fact that the words "solicitors" and "advice" were used more often than "Peter" and "Shilton" in McCauley's responses to Press questions, prevented the chairman from delivering the *coup de grace*.

Shilton made a brief statement which suggested he was determined to hang onto what little was left of his position as tenaciously as he used to grab hold of crosses. "I've asked the chairman to confirm to me what terms of my contract give him the right to [suspend me]," he said, looking genuinely confused.

It was a sad end to what initially appeared to be an inspired appointment and to a managerial reign which had promised so much, both in its anticipation and for one glorious nearly-season. There are those of us who would prefer to remember Peter Shilton as the planet's greatest goalkeeper, a dedicated – even obsessive – professional, the footballer who had it all, rather than dwell on the personal tragedy of the broken, broke figure who appeared in danger of ending up with nothing.

Steve McCall

On the day of Shilton's suspension, McCauley further outflanked his footballing nemesis by introducing his replacement: Steve McCall, the former Ipswich Town and Sheffield Wednesday midfielder who had twice been named the supporters' player of the season since joining Argyle for a bargain £25,000.

By appointing McCall immediately, McCauley had cannily filled a void during which supporters might have dwelt upon Shilton's departure and the causes behind it. McCall became a new focus for their attention, and the future assumed more importance than the past.

Because Shilton was merely suspended, McCall was given the title of temporary player-manager, although little can he have realised at the time just how temporary his reign was to be, and his first match in charge was at Nottingham Forest in the FA Cup. The final indignity suffered by Shilton is that he was prevented from returning to a stage which he graced so wonderfully as a player and where, under Brian Clough, he began to learn the management trade.

If this was a fairy tale, McCall would have immediately revived Argyle's fortunes and led them to safety, but the task proved beyond his limited experience. After 11 games in charge, Argyle had won just twice, and the defeats included reversals at fellow relegation-threatened sides Chester and AFC Bournemouth.

The concerned board suggested bringing in an experienced coach to work alongside him, but McCall declined their offer. Five games later, with no visible sign of improvement and the Third Division abyss looming, they gave him the same offer, this time a little more forcibly. McCall resigned.

His rejection of the take-it-or-leave ultimatum left Argyle in yet another fix. The board had not expected McCall to react so violently and so were left scratching around for someone to lead the team into the final vital nine games of the season.

"We did not go and talk to anyone else before [we saw McCall]," said McCauley. "Now we are in a bit of a cleft stick. There was nothing sinister about our intentions. We genuinely wanted to offer [McCall] some help and tried to do what was best. We wanted someone with experience in there with him but he felt he couldn't go along with that."

Ivor Jones added: "Myself and the chairman made great efforts to get him to stay but he just wouldn't. It's a sad day for the club. I personally thought Steve McCall had the potential to be an absolutely first-class manager."

McCall, who stayed on as a player, confessed to being "very disappointed" and added that he thought a joint-managerial approach undermined his position and was not the right way forward for the club. "The board kept on saying that I'd do well but they didn't exactly stick with me," he said. "They kept saying they needed experience but I've seen experienced managers relegated. They have now changed managers twice in three months and that is not good for the club."

McCauley expressed hope that an appointment could be made within 24 hours but one thing was sure: it would not be Dave Smith, who led Argyle to promotion from the old Third Division nine seasons previously and who had been the choice to work alongside McCall.

Smith, the popular "Ciderman", turned down their request for help because: "At 62, I feel my best days are behind me. Although my mind is as active as it ever was, the job is a very physically demanding one and I wouldn't have been able to do it justice."

With the end of the season looming, Argyle wasted no time in appointing McCall's successor and, for the second time since the new year, the board cast their eyes around the dressing room to find a suitable candidate before handing the poisoned chalice to Russell Osman.

The former England international centre-back had been at Home Park for only eight days, brought to the club by his one-time Ipswich Town colleague McCall on non-contract playing terms. The irony that it was McCall who had attracted Osman to Home Park was matched only by the fact that Osman had been a contender for the Argyle manager's job after David Kemp was sacked in February, 1992. On that occasion, of course, he was beaten to the position by another former team-mate, Peter Shilton.

In making the announcement, Ivor Jones said that Osman would have no title but would "be in charge of first-team matters until the end of the season", their reluctance to put a handle on his duties stemming from a desire to avoid complications that might arise for Osman, who was still in dispute with Bristol City after being sacked from Ashton Gate earlier in the season. Also for this reason, he was to be paid expenses only while he attempted to engineer Argyle's miracle escape.

In his first seven games as untitled, unpaid adviser on first-team affairs, Osman guided Argyle to two wins – against Swansea City and Shrewsbury Town – and three draws, but their own revival had been matched by similar determinedness from Cambridge United and, especially, Bournemouth. Survival looked unlikely. They had to win an away fixture at Wycombe Wanderers, who had been beaten just twice at home all season and were chasing a play-off place, as well as their final home match with Oxford United *and* hope other results involving their relegation rivals went for them.

However, Argyle supporters were spared a nerve-shredding 90 minutes on the last day of the season by a combination of the Endsleigh League fixture-list, the Dorset constabulary, and Bournemouth.

Despite winning 2-1 at Wycombe on the penultimate Saturday of their miserable campaign – becoming the third of only three teams to leave Adams Park with all three points during the season – Argyle had ceased to be masters of their own fate.

Their brave 2-1 victory, achieved through Richard Landon's 65th-minute prod past goalkeeper Paul Hyde, would have been more significant had not Bournemouth, their chief rivals for the one remaining place in the Division Two lifeboat, gained an equally improbable win.

The Football League, or, at least, the Second Division of it, was indeed upside down that

Saturday: at the same time Argyle were denying Wycombe a place in the end-of-season play-offs, Bournemouth were denting Brentford's chances of the championship by becoming only the second side to win at Griffin Park in 26 league games. To add further spice, the third side in the any-two-from-three-to-go-down relegation shake-up, Cambridge, shared a point with Neil Warnock's fifth-placed Huddersfield Town.

Now, if Bournemouth won their final game of the season against Shrewsbury at Dean Court, the Cherries would pip Argyle – and Cambridge – to safety, whatever result the Pilgrims managed in their own last fixture at home to Oxford. If Bournemouth lost, however, Argyle could still slip the hangman's noose.

Normally, the final matches of a season are all played at the same time on the same day, allowing supporters whose club's future depends on results elsewhere to experience the bitter-sweet agony of exhorting their own team to victory while at the same time keeping an ear tuned to radio reports from the relevant other matches.

This season, however, Argyle supporters would already know the score when *Semper Fidelis* heralded the Pilgrims onto the pitch for their final Saturday afternoon match. Bournemouth were due to complete their season earlier than the rest of the division, their game against Shrewsbury having been brought forward to the preceding Tuesday.

The date had been changed on the recommendation of the police, who had wanted to avoid any possible repeat of the chaotic scenes at Dean Court three seasons previously, when thousands of Leeds United fans had converged on the seaside resort on the last weekend of the season intent on seeing their team clinch the First Division championship.

Shrewsbury hardly represented the same threat to either peace or Bournemouth's chances of staying up. They had nothing to play for, were badly hit by injuries, and their form was so bad that, the previous month, they had been a rare home scalp for Argyle. Contrastingly, Bournemouth, who had appeared dead and buried at Christmas, had been showing promotion form since the return of Mel Machin as manager.

The form-book proved accurate. Argyle's proud record of never having played in the country's lowest division was effectively over 20 minutes into the game as two goals from Steve Robinson and another by Scott Mean gave the Cherries a 3-0 lead which they never surrendered or added to.

A crowd of more than 10,000 witnessed what was inevitably dubbed *The Great Escape* and not all were cheering the Cherries, as their end of season video of the same title shows. Among the crowd shots, it is possible to witness several characters in green and black striped shirts, all of who are holding their heads in their hands.

Dan McCauley was generous in defeat. "We were living in hope and died in despair," he said, "but really, Bournemouth have been playing better than any of the teams in the lower half of the table."

He promised the search for McCall's successor would begin immediately and outlined the criteria which the new man would have to fulfil. "We have got to go for experience," he said. "We have had enough first-time managers recently and it hasn't done us any good. At the level we will be playing next season, it is important we find a manager with a good track-record. There is no substitute for experience."

Among those in the game who fitted his identikit was Neil Warnock.

"PEOPLE WOULD THINK WE WERE IDIOTS"

NEIL Warnock's name had been mentioned as the man most likely to lead the Pilgrims during the 1995/96 season well before the 1994/95 campaign had ended.

It had long been assumed among Argyle supporters that the friendship between Warnock and Dan McCauley, which began when the former helped out as management consultant at Torquay United during 1993, would result in the pair teaming up at Home Park.

The fans were aware that they enjoyed each other's company to such an extent that McCauley and his wife Ann would spend time with Warnock and his partner Sharon whenever Argyle played in the North. On one occasion, the foursome had enjoyed a Barry White concert. The question now was: would the soul-mates be united professionally?

McCauley had been asked just that at a Fans' Forum in April and had denied there was any truth "whatsoever" in the rumour. Then again, with Warnock then employed by Huddersfield Town, he could hardly say anything else without running the risk of a high-level Football League question-and-answer session on the subject of manager-poaching.

Nevertheless, with complementary murmurings that all was not sweetness and light between Warnock and the then Huddersfield chairman Terry Fisher, the rumours persisted. And persisted.

The whispers continued because the matter could not be addressed head on until the end of the season and although Argyle's 1994/95 campaign had ignominiously petered out with a 1-1 home draw against Oxford United, Huddersfield's season had potentially another three weeks to run.

Warnock's Terriers had ended the season as the Endsleigh League Second Division's fifth-placed side, a feat which qualified them for the end-of-season play-offs. Having already won successive Wembley play-off finals while with Notts County, few doubted that Warnock would be unable to repeat the feat. While he did, Argyle's directors and supporters could only watch and wait.

During the three weeks between the end of the regular season and Huddersfield's promotion by way of a 2-1 victory over Bristol Rovers at Wembley on May 28, the Argyle board employed the normal tactics by a club seeking a new manager, superficially at least.

They advertised the position twice in the *Daily Express*, although sandwiched, as it was, in the Situations Vacant columns between enticing exhortations to become a driving instructor or gas-fitter, it is questionable how many suitable candidates it would have attracted.

McCauley declared himself "pleased with the response" and could not prevent himself from fanning the fires of rumour further, mischievously adding: "... but there are a few more people who I hope will apply." Warnock, he confirmed, was not among the official applicants.

Advertising the vacancy did, nevertheless, present the Press with an opportunity to indulge in their usual round of speculation as to who was among the applicants, even if most journalists believed the exercise was one in futility. The West Country was merely waiting for Warnock to take care of business with Huddersfield, shut up shop and head for Home Park.

The speculative Argyle managerial long-list of interested parties, out-of-work managers and former Pilgrims players included: Trevor Francis, Russell Osman, Mike Walker, Alan Smith, Brian Horton, Danny Begera, Gary Megson, Kenny Hibbit, Steve Perryman, Roy McFarland, Barry Lloyd, Frank Burrows, Tommy Tynan, Danny Salman and, for all most journalists writing on the subject really knew, Uncle Tom Cobley.

Meanwhile, as the good ship Pilgrim continued to drift rudderless, another list of names was being compiled – that of players who were reaching the end of their contracts and were stalling over signing new deals. Part of the Shilton legacy had been a higher than normal number of players' contracts expiring at the same time. If they all exercised their rights under freedom of contract legislation and left the West Country for new clubs, Argyle would be powerless to prevent them moving and whoever became manager would have a squad large enough only to compete in the five-a-side league at the adjoining Mayflower Sports Centre.

The players could not be blamed for at least waiting. It is always an anxious time when a new manager arrives at a club. In football parlance, he may not 'fancy' a particular player, even if he was the previous manager's pet (or, maybe, *because* he was the previous manager's pet); he may want to play a different, unliked, style of football alien to the player's instincts; he may be a complete and utter bastard in training; there are 1,001 good reasons for not signing and approximately one for signing – the clichéd cash offer that cannot be refused.

Winger Paul Dalton, and defenders Mark Patterson and player of the year Marc Edworthy all indicated early in the close season they would not be re-signing on the dotted line, but forward Richard Landon was the first to bail out, Argyle's leading scorer the previous season signing for Stockport County, and Craig Skinner was next to jump ship, to Wrexham.

Meanwhile, the West Country Warnock-watchers' attention turned to Wembley, where the man with the Midas touch at the Twin Towers extended his number of play-off final triumphs to three in five seasons when a goal from Chris Billy gave Huddersfield victory over Bristol Rovers and a place in the First Division.

To the rest of the football world, it seemed bizarre Warnock would turn his back on a side with which he had just won promotion, especially one with a spanking new stadium and a future seemingly as bright as its new fixtures and fittings.

McCauley, however, revealed more of his hand when he told the Press that he would be seeking out Huddersfield chairman Terry Fisher at a post play-off weekend meeting of Endsleigh League chairmen to speak about Warnock's "situation".

Argyle's own situation needed to be resolved quickly if the new manager was going to have anyone to manage. Edworthy had been signed by Crystal Palace – on the recommendation of former Argyle manager and Palace assistant-manager David Kemp – for a club record-equalling £350,000; Steve Castle and Martin Barlow had joined the contract *refusniks*; and record-signing Peter Swan, whose time in the West Country had been marked by a series of problems on and off the field, was on the transfer list.

Warnock's "situation" was resolved – at least partially – on Monday, June 5, eight days after Huddersfield's successful visit to Wembley, when the club announced he had resigned. His departure came after months of differences between himself and Town chairman Terry Fisher which, unlike similar *contretemps* at Argyle, had not been aired in public and did not involve Her Majesty's Inland Revenue.

Warnock said little on his departure, merely that he did not want to "jeopardise Huddersfield's future by staying on when, deep down, I know it is the right time for me to move on." He gave no indication where he intended to move on to but McCauley reacted to news of his resignation like a terrier that had seen a particularly juicy rabbit.

"We have got to talk to him," he enthused. "I will make great strides to ensure that we track him down and see if he is interested in coming to Plymouth Argyle."

Tracking down Warnock was not going to be an easy task, for the now ex-Huddersfield manager had taken himself and his partner Sharon on a fortnight's holiday to the Maldive Islands. However the fax machine in the Indian Ocean-based hotel was soon working overtime. Warnock became one of the few holiday-makers to receive, rather than send, a "Wish you Were Here" message and, a fax or two later, McCauley offered him a long-distance three-year contract.

"He wants a couple of days to think about it," said McCauley, but the fact that Warnock himself had opened that day's proceedings with a 7 a.m. wake-up call to McCauley's Exeter home in which he had made sure the Argyle chairman was acquainted with his hotel's fax and telephone numbers, suggested he had done most of his thinking.

"I have offered him a three-year contract, which was one of the things he was happy about," revealed McCauley. "It relaxed him." For which Warnock's loved one was probably grateful. When all you want to do is chill out and soak up the ultra-violet, you do not want to be doing it next to someone agitatedly twiddling with the straw in his pina colada or flicking pieces of coconut shell absentmindedly into the sea.

McCauley also brushed off suggestions that Fisher's removal as Huddersfield chairman by his fellow directors the same day might tempt Warnock back to the Sir Alfred McAlpine Stadium. "Why would he want to go back to Huddersfield when he can come to Plymouth Argyle?" he asked. "I don't think there's a cat in hell's chance of him going back to Huddersfield."

NEIL WARNOCK: *Dan McCauley knew I was unhappy at Huddersfield, because I spoke to him a couple of times and he also knew I was going to have interviews – he knew I spoke with Derby and Notts County – but I told him that if I had a choice to make, it wouldn't be* dependent on money. I loved Plymouth and he didn't worry me at all. People had told me about him but I had always got on well with him and his wife Ann, and Sharon and I thought a lot about him.

After the play-off final at Wembley, we went up to Scotland for a week. I hadn't been told that we could have gone around the town in an open-top bus and I had already planned to take the kids away for half-term. So we went up there and I said to the directors at Huddersfield that I wanted to wait until I came back off my main holiday to make a decision.

When I came back from Scotland, they asked me if I would help them out and my differences were then discussed, which they knew all about because I had been talking to them for six months about problems, and they asked me if I would consider making a decision.

Huddersfield vice-chairman Geoff Headey telephoned me on the Saturday night after we came back from Scotland and before we went to the Maldives said could he come over the next day. He felt that he needed a decision there and then.

I talked to Sharon and we both decided that, although people would think we were idiots, we would go to Plymouth. So we told the vice-chairman on the Sunday and they announced my resignation on the Monday as we left for our holiday.

Obviously I wanted to give them a bit of time to get a manager because I had no hard feelings at all. I had done my job and lifted us up to the First Division. We had a lovely new stadium and good players. They must have got three to four million pounds-worth of players on the pitch.

Before we went on holiday, I telephoned Dan to tell him that we had both decided to come to Plymouth. He obviously didn't believe us. He wanted to fax up a contract to Huddersfield to get us to sign it before we went on holiday. I said it was impossible to do that, he had to trust us. He said the other directors didn't think that I would stick to my word and they wanted to interview other managers.

I said I could only tell him how I felt and if he felt I was going to let him down then fair enough, but I gave him my word we wanted to come to Plymouth, no matter what anybody else offered us. If another club came in for me when we were on holiday, we wouldn't deviate from what we had said. Sharon went on the 'phone and told him that we wanted to go and nothing would change our minds.

However, he wanted to see us at the airport before we departed so we arranged to meet him two hours before we left for the Maldives. We had a chat and he wanted to get the contract signed but we didn't agree any figures. I left it with him that I would give him a ring when I got to the Maldives with a fax number and if he wanted to send me any details, he could, and we could have a chat while I was over there.

I said: "Rest assured, I have told them I am leaving Huddersfield now and I am going to come with you." He was obviously concerned that the other directors wanted to interview people and he said he had got two or three other people to speak to. I just said, "You must go ahead with what you think but I won't deviate from what we said and I think you have got to trust me. If I have given up so much, whatever happens – if anybody else comes in with a better offer – we are going to come with you."

And I told him what I would like to do in the next three years and I hoped it would be my last club – I would love to do the next 10 years down in Plymouth. Whether my heart would last that pace, I didn't know. I would love to put the smile back on to the Argyle supporters' faces and I felt I could actually make the club a happy place to be again.

I said to him it was important that people are happy – supporters, players etc. – and I was looking forward to the challenge.

We told Ann: "Don't let him worry about anything, we have given our word, we are not going to go back on it now, and we will see you when we get back."

So off we flew. I think it took us 12 hours to get there and, to be fair, it was just what we needed. It was super, really quiet and we were able to relax.

I telephoned Dan with the fax number and he asked me if he could send me a copy of my *agreement over and I said he could and he also faxed me the pre-season games they had got, and I tried to explain what kind of games I would want that weren't fitted in.*

We spoke every couple of days. He still kept asking me the same questions – to make sure I hadn't changed my mind. Sharon and I had a laugh with Ann, and we told him to stop wittering, which is a Yorkshire expression. I planned my pre-season. I got Dan to fax me the PFA free-transfer list of available players and I started planning who I would like to sign, knowing what we could afford budget-wise.

I was made aware of the players down in Plymouth – who wanted a new contract, who had refused contracts, which nearly everybody had. I knew I hadn't got to worry about players who were tied up for another year and then I had to find out where certain players were going.

Dan told me about Marc Edworthy. I was disappointed in Edworthy going although I was pleased for him. I spoke to Marc two or three times over the previous couple of years. I rated him highly and I had a couple of chats with him when he wasn't in the team at Plymouth. I tried to buy him for £100,000 at Huddersfield and I think it was Dan who refused it after I almost got Peter Shilton to accept that.

I spoke to the lad himself. He knew he couldn't get a regular game at the club and he was interested in coming with me. I told him that I would sign him at Huddersfield, but it seemed strange that I had already made up my mind that I wanted him to stay at Plymouth because he had a smashing attitude and was a nice lad.

When Dan told me the sort of money he was going to get for Edworthy, I just said he had no option but to sell him, because they had got relegated and I didn't think anybody should keep somebody if they could get decent money. We should just wipe the slate clean. I felt, having watched them a few times that season, he needed the slate wiping clean and a complete overhaul. I knew it would mean certain crowd favourites going but I told Dan that I would have to take the flak for that because that is what I have done in previous clubs.

So I set about my lists. There was a patch of white sand outside our room within about 30 metres of our hotel room and we just slumbered there each day. Sharon would sunbathe and I would have a dip and then look at the PFA lists, then the pre-season friendly games. I wanted to be on the phone but couldn't.

Although I was told about Micky Heathcote going somewhere while I was on holiday when I telephoned Mick Jones, I actually rang Micky from the Maldives and told him not to do anything until I got back. I wanted to speak to him personally, and he agreed. Incidentally, I didn't charge the chairman for that 'phone call, thinking about it.

I had two 'phone calls to my kids while I was on holiday, and when I came to get the bill it was £120 for three 'phone calls, which I just couldn't believe. I don't think I could work in another country, not with my telephone bills!

The agreement came through from the chairman for my consideration and we discussed certain things. He 'phoned me the following day to ask me what I thought. Although we couldn't agree anything totally, I just told him not to worry about it because I would agree something, whatever the circumstances, when I got back.

I still think he wanted to make sure that somebody couldn't get hold of me on holiday and then twist my arm around my back. But even if they had done, I wouldn't have gone anywhere else, not when we had committed ourselves like we had. Because I knew that so much depended upon us going now after the couple of years that Plymouth had had, I didn't want to let Dan or Ann down.

The two weeks did seem a long time on holiday, what with everything going on and Dan kept asking me if he could announce what was happening in the local papers. They were on to him all the time about what was going on and he was saying he was in talks with me.

When we were on holiday, we met another couple. They were the only couple who actually went to our island when we got dropped off by the plane but we didn't meet up with them until the second week.

They were called Mark and Helen. We had a couple of meals with them and evenings on the karaoke machine, can you believe it? Mark was telling us he had had a few problems over the past few weeks. He had found a lump and had been for tests and was diagnosed as having lymph cancer. He was having treatment and was going to have more when he got back.

You could see a deterioration in him during the second week, he was in quite a bit of pain. But we had two or three good nights and I think that helped him forget the pain.

He had just got engaged to Helen, and they were a smashing couple. He said that he was going to come to the first pre-season game against Chelsea. I invited him down. On the flight back, he took very ill. We kept in touch to see how he was doing and he went to hospital and they admitted him within a week. Three weeks later we were going to his funeral.

I think that really hit home to Sharon and me just how important your health is. You should never take it for granted. And I think there is more to life than football. Bill Shankly used to say football is more important than life or death. I don't think it is. I think your family's health is far more important.

The two weeks passed, Dan somehow got by, and we arrived back home, went up to Huddersfield, unpacked and arranged to go down to Plymouth the next day for the Press conference which announced my appointment to the world.

"I WAS THE ONE PERSON THEY'D BEEN LOOKING FOR"

NEIL Warnock flew into Gatwick Airport in the wee small hours of June 20 and some 56 hours later the worst-kept open secret in Plymouth Argyle's history became a secret no longer. Even the date of Warnock's appointment had been signalled long in advance: a bulletin issued by the club to supporters two weeks previously promised they would be able to meet the new manager at a Sponsors' Luncheon on June 23.

Warnock fairly breezed into Home Park on the bright, sultry morning of Thursday, June 22. That he was introduced as Plymouth Argyle manager in the Green Room, above which extensive renovation work was being carried out was somehow appropriate for he admitted that rebuilding the relegated, demoralised, fragmented club he had just joined would be the biggest challenge of his career.

Warnock had plenty to say on his first day but was studiously careful to avoid making any promises. Neither did Argyle's 24th manager mention "potential", nor did he use the words "long" and "ball" in close proximity.

He was, though, cautious only in these respects. Otherwise he charmed his way through his debut Press conference with an enthusiasm that augured well for the future. His 45-minute address – during which he needed around a dozen questions to stir his passion for his new task – was certainly the longest time the Pilgrims' chairman had been silent while awake and although Warnock is a qualified chiropodist, if he does not fancy facing feet for a living after leaving football,

Club photographer Dave Rowntree captures the beginning of a new era

he gave the impression he could quite easily talk professionally for England.

22

"I'd like to think I could put the pride back in supporters' hearts," he said, "but obviously I'm not naïve enough to think it's going to be a piece of cake. The only thing I can say is that, wherever I go, I work hard, give 100 per cent commitment, my staff do the same, and I expect total commitment from the players."

The fact that 13 out-of-contract players had yet to hint at that commitment was of no concern. "Many players will be leaving without me having a say. The lads that stay will enjoy their time with me, but the ones that want to go will be allowed to go," he said. "We will lose players who are crowd favourites but, on the other side of the coin, you've been relegated twice in three seasons so perhaps it's not a bad time for some of them to go." Two months later, when Argyle began the 1995/96 campaign at Colchester, their side contained seven debutants.

To the question which baffled most people in football – why had he moved from the First Division to the Third? – Warnock cited his friendship with McCauley, a fondness for the West Country which had developed when he was managerial consultant at Torquay United two seasons previously, and the challenge.

"I find every aspect of the job appealing," he said. "It would be tremendous to build a winning side in a place like this where you enjoy living. Dan appreciates more than anybody what I've given up to come down here and I appreciate the opportunity because Neil Warnock is not the type of person about who you can say 'he does this' or 'he does that' – Neil Warnock does what he wants to do and I wanted to be manager of Plymouth Argyle. I always think that when you want to do something and you love it dearly enough, you get more out of it. I think if you enjoy your job, you enjoy where you live, you enjoy your players, then you can get success. I'd like that and I'd like to put a bit back into the community because I feel that we're all in it together – the supporters, directors, players, the manager are all working for the same objective."

He was obviously aware that once someone throws mud, it tends to stick and, after a while, whiff a bit. Warnock's direct style of play employed at Notts County and Torquay was raised from the floor. He simply asked supporters to judge him – and his team – on what they would see.

"I like getting the camaraderie at the club right because in your windy winter months, when you go to some of the places we'll be going, you need people who will roll up their sleeves and have things under their shirts," he said, acknowledging the club already had a "nucleus of quality players" – Nugent, Castle, Swan, Patterson, Dalton and Nicholls. By the end of November, five of that sextet would no longer be at the club and one of them would have tragically died.

Touching once again on his friendship with McCauley, and aware of the chairman's strained working relationship with Shilton and McCall, Warnock admitted that McCauley was "similar to myself in that we both say what we think.

"But I'm hoping I can calm him down a bit," he carried on, conjuring up the image of someone attempting to extinguish a log-fire with a blow-torch. "I'd like to think that, if I do the job to the best of my ability and it doesn't work out, we would still get on, but I don't think like that. I'd like to think I can show Dan what a good decision it was to bring me to the club. I'm looking forward to it."

With that, Warnock left the reporters to their notebooks and tape-recorders, to pose for pictures and be interviewed for television on the pitch which would be his battle-ground for half the coming season. The sun shone as brightly as the smiles on everyone's faces and its warmth appeared to gradually melt away the memories of the trials and tribulations of the previous season.

NW: *When I arrived at Plymouth, I couldn't help but remember the initial Press conferences at the three clubs that I had taken over before. In just half an hour you could see the optimism in the room. I felt that I was the right person for the supporters and the club because I thought that the supporters could look at me and say "Bloody hell, he has taken Huddersfield up to the First Division, and he has come to Plymouth who have just got relegated to the Third Division; he has given up a lot and we have got to give him the best chance we can possibly can."*

I felt straight away that I was the one person they had been looking for and I felt ever so proud that the supporters felt like that. The first day I was there, and the following days, the number of people that came up to me and Sharon and expressed their gratitude for me coming down was phenomenal. I said to them all: "You shouldn't say anything yet until you've seen us play. Let's see if you will congratulate me in 12 months." Obviously, I was joking about it but I know football can change very, very quickly.

I knew it was the right place as soon as we went to a sponsors' luncheon the second day I was there, when I was invited to meet the day-to-day sponsors and the small sponsors who help the club every year. The warmth that welcomed me was second to none. Everybody couldn't do enough for you.

I know talk's cheap and anybody can say that when you go to a club but you could actually sense and feel that people were genuine, they actually meant what they said, they weren't bull-shitting. They weren't saying it because you were a new manager, they really wanted you to do well. They were really willing you to do well and because of that enthusiasm I was full of myself and the passion was burning inside me. I love to make people happy and I love to know that other managers don't want to play against my team, and I think it is a matter of putting pride back into clubs. I love that – even though I get criticised.

I think if people actually looked into what it takes to turn a club around, I don't think they would be as quick to jump on it. You have to get everybody and everything working in the same direction; you have to make sure you get the right players; you have to make sure the office staff are the right people to be with you; commercial staff; everything regarding the club.

That is what we started after the initial Press conference. Everybody wanted me to use the word "potential" which I avoided like the plague because that is all I had heard about Plymouth, every time I spoke about them.

"WHAT A LOAD OF RABBLE"

NEIL Warnock's initial weeks as manager of English football's most southwesterly outpost coincided with one of the most sultry summers on record, and the pre-season activity at Home Park was even hotter than July.

Within days of slipping into the manager's chair, Warnock had already lost the services of the first of the quality sextet he had identified at his first Press conference. Midfielder Steve Castle agreed terms with First Division Birmingham City and left to join the considerable contingent enticed to St Andrews by manager Barry Fry's patter and chairman David Sullivan's money.

Castle, who would have an early opportunity to renew old acquaintances with his now former team-mates in the first round of the Coca-Cola Cup, had been an inspirational captain in the 1993/94 season, when he scored 21 goals as Argyle narrowly missed out on promotion.

The following campaign had been as miserable for him as the previous one had been enjoyable. He lost the captaincy and his place in the side when Shilton reacted with pique to an eve-of-season transfer request, and then suffered a debilitating bout of jaundice which sidelined him for much of the doomed campaign.

Castle's move from the Greens to the Blues signalled the start of dizzying few weeks of transfer activity. However, Argyle's next import was not a player, but Norman Medhurst, the Torquay United physiotherapist who had struck up a friendship with Warnock during the latter's brief period as managerial consultant to the Riviera Coast club in the last few months of the 1992/93 season.

Medhurst, who replaced Shilton-appointment Paul Sumner, had recently been honoured with a star-studded testimonial after having worked with the England national team for 20 years. "I'm just delighted to have got someone of his calibre," said Warnock. "You want your own men and I was always impressed with Norman from my time at Torquay. I have explained to Paul that that's football, I'm afraid."

Another of Warnock's "own men" had already been confirmed as the Argyle number two. No surprise there – Mick Jones had served under Warnock at Notts County and Huddersfield as the perfect counterpoint to his long-time partner, being as quietly-spoken and unflappable as Warnock was sparky and excitable.

With Jones and Medhurst installed, Warnock went about surrounding himself with the players he believed would "roll their sleeves up and have something under their shirts."

Incidentally, the shirts under which their unspecified "something" would be revealed during the season would be of a new design, the change from the previous season's green and black stripes neatly symbolising the gathering wind of change which was sweeping through Home Park. Despite the exorbitant cost of street-essential replica kits, supporters were not the least bit sorry to see the demise of the stripes after little more than a season.

They were convinced the simple design design was jinxed and it was easy to see why. The strip was first worn in the Second Division play-off semi-final of 1994, when Argyle lost 3-1 at home to Burnley having done the hard part by previously drawing 0-0 at Turf Moor, and then during the subsequent relegation season. In little more than a year, the Pilgrims won only 25 per cent of their games in the "unlucky" colours.

Mind you, the 1995/96 livery did not meet with universal approval. The jazzy, fashionable, basically white shirts with green diagonal borders and black flashes were snapped up by more than 50 fans on their first day of issue, but others were less than enthusiastic. Bill Shepherd, in a letter to the *Sunday Independent*, expressed fears of a catastrophe because of the design. "Psychologically, it is accepted that diagonal stripes or anything on a slope is unbalanced," he wrote. "It disturbs the mind."

Meanwhile, Warnock's undisturbed mind was set on team-building. With millionaire McCauley willing to underwrite his manager's plans, Warnock could have been forgiven for thinking big and spending accordingly, but he proved more than prudent.

First to arrive in the West Country was Paul Williams, a 24-year-old pacy left-back who stepped down three divisions to sign from FA Premiership Coventry City for an initial £50,000. The fee was a whopping £250,000 less than West Bromwich Albion had been quoted for Williams's services after he had spent a spell on loan at the Hawthorns the previous season. Astutely, Warnock had realised Williams – whom he had also had on loan at Huddersfield – had slipped to third in the Highfield Road left-back pecking order after the arrival of David Burrows (former Pilgrim Steve Morgan was ostensibly Burrows' deputy) and had a hunch that City manager Ron Atkinson would welcome the chance to lessen the Sky Blues' wage-bill.

Next to arrive in quick succession were midfielders Ronnie Maugé, from Bury for £40,000, and Chris Leadbitter, a free agent after being released by Second Division escapologists Bournemouth at the end of the previous season.

Leadbitter, a key component of the Cambridge United team that won back-to-back promotions in 1990 and '91, had lost his place in the Bournemouth side – initially through a first-ever suspension – as Argyle were losing their grip on their Second Division status. The hard-working left-sided midfielder, now in his late 20s, had been considered by First Division Birmingham City. Then again, there had not been a player, available or otherwise, who had not.

Maugé was, said Warnock, to be Castle's replacement. "He is a strong attacking midfielder, who gets from box to box," summarised the Argyle manager, "and I think he can score many goals for us at this level."

It soon became clear that Maugé was what football managers like to call "a character". With two ostentatious gold false teeth, a confident swagger, and an air of chirpiness entirely in clichéd keeping with his Cockney upbringing, he did not strike you as the sort of person to be in awe of the limelight.

If Maugé's transfer went through without a problem, the pronunciation of his surname caused some initial difficulty. After starting out as the somewhat deathly "Morgue", it

somehow metamorphosed to the rather feline "Moggy" before the player himself sorted it out and "Mo-jay" it was. Warnock settled on calling him "Ronnie."

As two midfielders were entered into the Home Park equation, another was removed. Craig Skinner completed his move to Wrexham, putting another £50,000 in the credit column of Warnock's transfer dealings.

Two days later, Warnock succeeded in landing his prime close-season target. Most of Argyle's problems the previous season had stemmed from a deficiency in the goalscoring department and a regular contributor to the goals-for column was obviously paramount.

Enter Adrian Littlejohn, a 24-year-old Black Countryman whose contract at Sheffield United had expired. After much persuasion, the fleet-footed striker agreed to drop two divisions to spearhead the Pilgrims' promotion drive and rebuild a career which was foundering in the Yorkshire club's reserves.

A regular for a while at Bramhall Lane after Dave Bassett had snapped him up on a free transfer from Walsall, Littlejohn lost his place in the Blades' line-up following the sale of his strike partner Brian Deane to Leeds United and had fallen behind the international trio of Carl Veart, Jostein Flo and Nathan Blake in the United pecking order.

Once again, the player had been on the Warnock shopping-list for a while. "He is an exciting player and one I've wanted for six to nine months," said a delighted Warnock on the morning Littlejohn's signature was finally clinched. "I tried to get him before the transfer deadline last season at Huddersfield."

As befitted a player with experience at the top flight, Littlejohn did not come cheap, but good strikers are the rarest commodity in football and a maximum outlay of £200,000 for his services barely represented unbridled profligacy.

"I think the figure paid is realistic for a player who gives us an extra dimension," justified Warnock. "He worries defenders with his pace and that creates the space for others."

With pre-season training now underway at the Royal Naval Engineering College in Manadon, Warnock was still far from finished assembling his squad. Next to experience his cajoling tongue was Cambridge United captain Mick Heathcote, a 6 ft 1 in central defender held in the highest regard by most forwards in the lower divisions.

Heathcote, a 29-year-old Geordie, journeyed down from the Abbey to join the Pilgrims' West Country summer work-out and left after a couple of days to talk discuss a permanent move with his family.

"I've spoken to him and obviously I'd like him to join us," said Warnock. "He's the type of lad I like – he's a good leader, he talks a lot, and he's done it all before. He just wants time to chat to his wife."

Adrian Littlejohn

Mrs Heathcote obviously held no strong objections to uprooting herself and her family from Cambridgeshire and moving 300 miles across the country. Within a week, her old man had become Warnock's fifth new recruit, for an initial £70,000. The Argyle manager had effectively signed nearly half a team in 10 days.

NW: *On the first day's training, my first impression was "What a load of rabble." Long hair, earrings, jeans everywhere – they looked a bunch of scruffs, all looking down at the floor as they were talking, with the odd one or two looking up. As I was talking, I found myself thinking "I can see why you got relegated."*

We planned to do three days' training and after the first day's training on Wednesday I said to Mick [Jones]: "Mick, I think we should just train tomorrow and have the weekend off."

I was going up to Sheffield for a minor operation and was travelling up on the Friday anyhow and I said to Mick: "If I were you Mick, I would give everyone the weekend off. I cannot see the point of training these lads because there will be nobody here by the time we start in six weeks' time."

That's how I felt. I was so down. Obviously it was a big blow, realising what hard work it was going to be, especially having just had the euphoria of getting Huddersfield up. I mean, I wouldn't have been in Plymouth if it wasn't that I knew Dan [McCauley].

We came down for three months when I was helping out Torquay, we loved the area and I always thought that Plymouth was a massive club. I just felt like a challenge. Everybody in football – well, most of them – thought I was an idiot, and after that first day's training, I tended to believe them, but I thought "We will just have to wait and see."

I think there were three or four players when I saw the training early on, who I thought would end up playing for us. Mark Patterson was one, Martin Barlow another, Kevin Nugent, and I quite liked Hilly [Keith Hill], even though I didn't like his hair and earring. Once we started pre-season training, I also realised that I could get quite a bit out of Wayne Burnett.

I didn't see Paul Dalton during the first few days because he didn't turn up but came in the following Monday and I said to him obviously I would try and get him away, if that was what he wanted and even talked to him about staying. But he was adamant that his wife couldn't settle and she wanted to go back up North, so I said I would do my best and rang around a few clubs for him.

I got my old club, Huddersfield, interested in him, but I asked Brian Horton for a centre-half (Kevin Gray) and a left-sided midfielder (Paul Reid) in exchange and he came back and said he didn't want anybody to go at that moment in time, the dressing-room was good, which I knew – it was a fabulous dressing-room – and that he'd wait and see after a few practice matches.

With that, I went and signed Chris Leadbitter, who I knew could play the left-hand side position, on a free from Bournemouth. Leadbitter was just one of the lads who I thought would do me a job for a couple of years. He's a squad lad, he will never be a crowd pleaser, he's not going to beat people with skill and caress the ball, etc., but he is what every manager needs at a club. I knew that Chris was an honest lad and I thought "He's a smashing lad on and off the field, nice family as well, and he wants to come," so I gave him a two-year contract.

I got Paul Williams who I had on loan at Huddersfield the previous season, to come down from Coventry. He came with us to the play-off final at Wembley the previous season, and I said to him coming back on the bus that, wherever I was the next season – whether it was Huddersfield or anywhere else – I would sign him the following year, and I meant it.

So, naturally, I rang him as soon as I got the Plymouth job and told him that there was no-one else interested in him, there was only one manager he could play for, and he was going to Plymouth!

Paul and his wife Jane came down with his child, and they liked the area and although we had to iron out certain financial things, we sorted all that out in a couple of days, and he put pen to paper for a three-year contract.

I was looking for midfield players and I had a call from a guy mentioning two lads at Bury, Ronnie Maugé and Roger Stanislaus, the left-back. Bury had knocked us out of the Auto Windscreens Shield that year and I remembered Ronnie Maugé. He only played the first half before going off injured, but we had a very strong midfield at Huddersfield and he dominated them and I liked him.

When I got the 'phone call, I said to the agent I would be interested in talking to Ronnie to see how the land lay because he was the type of guy I was looking for and I had been given a price of £40,000 or £50,000, which was well within our budget. So I asked if he could send him down to have a chat.

He turned up on my doorstep with his gold teeth flashing away and I immediately thought what a likeable rogue he was. You know, one or two people had given bad reports about him and one or two – Sam Ellis, his previous manager at Bury, in particular – had given good reports about him. Sam said he was a jewel and said we would have no problems at all in handling him.

I liked him right away, really. Money wasn't the motivation at all. He said that he wanted to win things, he had got the opportunity to stay in Lancashire with two or three league clubs, but he wanted to give it a go with us. We never really discussed money until he was signing his contract.

I always like that type of thing from a player. Usually the first thing they say to me is "What sort of contract can I have?" or "What is in it for me?" If that is the opening remark or comes within the first five minutes, I go straight off players, because obviously they are going to come for the wrong reasons.

In the end I asked Ronnie what he was looking for and he told me. By that time, he had met the chairman and the chairman, like me, thought he was a likeable rogue and got on quite well with him. I had made up my mind what I was going to offer him and asked Ronnie what his minimum request would be. He told me, and I said "Well I'm not giving you that." His mouth opened and he looked a bit shell-shocked and I said "No I'm giving you more than that." Then we both smiled.

I have always been like that. If I've thought a player is worth more than I could get away with, I will give it to him – up to a point. His commitment in wanting to play for us really impressed me. I just thought, "Well, this guy wants to play for the club and they are the type we need."

I think I gave him about £50 a week more than he wanted. He looked around my office. I had a picture of the championship winning Scarborough side of 1986 on the wall, two of Notts County's promotions, and Huddersfield Town's promotion, and Autoglass Trophy appearance at Wembley. I asked him what sort of money he was looking for and he said: "I want some of this, boss, I want some of this. I want to win." I just had this feeling about him.

Micky Heathcote was a player who we played against Cambridge at the end of the previous season and Andrew Booth, who is worth £2m, absolutely battered him with his head. There was blood everywhere. Micky Heathcote wouldn't come off because it was a vital game for Cambridge. All his head was bandaged up. I went on the pitch after the game and said to him: "Wherever I am next season, I'm going to sign you" and shook his hand.

I remembered him and thought "What a brave lad he was, I wish I could sign him," but to get him to come down was a battle. Eventually, I got him down with his wife to have a look around and I knew there were only a couple of clubs in for him because he'd got a history of a bad back – he had an operation when he was at Sunderland – but if anything, I am glad he had got a bad back because if he hadn't, it wouldn't have put anybody off signing him and I knew what I was getting.

I was determined to try and sign him because I wanted him as my captain. It took

Mick Heathcote, bleeding but inspirational

about two and a half weeks to actually get him to sign, but he was so vital to us. I told him that I would have signed him whatever division I was in and I think he believed me.

I also said to him, as I said to them all, that I wasn't at Plymouth just for a nice quality of life, that I'd thrown two divisions away – I had just gone up to the First Division with

Huddersfield – because I loved the challenge of building a club from scratch and filling the ground with supporters, and that with the supporters at Plymouth, I could do that.

I told Mick that he would be very important and he hadn't won much in his career, as indeed most of the lads I signed hadn't.

When I tried to get Mick to sign, I couldn't agree a fee with Cambridge. They were adamant that they wanted £150,000 for him, because I asked about Carlo Corazzin as well and they talked about £350,000 for the both of them.

I decided I wanted to try and get Adrian Littlejohn at that particular time, so I wanted to wait to see if I could get Micky Heathcote for less than £150,000 even though I thought he was worth that. I offered £70,000 originally and they said "No" but we knew that they were short of money and just kept at it.

I spoke to Mick a couple of times and I think he was disappointed that Cambridge didn't make a sustained effort to keep him. I think they wanted to sell him but eventually I gave them an ultimatum that I would give them £70,000 and £30,000 based on appearances and promotion and they had to give me a decision within 24 hours. They came back and said "No."

Michael Evans

I told Micky the deal was off because they were asking £150,000 and he told me that the manager had told him that they would let him go for the offer we had made.

I went on to Adrian Littlejohn, who I was trying to sign. I offered £150,000 for him on deadline day at Huddersfield but they wanted £300,000 at that time. I rang him and he hadn't had many people speaking to him and obviously the biggest part for me was trying to tell him that Plymouth was a progressive step for him.

We decided that the only way to get him interested was get him and his family down with the two kids. We got him down and they stopped in a hotel overlooking the Hoe. Thank goodness for the glorious summer we had because in the six weeks before the season started, I must have put everybody up – every Tom, Dick and Harry and their dogs at these hotels on the sea-front.

With the weather being what it was, Sharon used to talk to the wives or girlfriends, while I went on to the players about the city. They could see for themselves what a fabulous place it was just by looking around, and I was telling them that it had all the amenities anyone could wish for. To the ones that had kids, I stressed what a beautiful part of the country it was for the kids.

I spoke to Adrian for a couple of hours on the Hoe, and Sharon went down to the playground below with the kids, including his young lad Reece, who is only about five, and had a game of football with Reece in the park.

I worked on him like I've never worked on anybody else, really. Same with the chairman. The chairman and I had healthy discussions about him – whether we could afford him, whether we could buy him – and the night before we agreed terms, it was decided we weren't going to sign him. I had one more go at the chairman, asking him to help me. I thought we needed Adrian Littlejohn at the club. I spent all night up trying to think how I could convince the chairman and he finally agreed. He was as good as gold, really.

He said "Okay, go and get him then" and I told him he wouldn't regret it and that he would score 15 to 20 goals, to which I think he said "Yeah, in his dreams."

Micky Evans had done well in training as well but had not figured in my first-team plans as such. I could see why people had told me that he had been to Blackburn. I was told he was the best sub at the club. He worked hard in training and I liked his attitude, but with him being under contract I didn't have to worry about him, so he was the least of our worries.

Dave Bassett had gone abroad so I spoke to Brian Eastick, who was in charge while he was away and he told me that they were looking for £150,000, so all our figures when we talked to Adrian and his agent were geared to that. Then I got a telephone call saying that their valuation was a lot higher. Derek Dooley, the chief executive, said to me that they wanted £350,000, they couldn't let him go cheap. In the end we agreed on £200,000 which I thought was £25,000 over what he was worth, but if we had gone to a tribunal, we might have got stung for £250,000 because he had played in the Premier League, and had scored goals.

At tribunals anything can happen, so the chairman and I talked about it and decided not to get stung and go for the £200,000. I said to Dave Bassett "You are not going to get any more than £200,000 at a tribunal" and we agreed without going to one. I was relieved, to say the least, when he signed.

I didn't tell the players anything that I didn't believe. I have always tried to be honest with players, even though managers are two-faced – they've got to be. I have always said to players that I will get them whatever I can in football, but if they cross me once, then I will finish with them as quickly as they came to the club.

I just warn them once – they only have to let me down once and I have had enough. They won't see another day.

Before putting his new-look Pilgrims out in competition, Warnock had to attend a meeting of Football League Appeals Committee – known colloquially as the Transfer Tribunal – who were sitting to fix the transfer prices of Steve Castle and Richard Landon.

After hearing submissions from all parties, the tribunal ordered Birmingham to pay a flat fee of £225,000 for Castle, and fixed Landon's price for his move to Stockport at an initial £30,000. Both valuations were lower than Argyle had been seeking – they had asked £750,000 for Castle – but neither deal left them out of pocket, either.

"I am a little bit disappointed," said chairman McCauley afterwards, "but we had a disappointing season and I guess the players have been valued with that in mind. We were talking about £400,000 for Castle when Coventry were interested a couple of years ago."

NW: *The chairman and directors thought I should get about £350,000 from Birmingham to start with, but it was obvious that we weren't going to get that sort of money and we decided that if we could get £300,000 without a tribunal, then we should go for it.*

Barry [Fry, the Birmingham manager] and I got together and Barry agreed to give us £250,000 and £50,000 after 35 appearances, so I reported that back. Although we thought we wanted a bit more, we decided to try and go ahead with that.

I spoke to Barry the next day and his chairman had come back to him and said he had got to offer £100,000 because Castle couldn't be worth £300,000. He was three years older than when he came to Plymouth, and although they had paid £195,000 for him, he had got to be worth a lot less than that.

He didn't take into consideration how many goals he had scored the previous year and Barry was a bit embarrassed, but it was his chairman and there was nowt he could do, so it might have to go to a conditional tribunal if they couldn't agree. I spoke to Steve Castle and I said I thought he was too good a player to go to a conditional tribunal. They should either sign him or not.

We hadn't had anybody else in for him so he didn't really have that many options, but Steve went to speak to Birmingham and decided to sign for them on condition the deal would go ahead only if Birmingham were happy with the tribunal.

The chairman, Ivor Jones and myself had to go all the way to Lytham. We put our case, Barry put his case, then they came back in and said £200,000. So Barry went out, telephoned his man, and came back five minutes later and said we had got a deal.

Then we had the Richard Landon tribunal on the same day, a lad I didn't really know but I could tell from the evidence that we weren't going to get much for him – we got him from non-league and hadn't offered him much of a contract. Stockport put forward a good case, and in the end I think we got £30,000 for him. He was only going to be a squad player for them, so I couldn't really argue with that.

On the same day as the tribunal, Argyle played their first pre-season friendly, when a decidedly second-string looking line-up easily beat Jewson Wessex League Swanage and Herston 4-0, with goals from Micky Ross, Sam Shilton, Martin Barlow and Michael Evans.

"IF YOU MESS ABOUT LIKE YOU ARE DOING, ME AND YOU ARE GOING TO FALL OUT"

THE first opportunity Argyle supporters had to see Warnock's new signings in action came on July 21. Fewer than eight weeks after the new manager had been appointed, a Pilgrims' side containing five fresh faces strolled to a 3-0 victory over Great Mills League champions Tiverton Town at Ladysmead. One of them, Ronnie Maugé, celebrated Argyle's new beginning with the opening goal in the 38th minute, with Kevin Nugent and substitute Michael Evans adding the others.

Kevin Blackwell, who had come to Home Park from Huddersfield to take charge of the Pilgrims' largely-lapsed youth development pro-gramme, played in goal because of injuries to Alan Nicholls and James Dungey. Warnock had intended to use the game to run the rule over Nicky Hammond, who was down from Swin-don Town on trial, but, with the sort of misfor-tune that was destined to typify the goalkeeper's brief Home Park career, Hammond missed the game with a thigh strain.

In Blackwell, Warnock not only had a goalkeeping option available to him, but also another trusted long-time colleague. The 36-year-old had followed his mentor from Scarborough to Notts County and Huddersfield – where he ran the Terriers' successful youth team – before once again linking up with him at Plymouth.

In addition to Maugé and Blackwell, Argyle bows were made by Chris Leadbitter, Adrian Littlejohn and Mick Heathcote, who captained the side at Ladysmead, as the jinxed Peter Swan had done precisely 12 months earlier. Within a year, Swan had gone from record-signing to surplus-to-requirements and was now on trial at Second Division Burnley.

Kevin Blackwell

Other notable absentees from Warnock's first Argyle team-sheet included injured defend-ers Keith Hill, Mark Patterson and Paul Williams, and winger Paul Dalton, whose last known movements had him playing in a testimonial match with previous club Hartlepool in preference to joining Sheffield United's pre-season tour of Sweden.

Warnock professed himself delighted with "an excellent work-out" and promptly continued his search for the perfect promotion-winning squad by taking Sheffield United's Australian central defender Doug Hodgson, Bury goalkeeper Lee Bracey and Peterborough winger Liburd Henry on trial. Paul Dalton returned to Home Park from wherever he had or had not been and promptly injured himself by stubbing his toe in training.

Summer signings Nicky Hammond, Mick Heathcote, Adrian Littlejohn, Ronnie Maugé, Chris Leadbitter, Paul Williams and Mark Saunders

NW: *I tried to sign a couple of centre-halves to no avail, so I got Dougie Hodgson down from Sheffield United and he made a pretty reasonable contribution, but if I'm honest, I couldn't make my mind up about him although the lad himself was a smashing lad.*

During pre-season Hilly played there and he didn't do badly. I must admit I changed my mind a little bit about him. He got his hair cut as well. His attitude was good, so I said to myself "Who knows? Certain players change your mind, so I'll give him a chance." I had to try and instil one or two things in him, like I had to do with most of the lads who were already there because they wanted to play football in the wrong places and I had to get my point through, because for me it was dicing with death.

The itinerant Dalton missed Argyle's second pre-season game at Yeovil four days later, as did Maugé, who was on antibiotics after grass-burns on his leg turned septic, a problem unlikely to be encountered again during the coming winter months.

Patterson and Williams played, however, as did Bracey, Hodgson, Henry, and former Home Park winger David Byrne. At 34 and based in Scotland, Byrne was looking to return to the West Country, where he still had a home after a two-year spell at Home Park during Ken Brown and David Kemp's management. Of the six, Hodgson made the biggest impact on the game, with referee Keith Cooper asking Warnock to withdraw his defender after a quarter of an hour following an earthy challenge on Chris White, the implication being that Cooper did not want to have to send him off.

ICIS League Yeovil scored from the resultant free-kick through 36-year-old player-manager Graham Roberts, the former Tottenham and England defender equalising Nugent's early opener, and it was not until the final 10 minutes that Argyle secured a 3-1 victory with late goals from Nugent and Littlejohn.

"I am glad we have still got nearly three weeks to go before the start of the season," was Warnock's blunt verdict on the match. "We are still miles away."

He had reason to feel he was a little nearer four days later, when Argyle travelled to Cornwall for a match with the Duchy's cup-holders, Jewson South Western League Truro City.

Truro manager Leigh Cooper, a loyal servant to the Pilgrims who played more than 400 games for the club and led them in their finest hour-and-a-half – the 1984 FA Cup semi-final – was delighted his present club was hosting such a prestige game.

The jaunt into Cornwall, which was also to take in a visit to Falmouth, had been arranged by Dan McCauley with Warnock's agreement before the new manager's appointment. The Argyle chairman was aware the Pilgrims had often ignored Cornwall during their pre-season build-up, and equally aware of the large fan-base in the Duchy, so he promised to take Argyle to their loyal Cornish fans.

Warnock, who had set up home in Cornwall, was equally as happy as Cooper. "I spoke to some Cornish fans and they told me they had been a little bit neglected," he said. "I told them we'd look after them."

Truro, and Argyle's Duchy supporters, reciprocated by looking after Argyle with typical Cornish generosity. After the match, the Argyle players attended a beach barbecue at Crantock organised by the Cornish Supporters Association, at which they entertained the supporters with an impromptu game of beach-cricket that was unfortunately cut short by the incoming tide.

The players appeared a happy bunch – Swan showing a nice line in beamers and Hodgson reminding everyone which side held the Ashes – and they had every right to feel pleased with themselves, having left Treyew Road with a handsome 6-0 victory under their belts.

In truth, it was probably a little too easy for Warnock's liking. Argyle looked good but, as they say on the Newmarket gallops, all horses run fast past trees, and the canter in the sunshine gave little indication to the Argyle manager as to how his team would shape up in the Endsleigh League Division Three opener at Colchester two weeks later.

Warnock, who included triallists Hammomd and Hodgson, started with what appeared to be his first-choice line-up – injuries notwithstanding – and Argyle were far too strong for their non-league opponents. Wayne Burnett opened the scoring from the penalty spot after Maugé had been clattered clumsily by Tristan Wood in the 10th minute, and two goals in the 13th minute, from Maugé and Littlejohn, allowed Argyle to enjoy a stroll in the summer sunshine.

Littlejohn increased the lead five minutes before the break when he pirouetted around two gallumping tackles before planting the ball past goalkeeper Dennis Annear, by which time even Truronians were wishing the Pilgrims well. Truro might be their local team but, as the match-day programme pointed out, Argyle are the Football League club for the county of Cornwall and everyone west of the Tamar wants them to succeed.

Michael Evans and Chris Twiddy completed the scoring in a second half during which both managers made numerous substitutions. Among those who made their pre-seasonal bows for the yellow-shirted Greens were Swan, back in the West Country after failing to agree terms with Burnley, and Tiverton Town midfielder Mark Saunders. Paul Dalton was about to start a week's trial with First Division Ipswich.

The one-sided nature of the Truro game meant Hammond did not have much opportunity to impress Warnock but the Argyle manager had apparently seen enough to make up his mind and the following Monday paid Swindon £40,000 for the 27-year-old ex-Arsenal goalkeeper.

"He has always been my number one choice," said Warnock. "He is a smashing lad and very professional, which impressed me."

NW: *We had two or three goalkeepers. I decided to give Alan Nicholls a chance and I spoke to him when he was working hard with [physiotherapist] Norman Medhurst. Nicholls had an operation or injury before the end of last season and had done no rehabilitation whatsoever, so the first day we trained, he pulled up with an injury. That was the last I ever saw of him on the training-ground.*

I wanted to persevere with him because I have never been a manager to duck troublesome players. You get them everywhere, and I thought it would be nice to get him going for me. He seemed a good lad regarding working. Norman said he was a good professional regarding his rehabilitation, that he worked hard.

It was just one of those things that whenever I spoke to him, he promised this and he promised that, but he was always going to let you down. I put up with it for two or three weeks, maybe even six weeks, and thought he would just get back in time before the season started and then two or three things happened off the field, nothing to do with football.

So I decided it just wasn't worth the hassle. I was doing things off the field spending personal time with Alan which really I needed to spend on team-work and I wasn't getting anything back. So I decided there and then that I needed a goalkeeper.

We had two or three 'keepers down for trials with us and in the end I found Nicky Hammond. Well before that, Alan went absent without leave again, and got done for drinking and driving, so I just washed my hands of him. I couldn't really stick up for him anymore. I tried to, but we decided to cancel his contract and really let somebody else have the trouble.

It's sad that someone with his ability just let himself down time after time. I just felt that Gillingham, who eventually signed him, could get him straightened out and back to what he was good at, and that was playing football.

Pre-season saw us also ask the Saunders brothers to come down from Tiverton and have a game. We were short of bodies. I must admit my first impression of Mark was that he wasn't too bothered really. He had just come back from honeymoon and hadn't done any training. But after that I liked him, especially his attitude on the pitch.

I thought he would be a good asset to us in the squad. He was very good in the air. I could see if Ronnie Maugé got injured, him getting in the box and back again so we signed him and ended up paying £5,000. His brother Neil also came down but we decided against taking him because we already had enough cover at left-back.

Further evidence that the squad was beginning to settle down and take shape was provided by full-back Mark Patterson, who finally signed a new two-year contract after stalling for most of the summer.

NW: *All this time we were trying to get Mark Patterson to sign a new contract. The chairman and directors said he had had a good season, he was a good player but he was trying to get a contract out of me which I decided was probably a bit more than his value. It didn't help that he was injured nearly all through pre-season and we didn't really get a good chance to watch him train properly or play. Having lost a number of players during the summer, the chairman and I decided we ought to try and get Mark tied up but I think Mark had had enough of trying to get a contract out of me and decided to go.*

At one of the pre-season games, I said to Patto: "You will not get it out of me, but the chairman likes you as a player so you can try getting it out of him." He came to me at the end of the game and said he had agreed terms with the chairman and he was going to sign a new contract. I thought that it was the chairman's money so it was up to him. So he agreed to sign a two-year contract on the assumption that if we didn't go up, he could go to the first club that paid £200,000 for him. I felt that if we didn't go up he would not be worth two-hundred grand, so I just agreed to it.

At the same time, I was trying to get Kevin Nugent to sign a new contract. I had a look around and there weren't many big lads about, and although I knew we could get decent money for Kevin – even if I had not many offers. I decided to try to talk Kevin into staying with us. When Adrian Littlejohn signed, I told him that Littlejohn's pace would make it a lot easier for Kevin up front. In the end, he decided to throw his lot in and sign a two-year contract though he, too, had a provision that if we didn't go up, he could go for £200,000.

Hammond and Patterson both missed Argyle's second Cornwall friendly against Falmouth on Tuesday, July 31, when another largely second-string side narrrowly triumphed 1-0 at Bickland Park. A 21st-minute own goal from Nigel Rowe settled the game, but the Jewson South Western Leaguers were unlucky to find the Pilgrims' England junior international goalkeeper James Dungey in such fine form.

The second-year YTS player made three saves to deny the Street brothers, Adrian and Andrew, and the unfortunate Rowe, and drew praise from his manager. "He is as brave as a lion," said Warnock, after Ray Nicholls' outfit had provided the stiffest test so far for his side.

Argyle also included brothers in their line-up, with Neil Saunders joining brother Mark despite not having kicked a ball in anger since the end of the previous season. The pair had been due to join GM Vauxhall Conference side Bath City from Tiverton, but Mark had put the move on hold following Warnock's obvious interest.

A 12-month full-time professional contract beckoned, provided Warnock could come to a suitable arrangement with Tiverton. "I don't think that will be a problem," he said, and why should it be? After all, he was on pretty good terms with the Great Mills League side's president – Dan McCauley.

Also on the brink of committing his immediate future to Argyle was forward Kevin Nugent, another of the summer's contract stallers, who was one of the few players at Home Park to avoid a pre-season injury. Training on the eve of the Pilgrims' prestige friendly against FA Carling Premiership Chelsea on Thursday, August 3 was cancelled. There did not seem to be much point in holding a three-a-side session.

It was against this background of an injury-list that would keep a whole series of *Casualty* going that Warnock returned to to Swindon to borrow central defender Adrian Viveash, a long-term interest of the Argyle manager who had fallen out of favour with Robins' manager Steve McMahon.

"Whoever's fit is playing," declared Warnock as he prepared to face Glenn Hoddle's Londoners. "You never know, I might even be on the bench myself." Since his last serious outing was as Crewe Alexandra's number 11 in a 2-1 home defeat by Rochdale in 1979, it was safe to assume he was joking. Nevertheless, it was a measure of his managerial approach that he could enjoy a laugh at a situation which would have many of his peers tearing their hair out.

On Thursday, August 3, Argyle's pre-season preparations were given a rude awakening. Or rather, a Ruud awakening.

Ruud Gullit was in town and, for the first time in living memory, people were locked out of Home Park as fans flocked to see the Dutch master's artistry, with Warnock's Pilgrims rather incongruously second on the bill in their home bow.

The doors were locked on a full-house, though the gate was limited to a little more than 13,000 because of on-going renovation work to the main grandstand, as Gullit-inspired Chelsea eased to a 2-0 victory with goals from Craig Burley and Mark Stein.

Argyle, without a clutch of injured potential first-teamers, showed few signs of being overawed by the Premiership side. Former Tiverton midfielder Mark Saunders had signed a contract earlier in the day and found his first professional job was to mark England international Dennis Wise. His performance was all the more commendable given that he must have spent half the time pinching himself to check he was not dreaming.

After the match, Warnock declared himself pleased with just about everything.

"It was a marvellous crowd and a great atmosphere," he enthused. "It's a good decision to come down here when you see a crowd like that. It's got to make you want to fill the ground regularly. You know what you have got to do here. We have got to aim to win these fans back week in, week out. I thought we created problems and had chances. I thought we got more out of the game than Glenn Hoddle. Certain lads showed me what they can do."

Whether the description "lad" suited veteran midfielder and immediate past manager Steve McCall is open to question, but his surprise inclusion in the starting line-up, given that he had made no secret of his desire to leave the club, indicated he was not completely out of his successor's thoughts.

"In the situation we are in, I have said to him that I have no grudge to bear," said Warnock. "If he wants to play and he's good enough, he's in the side."

Meanwhile, two other want-aways appeared to be nearer achieving their aims: Peter Swan returned to Burnley on a month's loan and Paul Dalton fixed himself up a trial at Warnock's previous club, Huddersfield.

NW: *I offered Wayne Burnett a new deal, but he thought he was worth more, so we left it at that and said we would see how it went and I tried to play him in different areas. I tried him as sweeper in front and behind the back four where he could play to his strengths.*

I couldn't make my mind up about a new contract for Martin Barlow, so I said to him we would see how things went in the first four or five weeks.

Then there was the biggest problem – Peter Swan. Peter obviously thought he was bigger than the club. When we finished a run or training or whatever I did, he would walk off on his own, away from the lads.

I had already met him up in Huddersfield and he told me he didn't want to stay in Plymouth and what he thought about the team, the players, the club itself, supporters, you name it. I said to him, "If you're straight with me and give me everything, I will do my best to get you away because I never have anybody who doesn't want to play for me or the club. But if you mess about like you are doing in training at the moment, then me and you are going to fall out and as far as I am concerned you can train with the reserves and just stay and rot here. So you've got two choices."

He said he would give it a try. I was trying to get him away and I knew Burnley were going to sell Steve Davis for big money to Luton on I got on the telephone and told Jimmy Mullen that I thought he would do a decent job for them with Winstanley, the lad they had signed the year before, who I also recommended to Jim.

I said to Jim "Instead of taking him straight away, have him for a week and take a look at him." He did that and liked him and I told him to keep him for a second week. Burnley were having a disastrous pre-season so I thought they would have a good chance of signing him.

They would go for Swan, and they would give us £175,000 only on the condition that we kept it under wraps until Davis had gone to the tribunal so no-one would know they had another one lined up to replace him.

I agreed and we eventually got £200,000 for him, which I thought was a cracking deal. I personally didn't think he was worth more than £100,000 at the time. Although the club lost a lot of money, the chairman agreed to let me do the best deal we could.

His influence around the whole area was one of contempt, really, and although I pulled him up in front of the lads one day to let him know who was boss, the sooner I got him away, the better, because you could see why the dressing-room was poisonous the year before.

I'm not saying it was all Swan's fault, because having met some of the other players that were already here, I could see that their hearts were not in the right place. I don't think they were really worried about dying for Plymouth Argyle, if I'm honest.

Swan was, therefore, absent from Argyle's official photocall – marshalled by Warnock with breathtaking efficiency – two days after the Chelsea defeat, as were goalkeepers Alan Nicholls and Martin Hodge. Adrian Viveash, who had played against Gullit & Co, was definitely in the picture, as was confirmed two days later, when he took his place in Argyle's starting line-up for their final serious warm-up match against Spanish First Division side Real Oviedo.

Say whatever you like about Argyle's preparation for the 1995/96 season, it had not lacked variety, and neither had Neil Warnock's selections. In eight meaningful matches under his management, Argyle had fielded 42 players and still no-one, including the manager, was sure which of those were going to comprise his starting 11 at Layer Road on August 12.

Oviedo triumphed 4-1, which was not surprising seeing as their last league triumph had been a 3-2 success over Real Madrid. They worked on the principle that if Argyle did not have the ball, they could not do a whole lot with it and for much of the match the Pilgrims' midfield resembled the pig in a game of Piggy in the Middle.

Still, there were signs that the Warnock hallmark had been stamped on his new side. They looked like a team of battlers, filled with the sort of players for whom a wet November Wednesday evening on a Wigan mudheap is positively paradisal, which boded well.

NW: *When we did the pre-season games, I made sure we went down to Cornwall because*

I had been told that we had neglected people down there in the past, but it was too late to get any other games at home. We had Chelsea lined up and I wanted a game against a club from a division higher than us, but found it impossible to get anybody the week before. So I decided to go for Real Oviedo just to get a run-out really, because I didn't think we had enough games.

That was to prove a disaster, not because we got beat easily, but it served no purpose whatsoever in our build-up. They play totally different football to what we expect. It was a wasted exercise. I would have got more out of just a training session.

The trip down to Cornwall was good, although a couple of tackles left a bit to be desired. But it was a good work-out.

Chelsea had beaten Torquay 4-0 and I will never forget my first impression as we got to the ground for my first home match. One of the stands wasn't open because of the renovation work and yet 13,500 filled the ground – what a sight!

I remember watching Ruud Gullit play the first half an hour and thinking that the entrance fee alone was worth it just to look at him. His professionalism and his ability just outshone everyone on the pitch. He was just head and shoulders above everybody. I thought what a plus it was for English football to have someone like Gullit coming to England at the end of his career.

We were unlucky not to score and lost the game but we had a few chances and I thought, generally, it was a good performance and we played well.

Warnock's final week of planning for the new campaign was undermined slightly by Swindon manager Steve McMahon, whose six-figure transfer valuation of Viveash was not in line with Warnock's assessment of his worth. Viveash returned to the County Ground and Warnock returned to Sheffield United for the temporary services of Doug Hodgson.

He followed that piece of business by offloading Paul Dalton to Huddersfield in exchange for £125,000 and two midfielders, Gary Clayton, a 32-year-old who first played for Warnock at non-league Burton Albion, and Chris Billy, 22, who scored for Huddersfield in the previous season's play-off final.

Billy was the key to the deal, and decided to leave the First Division for the Third only after encountering Warnock at his most enticing. "He's the one that I wanted," said Warnock, after spending three days persuading him to climb aboard the Pilgrims' Express. "He's a very talented player."

NW: *This was at a time where I was still talking to Huddersfield about Dalton, who had also had a game for Sheffield United against Boston, in which he scored.*

Huddersfield were quite keen on him. They talked to the lad and he was keen to go there and I said the only way I would allow that was if I got Chris Billy and a lad called John Dyson. Brian Horton came back and said that he couldn't do that and how much did I value Chris Billy at? I said I wouldn't give more than £100,000 for Billy, who is a lad I think could be worth a lot more money than that.

They wouldn't sell Dyson either, so I suggested that they gave me £125,000 plus Chris Billy and Gary Clayton. Gary wasn't worth anything in the equation for me – probably £10,000 at most, but I don't think you can put a price on Gary Clayton's contribution to the dressing-room on and off the field. I like him wherever I am because of his contribution, not just on the pitch, but off the field.

He's a tremendous dressing-room lad and he has been with me for many years. He's had his ups and downs but I was quite pleased when Huddersfield came back and said that they'd do it. I was also aware, as I said to Brian, that Chris Billy got certain stick from parts of the crowd at Huddersfield with him being a local lad. After the first couple of pre-season games didn't go so well, I heard that one or two of the crowd were having a go at him. So, I just took the opportunity and it worked.

Huddersfield came back and said they would like Paul Dalton and would do a deal. The biggest problem for me then was talking to Chris Billy, who four weeks before, had scored the winner at Wembley to take his local club up to the First Division – talking him into coming to Plymouth Argyle, which must have seemed like the back of beyond for him.

I had seen him in the summer at a garage after he had had a little bump in his car and I said to him "I'll be after you, you know," and just laughed at him. I am sure that he didn't think that Huddersfield would ever contemplate selling him after what he had just done, but you've got to take every opportunity and when Huddersfield agreed, I immediately got Chris to come down with Gary Clayton. I don't think he would have come on his own, but I told Gary Clayton, who was dead keen to come, that I wanted him and Chris and they both came down. I think it took them six hours.

I made them come to our house near Callington, in Cornwall, because it would be late at night when they arrived and I spent three hours, well into the early hours of the morning, trying to talk Chris Billy into convincing him it was the right move.

Even though, underneath, I knew that I wouldn't come to Plymouth if I was in his situation, not when you'd just scored the winning goal for your home-town club and they were going into the First Division, I obviously emphasised to him that you play for managers not clubs, and for Brian Horton to consider selling him meant that he wasn't really in his plans.

My big plusses were that Plymouth was a fabulous part of the country to live in and that he could establish himself in the team over the next few years. He already knew me and I think he is the type of lad that needs to work for somebody he knows. I told him I thought I could help his career and I wasn't down in Plymouth just to grow daisies – I had also dropped down two divisions and I was hoping to get a type of player who would enjoy playing for me for a few years.

He agreed to listen. I don't think money was a problem – Chris is not motivated with money – and I think it was about 2.30 in the morning when we eventually went to bed. Gary Clayton laughed, because I only spent one minute with him whereas I spent three and a half hours with Chris. I think it was obvious to Clayts that I could have him whether I wanted him or not, but I also stressed to Gary to try and do the best he could to push Chris to come because it would be better for them both to come down together in the deal.

The ongoing thing with Paul Dalton carried on. Ipswich Town came in for him, with George Burley wanting him to go on a pre-season trip and I said as far as I was concerned he could go abroad with them.

I told Huddersfield he had gone up there and it must have just quickened up their minds a bit, because Horton came back and said he wanted to speak to him again and would I make sure he didn't sign for Ipswich?

He also asked if there were any other players that he and I could do a deal with, because I knew by then he was thinking that he didn't know whether it was right to let Chris Billy go. But I stuck to my last and said "No it's got to be Billy or nobody."

I knew that if he got into the season he wouldn't let Chris Billy go, because he was too good a player, but I also knew that the crowd at Huddersfield didn't like Chris, and he only had to make a mistake early in a match for them to crucify him. I stressed that to Brian, knowing that the Huddersfield directors felt the same way. I decided if Dalton wished to go to Huddersfield, I was going to stick out for Chris Billy. They rang me back and asked if they could have Paul Dalton to play against Blackburn Rovers in a friendly game. I telephoned Paul to say they were very keen. He was keen as well, because he wanted to stay living in Middlesbrough, and he thought Huddersfield would allow that. I wasn't bothered as long as I got Billy.

Argyle went into their first game as just about everybody's favourites to win promotion. With some bookmakers, they were as low as 10-3. Warnock accepted the compliment, but not the odds.

"Put it this way," he said on the eve of the visit to Colchester. "There's no way I would put any of my money on us at the odds we've been quoted and I wouldn't expect our supporters to, either. I hope the bookmakers are right – they don't normally chuck their money away – but it's a good job they haven't been with me for the last couple of weeks.

"All I ask is that players put as much work into their Saturday afternoons as I put into my job during the week," he said, stifling a yawn which suggested his charges should be prepared for some busy 90 minutes during the forthcoming 36 weeks. "I know that if it comes to working hard, we will be among the top sides because I work hard and I expect everybody I work with to work bloody hard."

Warnock chose the eve of the season to address the two previously unmentioned issues that had been on the minds of supporters since his arrival. Would his playing tactics embrace the direct methods of the David Kemp era, and would his friendship with chairman Dan McCauley hold up under the strain of a promotion bid?

"Whatever happens, I will be classed for the rest of my career as a long-ball merchant," he conceded. "I'm going to get tarred with that brush, whatever I say or do. I like to let people make up their own minds, but put it this way: I like to see goalmouth action; I love to see goals and chances, crosses, shots and saves. I don't like to see the right-back pass to the centre-half, to the other centre-half, to the left-back. I don't see the point of that. I like to see us get the ball in the other half of the field as quickly as possible and then play football. I like to see wingers take players on; I like centre-forwards to turn and dribble; I like midfielders to make breaks and get in the box and pass or shoot. I do not tell players to lump the ball, whack it up there, aim for the corners, whatever. Just get it over the halfway line as quick as possible and play from there."

Warnock was as unequivocal over his relationship with McCauley, an understandable area of fans' concern. Any fall-out between the pair could precipitate a bigger crisis than that of the previous season between McCauley and Shilton.

Warnock said: "The thing about Dan is that I know deep down he really loves this club and has thrown away a lot of money because of that love. I know he wants me to do well and I also know he knows just what I have given up to try and take Argyle back up – and I have given up an awful lot. I know we'll have arguments because of the nature of the two animals but I also know that within a couple of minutes we'll be able to pick up the 'phone. In this game, you can't have grudges. It excites me more than it worries me because I won't be successful unless Dan backs me all the way and I know Dan will give it everything if he sees it's going in the right direction."

After using 42 players in eight pre-season friendlies, Warnock was satisfied that matters were progressing in the right direction, although he conceded the Piccadilly Circus approach to the campaign – caused by the lapsing of so many players' contracts – was not ideal.

"Someone had to do it, though," he said. "One thing's for sure – it won't happen at this club again. Imagine if I'd still been at Huddersfield. There's no players out of contract, they've just won promotion, everything's going forward – I'd just look for the icing on the cake. Here, I haven't even finished mixing the ingredients, let alone thought about the icing. It's been the most difficult time of my career, I'm not exaggerating."

"THE TIME TO JUDGE US IS AT THE END OF THE SEASON"

PLYMOUTH Argyle's reaction to another new dawn was depressingly familiar: a quick peek through a chink in the curtains, a couple of startled blinks, and then slump back into bed.

There have been less auspicious starts to a successful promotion campaign than a 2-1 defeat at Colchester, but the impressive Green Army which marched on England's oldest town in 90-degree-plus heat must have been hoping for better.

Neil Warnock's new-look Pilgrims possessed the better individuals but were the poorer team: to carry on the manager's cake analogy, what emerged from the oven that was Layer Road was a cream-filled effort that failed to rise to the occasion.

With seven debutants in a side that had never played together – Nicky Hammond, Paul Williams, Ronnie Maugé, Adrian Littlejohn, Chris Leadbitter, Chris Billy, as well as substitute Doug Hodgson – it was unsurprising nothing really clicked. Billy had been a Pilgrim for less than 48 hours.

Warnock's unfamiliar side displayed some all-too-familiar failings as they contributed to their own downfall. The first goal came from a free-kick needlessly conceded and badly defended; the second resulted from some non-existent marking.

Chris Leadbitter at the centre of things against Colchester

It took Colchester 15 minutes to deflate the pre-season bubble of optimism after Keith Hill gave away a free-kick on the edge of the Pilgrims' penalty area. While Hammond was still organising his defensive wall, Colchester defender Simon Betts fired the ball home.

Nevertheless, Argyle bossed proceedings and the game appeared to swing to their advantage 10 minutes after the interval. First, Colchester were reduced in numbers when their captain Tony English was dismissed for a second bookable offence, then Littlejohn equalised in the 55th minute, seizing on Leadbitter's perceptive pass to slip the ball past goalkeeper Carl Emberson.

Within three minutes, though, Colchester re-established a command that was to prove decisive. Adam Locke, pushing out of defence to cover for English, latched onto a midfield breakdown and blasted home a 30-yard drive that Hammond should have had covered.

Despite their superiority of numbers, Argyle could find no way back into the match, although Wayne Burnett was desperately unlucky not to salvage a point when Emberson instinctively plopped on his point-blank drive to smother the ball on the goal-line. Earlier, the impressive Burnett had almost embarrassed Emberson from the second-half restart with a lob from halfway that caught the goalkeeper out of his ground. The ball dropped just over the crossbar as the furiously backpedalling Emberson tumbled into his own net, much to the amusement of his substitute team-mates warming up nearby.

There was precious little laughter in the Argyle dressing-room afterwards as Warnock sent his players to the team-coach with a rather large flea in their collective ear.

"If the lads had done the things they were told to do, there was no chance of us losing," he said. "The game was a lesson to everybody – we're going to have a hard game every week – but I saw a lot of promising things. I know it sounds daft, but I'm quite pleased with the way things went because I know we haven't got owt to fear. As I said to the lads after their rollicking, I know which dressing room I'd rather be in. We've just got to work a bit harder, which we can do now I've got everybody together. The time to judge us is at the end of the season."

No doubt the managers of Preston and Bury, who also succumbed to opening-day defeats, were telling members of the Lancashire Press fraternity something similar.

Despite his assertion that he now had everybody together, when judgment time did eventually arrive at the end of the season, only eight of the 14 players who began the 1995/96 Pilgrimage to Wembley would actually have made it to the Twin Towers.

Another Argyle player who had missed out on Wembley appearances three times in the past – through injury and being cup-tied – made his debut in the next match, a midweek Coca-Cola Cup first-round, first-leg tie at Birmingham City, the previous season's Second Division champions.

Given that the two clubs had invested in 18 new players between them during the summer, it was a mild surprise that Gary Clayton was the only player who had not previously shared a post-match shower with his team-mates. Leadbitter was dropped, giving substance to the speculation that Warnock held him responsible for allowing Locke to score Colchester's winner three days previously.

They say managers create sides in their own image so it was therefore no surprise to see Barry Fry's Birmingham line up with two fast wide-boys – Ricky Otto and Louie Donowa – to which Warnock (alerted by Fry announcing his intentions in early editions of the *Birmingham Evening Mail*) responded by selecting Wayne Burnett in front of the back four.

The conversion of Burnett from a prissy midfielder who had trouble tackling a bowl of cornflakes for breakfast into a deep-lying midfield dog of war had been one of the revelations of Argyle's pre-season and he continued to revel in his pivotal role at St Andrews.

Nevertheless, Burnett was one of the players at fault when Birmingham defender Gary Cooper collected the ball on the halfway line a minute before half-time and rode through some half-hearted tackles before planting the ball firmly past Hammond for the only goal of the match.

Hammond never looked like being beaten again. In what was to turn out to be his finest hour for the Pilgrims, he made several splendid saves which, combined with some backs-to-the-wall defending in the face of extensive home pressure, ensured the enticing possibility of a cup upset in the second leg.

Off the field, Warnock continued to do business. Peter Swan, the club's £300,000 record signing the previous summer, left for Burnley for two-thirds of his original fee, and Chris Twiddy signed a new one-year contract.

Swan, plagued by injury, lack of form and personal misfortune since being signed by Peter Shilton, had made no secret of his loathing for Plymouth, forcing the issue by appearing on television to express those sentiments.

"I knew from day one that the move to Plymouth was totally wrong," he said later. "The whole atmosphere about the place was really poor. It was the worst mistake of my life joining Plymouth Argyle. I started to blame everything on Plymouth. My two dogs died when I was down there and I smashed my cheekbone badly in one match. I was made captain by Peter Shilton instead of Steve Castle. The crowd did not like that and they were on my back straight away. The whole thing was a nightmare and by Christmas I had moved home to Staffordshire. I used to stay down in Plymouth during midweek and travel home after a match just to get away from the place."

"Once Swan had made his intentions clear, there was no point in trying to keep him," said Warnock.

The decision of teenager Twiddy, who made 19 appearances the previous season, to commit himself to the club, left Martin Barlow, Wayne Burnett and injured centre-back Andy Comyn as the only Pilgrims on weekly contracts.

Argyle's first home game of the new campaign could not have been a tougher fixture. Preston, conceded Warnock before the encounter, should have been made favourites to win the division ahead of his own side. Not for the first, or last, time during the season, his reading of the division proved to be entirely accurate.

Warnock further stamped his mark on Home Park by insisting the players took to the pitch to the strains of Tina Turner's power-ballad *Simply the Best*, a song much beloved of football managers.

The change meant ditching Argyle's traditional long-serving club theme *Semper Fidelis*. When the same move had been instigated two seasons before, the club's commercial department, whose idea it was then, quickly restored the ever faithful standard after emerging from under a mountain of critical mail.

Warnock said: "I've got to take the blame, but every promotion season I've had, we've run out to that." For someone who had yet to send out a winning team, he might have been considered at best cheeky to insist his side took to the field to a lyric proclaiming they were "better than all the rest".

"We need a win now, to get the ball rolling," he maintained, "but if it doesn't come, we've just got to keep going until we start. Over a season, the best sides usually go up and I'm more than happy with what I've got. All we have to do is make sure we're there or thereabouts after 46 games."

After two games, they could not have been further away from being there or thereabouts. Following Preston's easy 2-0 win at Home Park on August 19, the incontrovertible evidence of the Endsleigh Third Division table was that Argyle were, on paper, the worst professional team in England. Even harder to bear for most of their supporters, they were the worst professional team in Devon.

If Argyle were going to live up to their pre-season billing as championship favourites, they were now going to have to achieve the title the hard way, by overtaking every other side in the table. Quite a challenge, even for a manager who is fond of pointing out he has never had things easy throughout his career.

The atmosphere before the first home game of the season was strangely reminiscent of 12 months previously as giddy expectation crashed head on into harsh reality and hope was pronounced dead on arrival. At least no idiot prattled on afterwards about things only getting better.

More lamentable defence contributed to the Pilgrims' downfall. Nicky Hammond, the saving saviour of St Andrews, went from hero to zero in the 64th minute when he collected Jamie Squires' corner and then – under no pressure whatsoever – inexplicably threw the ball into the net behind him.

Twelve minutes later, Preston doubled their margin when Ian Bryson sauntered into Argyle's penalty area blissfully unmarked to collect Steve Wilkinson's cushioned header and calmly slide the ball past Hammond.

Despite creating a comfortable number of opportunities in front of goal, Argyle still managed to give the impression they would find it hard to score down Union Street on a Saturday night.

"It's just confidence," insisted Warnock. "If you are not creating chances, you worry, but we are creating chances. It does put pressure on the back lads, though, because somebody makes a mistake and it costs you the game."

Unfortunately, in Nicky Hammond, Argyle had someone only too able to make a mistake. Warnock, though, gave his under-fire goalkeeper a conditional vote of confidence before the Coca-Cola Cup return with Birmingham.

"I said to him that I know, and the whole team knows, the first goal against Preston was his fault, but if we're going to get promotion this season, he's probably going to be the one to win it for us. I wouldn't swap him for anyone in our division."

Neither party believed then that Hammond's Argyle career was approaching its end but Hammond's stock amongst manager and supporters depreciated further as Birmingham took advantage of his frailty to win the Coca-Cola Cup second leg match 2-1, the first-round tie 3-1, and set themselves on the way to the competition's semi-final, where they would eventually lose to Leeds United.

Pilgrims' captain Mick Heathcote briefly levelled the tie in first-half stoppage time but goals from the Blues' Andy Edwards and Jonathan Hunt in the 52nd and 54th minutes ended the Greens' interest in the tie.

Like the Saturday before, the game's killer moment – Hunt's strike direct from a corner – was the result of an unforced error at the near post, goalkeeper Hammond and defender Wayne Burnett leaving each other to deal with a ball which slid between the pair of them.

It was a pity. Victory over a Birmingham side containing two former Pilgrims (Gary Poole and Steve Castle, making his Blues' debut) and the only player in either starting line-up born in Plymouth (former Exeter City midfielder Scott Hiley) would have been sweet.

Unlike the fans, Warnock exonerated Hammond from blame for the goal. "Wayne was there on the near post, but he thought the ball was going out," he said. "I have told him to get his hair cut."

Argyle's failure to pass the Coca-Cola Cup fizzical was of less concern than their league form – two defeats, one goal scored – and their preparations for a potentially difficult trip to Chester were not helped by further off-field problems.

Two days before the visit to the Deva Stadium, the club sacked goalkeeper Alan Nicholls halfway through his two-year contract. The talented, but wayward, former England Under-

21 player who had been dogged by a long-standing knee injury, was dismissed after being twice pulled up over his conduct and warned about bringing the club into disrepute.

An incident which led to Nicholls being charged with drink-driving proved the last straw.

"The boy has got to come to his senses," said Warnock, who had been talking to Gillingham about a possible move before Nicholls' final indiscretion. "His ability is not in question. From a personal point of view, I think he needs to get away from Plymouth and start again."

Chairman Dan McCauley was in agreement. "He could have the world at his feet," he said, "but he has not even got his feet on the ground."

The same accusation could easily have been levelled at Argyle's remaining staff after their visit to Chester completed an unwanted hat-trick of Saturday afternoon league defeats.

"It's getting ridiculous," ranted Warnock after two goals from midfielder Eddie Bishop and a late strike by veteran forward Cyrille Regis gave the home side a 3-1 victory. Paul Williams scored Argyle's lone goal, which briefly levelled the scores early in the second half.

"We are too nice and a soft touch," continued the Argyle manager. "Other teams should be wanting to rearrange games to play us at the moment. We

Keith Hill

are bottom of the league. We have reached the pits. We should be burying teams like Chester but it is not hard to see why Plymouth were relegated last season. Some of the players were just not up to it. You will see exactly what I thought of this performance by the team I pick to play Hereford on Tuesday. My job is to make sure we have 11 lads on the field of play who are willing to die for the club," he continued, ignoring the fact that more than a few supporters would have considered death too good for some of the players.

Warnock went through with his threat to clear out the team he inherited. Wayne Burnett, Chris Twiddy and Keith Hill all failed to dodge the swinging axe, leaving forward Kevin Nugent as the sole survivor from

Kevin Nugent

Peter Shilton's reign when the team took to Home Park to face Hereford.

In came Chris Leadbitter, Doug Hodgson (still loaned from Sheffield United) and Tiverton product Mark Saunders, making his debut at right-back.

New faces, old failings. Once again, Argyle lacked forward penetration and ironic cheers greeted their first shot on target, a 40th-minute long-range shot from full-back Paul Williams which scarcely tested the opposition goalkeeper Chris Mackenzie.

By then, Argyle were in arrears to the goal which eventually decided the match and condemned them to a sixth successive defeat. Once again, Hammond was at fault, flapping hopelessly at a long throw-in by Richard Wilkins, allowing Neil Lyne's flick-on to find the predatory Steve White for a routine tap-in.

Hammond's confidence had by now completely evaporated and it required some desperate defending by Hodgson to prevent Lyne scoring from a Nicky Cross header which rebounded from the crossbar while Hammond remained rooted to the spot, bamboozled by what was going on around him.

Nugent was replaced at half-time by Michael Evans but it was a midfielder – Chris Billy – who came nearest to opening Argyle's home account when he smashed a drive against the crossbar in a frenetic finish. Too little, too late.

Despite the result, Warnock insisted it "was not a night for rollickings. The players gave me 100 per cent and I will not have a go at them if they give me 100 per cent and it does not come off."

However, 100 per cent effort had still done nothing to improve on a 0 per cent return during the month of August and it was unlikely that Bury were shaking in their boots as Argyle prepared for their subsequent gig in Greater Manchester at the weekend.

NW: *I decided to go into the first game with a sweeper. I had looked at the situation and I thought Wayne Burnett was better with no responsibility of marking so I gave him the freedom to come forward or go behind whenever he wanted and link up with the midfield and forwards.*

Obviously, I had to work on the full-backs. They found it strange, especially Mark Patterson, to play in a back five where they didn't have any responsibilities for covering around centre-halves. I found that Mark and Paul Williams didn't get tight enough further up front. I actually wanted them to play further forward than full-back.

We had a lot of the play at Colchester and I think we should have been two or three up before we conceded a stupid goal from a free-kick. To be fair to Nicky Hammond, I think he just gave himself a yard to cover the wall, rather than looking after his own half of the goal, and the lad sneaked it in. We clawed our way back to equalise with a cracking goal in the second half and I thought we would just go on and win it. Then, once again, our defenders Mick Heathcote and Mark Patterson didn't shove up tight enough and let a man forward. You couldn't blame anybody regarding the shot – it just went flying into the top corner – and then we were up against it and ended up losing.

We went to Birmingham in midweek for the first leg of the Coca-Cola Cup and we had by far the best chances during the game and ended up losing 1-0 with another goal just before half-time. The full-back [Gary Cooper] made a run, Chris Billy left him, and he ended up slotting it past Nick. But Nicky played super that night and the chances we had were unbelievable. We are talking about tap-ins from two or three yards out. I thought it was so pleasing at that time to be making the chances.

Then on to Preston, our first home match. I knew it would be a good crowd and I knew Preston would be strong, but we went at them and once again we had a number of chances, four one-on-ones with the 'keeper, but it wasn't going for us. We weren't scoring. In the second half, we sat back a little bit and then Nicky made an obvious clanger. He was that keen on getting the game going, he collected a corner at the near post and wanted to throw it out before he had control of it to start an attack, and he ended up throwing it in the net.

There was nobody near him. So, we were back up against it really and heads went a little bit. We conceded the second goal with 10 minutes to go and that was the end of the story.

The Coca-Cola Cup second leg attracted another good crowd and Micky Heathcote missed an absolute sitter to level the tie and then scored just before half-time to make it 1-1. Really, we should have been two or three up again in that tie.

After five or six minutes of the second half, Birmingham had a corner. We didn't clear the corner and it went back in and Micky had lost his man, which allowed them to equalise. Then, within two minutes, they scored direct from a corner. I think Wayne Burnett thought it was going into the side-netting so he left it; Nicky couldn't get across in time and it went straight in.

So we lost the game and we went on to Chester. It was a red-hot day at Chester, they had started the season by winning every game and we played like we were top of the league and they were at the lower end. Chance after chance again, it was just like a repeat of all that had gone on before.

We couldn't score and chances went begging. We went into the second half and then Paul Williams got an injury. The referee had let two of their lads have treatment during the first half, but Norman went on to see him and the ref wouldn't let him have treatment and told Norman to take him off because he had a cut.

Paul Williams came off and they took the free-kick while he was just leaving the pitch and went down the right wing and crossed it and scored, while Williams was off. Paul came back on a minute later. Norman apologised to me later but he should have just bandaged him up on the pitch and sod the referee.

Then they scored at the death to make the scoreline flattering really. We got a cracking goal back from Paul Williams but they scored near the end to make it 3-1.

So, it came to Hereford at home and I thought "This is it – the last chance for my spare-man system." I thought it didn't matter what system you played, the players will make it, and we had created a load of chances in every game. Once again, we absolutely battered the opposition. I think it was probably the most chances we've had in a game – off the bar, our own men missing chances, you name it. It was quite unbelievable really.

Then they had a long throw on the half-hour. Nicky came for it, trying to make amends, and missed it and the lad just tapped it in. We couldn't get back and it ended up 1-0 again. That was difficult to digest, because they were poor. I could cope with losing the other matches, but I couldn't believe how we could have lost that particular game.

I decided on the night that I was going to leave Nicky out, so I told Kevin Blackwell that he would be playing on the Saturday. I also told Micky Evans after that game that he would be starting up front for me at Bury on Saturday and that he was going to play indefinitely. He didn't have to worry about being dropped because I was going to play him for the next few games irrespective of how he played – all I wanted him to do was to enjoy it. He had been enjoying training, he had been doing well up front but because of Kevin Nugent I had not had a chance to play him with Adrian Littlejohn.

I have got to admit that at the start of the season Kevin was disappointing me, really. He couldn't get an understanding with Adrian and really found it hard work to make headway, although it wasn't for lack of trying. The lad was a super lad and he tried and worked very, very hard in training but just couldn't get a spark.

I had a bath with the players after the Hereford game and Micky, who had been substitute, was the first in the bath with me. I said to him: "You are playing, Saturday, son and you will be playing for a few weeks, so it's up to you." He was obviously chuffed and thanked me and said I wouldn't regret it.

If he played badly on the Saturday at Bury, he wouldn't be dropped. I was going to give him a run in the team when he could play a few games and know he wasn't going to be dropped, whatever happened. I wanted him to go out and enjoy the games like he did the training because he was a credit on the training-ground. He always had a smile on his face and he always did his best.

"I HATE SATURDAYS WHEN THE SUNSHINE IS OUT"

Warnock had already decided to give striker Michael Evans his first start of the season at Gigg Lane on Saturday, September 2 after using him regularly as a substitute during the opening weeks of the spectacularly unsuccessful season.

"I want to have a look at our side with him in," said Warnock of the Plymothian who thought he had done enough to make the number 13 shirt his own, "because with Nugent in, we are playing the ball too long. I want to see us play it more to feet."

While one local lad was back in favour, another seemed as far from Warnock's plans as possible. Martin Barlow, runner-up to Marc Edworthy in the fans' poll for the previous season's player of the year, was having talks with Argyle's Third Division rivals Cardiff City, with Warnock happy to let the out-of-contract midfielder depart.

Warnock also decided to make defensive changes. Mark Patterson, who had been out of touch and out of favour, was restored to the right-back berth in favour of Saunders, and the Argyle manager finally bit the bullet and dropped the hapless Nicky Hammond.

With lack of confidence spreading through the team like a viral epidemic which stemmed from the diseased and diseasy very last line of defence, Warnock knew he had to act swiftly. Out went Hammond and in came Kevin Blackwell.

Blackwell was celebrating his 10th year with Warnock, having first teamed up with the Argyle manager at Scarborough, and had been brought to Plymouth to help establish the youth-team set-up alongside another veteran goalkeeper, Martin Hodge.

At Huddersfield, he had guided the Terriers' young pups to success in the Northern Intermediate League Cup, where they beat Newcastle, as well as providing cover for first-team goalkeeper Steve Francis.

Warnock later confessed that he had not planned for Blackwell to play first-team football for Argyle except in emergencies, although there were many who felt Hammond's form and Argyle's league position before they met Bury constituted more of a crisis than an emergency.

As it turned out, Argyle could have played a green and black pussycat between their posts at Gigg Lane and still come away with all three points. They were 3-0 up by the interval, with goals from Evans, Gary Clayton and Chris Billy, and Blackwell had still not touched the ball by the time Bury defender Ian Hughes was dismissed for a so-called professional foul on Adrian Littlejohn.

Against 10 men, Argyle rubbed in their numerical advantage. Evans, again, and Littlejohn completed the rout. The margin of victory was even more stunning given that Bury had not lost one of their previous 22 home games and it cost the Shakers' manager Mike Walsh his job after five years in charge.

The key to the victory lay in some subtle pre-match psychology by Warnock, who read some unwise bragging by Bury midfielder Shaun Reid in the *Manchester Evening News*. Reid, who had lined up the previous season alongside Ronnie Maugé, claimed he would not allow his former team-mate a kick.

Not only did Warnock throw Maugé a copy of the paper during his pre-match team-talk, he also made him captain for the day in front of his former home crowd. The twin tactic worked to perfection. Maugé was inspirational and it was Reid, rather than the man he had promised to nullify, who failed to make a meaningful contribution.

Maugé put the skids under his old colleagues in the 28th minute when he hooked over a cross that Evans plunged forward to meet; five minutes later, Clayton drove spectacularly past home goalkeeper Lee Bracey whom Warnock had looked at during the previous summer; and in first-half injury time, Billy lifted in the third goal after Littlejohn had headed on a superb cross by full-back Paul Williams.

Hughes departed midway through the second half and provided Argyle with the incentive to go for Bury's jugular. Evans audaciously lobbed Bracey from 30 yards for the fourth and Littlejohn powered home an injury-time shot to complete the nap hand.

Afterwards Maugé, having stomped over his colleagues on his old stomping ground, summed up the Argyle players' determination to right the wrongs of the previous few weeks. "We have the best manager, the best fans and the best team-spirit in the division," he said. "We are determined to win promotion and we see nothing to fear despite our poor start. Plymouth is a big club with big ambitions and we aim to fulfil them."

Maugé's reward for leading Argyle to their overdue first three-point return of the campaign was to be appointed on-field captain by Warnock "every week until we lose."

He said: "Micky Heathcote will be captain in every game whether he has got an armband or not, because he is that kind of player, but Ronnie will wear the armband and take the toss-up. It's been too much pressure on Mick, calling heads or tails," joked Warnock. "He wanted relieving of that sort of responsibility."

Warnock was satisfied enough with his team's up-turn in fortune to allow Wayne Burnett to leave Home Park for a trial at FA Carling Premiership Bolton Wanderers during the following week, at the end of which one of Burnett's former clubs, Leyton Orient, headed West.

Despite the stunning victory at Gigg Lane, Argyle had remained rooted to the foot of the Third Division table but there was every reason to suppose they would be able to double their points tally against the Orienteers, who had not won a league game away from Brisbane Road for nearly two years.

Maugé, having convinced Argyle supporters he had not come to Plymouth to understudy for the Claude Rains role in a Theatre Royal production of the *Invisible Man*, led out an unchanged side to the slightly more believable strains of *Simply the Best*. Up until the previous week, the Pilgrims' punters had been trying to fathom whether the second line of the chorus really did continue "at cocking things up rather spectacularly."

Not for the first time in history, the high expectations of a Home Park crowd were misplaced. Argyle stuttered to their first home point of the season thanks to Michael Evans' 19th-minute goal in a 1-1 draw, and if the fans were unhappy, Warnock was apoplectic.

The Argyle manger vented his spleen against referee Clive Wilkes, whose perceived misdemeanours were to award a penalty against Argyle and then fail to punish a late piece of foul play by Os' goalkeeper Peter Caldwell, and against his players, whom he accused of turning in their worst performance since his arrival.

Wilkes awarded a penalty against Heathcote, for a foul against Danny Chapman in the 65th minute, but Warnock insisted: "He didn't touch him but I knew [the ref] was going to give it before he went down."

The second moment which had the Argyle manager off his feet and going ballistic occurred in the dying moments as Argyle threatened to escape with a victory they did not deserve.

Chris Billy was played through, only to be apparently fouled by Caldwell. No offence was registered by Wilkes, who compounded Warnock's anger by almost immediately blowing for what seemed to be a lesser challenge on Chapman.

"The ref said afterwards that it was a foul but that Billy had dived," raged Warnock. "What difference does it make? If you pirouette or whatever, it's still a foul. It's a sending-off offence, is that."

Chris Billy, about to be upended by Orient's Peter Caldwell

The irony is that neither incident made a difference to the result: Colin West's penalty was brilliantly saved by the blameless Kevin Blackwell and the foul on Billy took place outside the penalty area. Even if Caldwell had been sent off, the way Argyle attacked in the second half would not have threatened the Orient goal enough to concern any temporary goalkeeper.

"We can't afford to play without Billy, Leadbitter and Littlejohn," said Warnock, turning his anger on his own team. "No team's good enough to win with eight players and we had eight players out there today."

The eight players were not enough to prevent substitute Mark Watson, a loanee from West Ham, scoring within seven minutes of coming on for Alex Ingethorpe in the 74th minute. However, all eight appeared to have a chance of clearing Roger Stanislaus's corner before Watson hooked the ball in from two yards.

Nevertheless, for the first time in the season, Warnock and his players were able to buy a Sunday newspaper in which the Third Division League table did not have Argyle at the very bottom. The point had been enough to raise them from 24th place to 23rd. The Pilgrims were progressing at last. Slowly, but they were progressing.

The same could not be said for Burnett's trial at Bolton, which Warnock cut short after learning that Billy and Gary Clayton had picked up injuries in the draw with Orient. Thus, instead of walking out for the Trotters' midweek reserve game against Sheffield United, Burnett was restored to the Pilgrims' line-up for the visit of Doncaster Rovers.

In a similar reverse move, injury-hit Sheffield United recalled centre-back Doug Hodgson from his loan spell at Home Park, meaning an Argyle call-up for Keith Hill, who had registered his frustration at being on the periphery of Warnock's plans by requesting – and being granted – a transfer.

The two former Blackburn players contributed to Argyle's first home victory under Warnock. It might not have been the most sparkling performance, but the 3-1 win continued the Pilgrims' rise up the Third Division table and the final goal alone was worth the price of a season-ticket.

It was a training ground set-piece speciality which came with five minutes to go and Argyle holding on to a precarious 2-1 lead, given them by goals from Michael Evans and Chris Billy.

The Pilgrims won a fortunate free-kick on the edge of Doncaster's penalty area. Burnett shaped to shoot but instead dummied and played a short pass to Evans which totally befuddled the opposition. While Rovers' defenders scratched their heads, Evans played in Adrian Littlejohn behind the wall for a simple conversion. Game over.

It is fair to say – as many lucky managers do – that you make your own luck in football, but Warnock's two enforced team changes had worked in his favour. Burnett had played well (hoping, no doubt, Bolton would take note) and Hill, despite an early *faux pas*, earned praise for his play, and for visiting the barber's in midweek.

"Apart from his mistake, I thought it was the best game I have seen him play," said Warnock, before returning to a theme close to his heart. "I must admit, I like his new haircut. I think it makes him run a yard faster."

The night had not begun so well for the newly coiffured Hill, as Argyle went behind in bizarre fashion in the 11th minute. Ryan Kirby's through ball towards Steve Brodie was comfortably wide of its intended mark for Burnett and Hill to content themselves with merely policing the ball back to goalkeeper Kevin Blackwell.

The policing quickly turned into a Keystone Kops undercover operation as Hill, with impeccable comic timing, waited until the precise moment Blackwell cocked the trigger to boot the ball away before toe-poking it past him into the net.

The set-back merely spurred Argyle's endeavours and they metamorphosed from a shapeless disorganised mess into a potent attacking force. Evans superbly held off Matt Carmichael to finish off Mark Patterson's looping cross; Littlejohn then seized on a splendid forward ball from Chris Leadbitter and squared a low cross from the bye-line which goalkeeper Perry Suckling made a pig of, allowing Billy, who had all-but given up the cause, to convert the chance sitting on his backside in the centre of the goal.

After that, it could have been anything-1 before Littlejohn's late *coup de grace*. "We played with a lot of passion, as well as a lot of skill, craft and class," said a proud Warnock afterwards. "I said to the lads at half-time: 'That's the way Neil Warnock's teams play for 90 minutes.' I think we managed it for nearly the full 90 minutes."

The Pilgrims' bandwagon continued to gain momentum against Barnet the following Saturday, when a 2-1 victory lifted them to halfway in the Third Division table. Burnett was at Barnet, prior to another trial at Bolton, and Hill also took his place at Underhill.

The first half of the game was even; the first 20 minutes of the second even worse before Michael Evans broke the deadlock from the penalty spot in the 69th minute after Chris Billy had been upended by David McDonald. Parity was restored six minutes later when Mark Cooper, sent through by Alex Dyer, lobbed goalkeeper Kevin Blackwell for the equaliser.

After the fuss created by Warnock sacrificing *Semper Fidelis* on the altar of pop, perhaps he would have given some thought to ditching Tina Turner for Vanessa Williams's *Save the Best 'Til Last*. Against Bury and Doncaster, Adrian Littlejohn had produced last-gasp goals of stunning quality and the dose was repeated at Underhill as he linked effectively with Evans to send the Argyle fans back down the M4 bubbling with excitement.

Big defender Linvoy Primus, prematurely celebrating the announcement of his man of the match award seconds earlier, lost the nippy striker for the first time in the game in the 88th minute. Littlejohn was goal-bound in a flash and that was that.

A 1,000-strong Green Army, swollen by a dozen members of the Plymouth-based Bruce Forsyth Appreciation Society, had endured torrential rain but went home happy. After the drenching, it was nice to see their team win. To see it, nice.

Despite a 'flu-bug that swept through Home Park during the subsequent week, Warnock was able to send out an unchanged side for the Pilgrims' visit to Wigan the following Saturday.

They came away from Springfield Park with a 1-0 victory from a match which the manager beamingly described afterwards as "a typical Warnock game" without bothering to elaborate on what he meant.

What he might have meant was that Argyle defended superbly under the cosh, smothered the midfield, and ram-raided the opposition's goalmouth for all three points with little more than 10 minutes remaining.

The game turned on a turbulent four minutes late in the second half. In the 75th minute, Isidro Diaz turned in the box and was flattened by Mark Patterson. Every green shirt froze, waiting for the referee's fickle finger of fate to point to the penalty spot but Wrexham official John Lloyd, clearly unimpressed by the earlier diving antics of the young Spaniard and his countryman Roberto Martinez, gave Patterson the benefit of doubt and Argyle breathed a collective sigh of relief.

The Pilgrims capitalised on their good fortune within minutes when Paul Williams' lofted free-kick fell kindly for Michael Evans. Evans' drive was blocked by goalkeeper Simon Farnworth but Adrian Littlejohn was on hand to snaffle up the loose for his fifth goal in nine league games.

Although the Latics were left counting the costa not having anyone to finish off the approach play of Diaz and Martinez, the Argyle back four did enough to leave goalkeeper Kevin Blackwell thinking he would have been more fully employed spending an afternoon in his garden.

For the first time since the season had kicked off, Argyle, having collected 13 points from the previous 15 up for grabs – nine on their travels – were in the top half of the table.

NW: *We went up to Bury with everybody tipping us to get beaten. We had now gone from 10-3 favourites to something like 14-1 with certain bookies. You could understand why – we were already 12 points behind Gillingham.*

We went up to Bury and I decided to make Ronnie Maugé captain because he had a lot of supporters who liked him at Bury, some of who didn't want to see him go, and I thought it would be a nice gesture for Ronnie to lead the lads out. Not only did we play differently to any other game, our chances went in. Micky Evans' first goal came from a cross when he slid in. We had never had anybody sliding before.

The second goal was a cracking goal from Gary Clayton, a volley from a full 30-yards-wide position. He knew exactly what he was doing and it was a cracking goal. After that we just took off and enjoyed every minute of it. We scored five but it could have been more.

I brought Wayne Burnett back. The week after the Bury game we played Orient and, if I am honest, I think that that was our worst performance of the season. I thought it was very drab. It was quite warm again – I hate Saturdays when the sunshine is out – and it was a nothing sort of game. There wasn't a lot of passion and it was like a typical end of season game.

We managed to get in front and I thought it would be nice if we were lucky and could get a 1-0 win but they equalised. Dougie Hodgson made a cock-up clearing his line and they equalised. Then they almost went and snatched their first away victory in 40-odd games but we hung on for the point.

That was Dougie Hodgson's last game for us. He had played a few games on loan for us when Sheffield United called him back. I was going to try to sign him but they changed the figures again – the same as they did with Adrian Littlejohn. I was told they wanted to get their money back, which was around £30,000, and then I had a telephone call from Dave Bassett, who was abroad. He wouldn't take less than £80,000.

I said that I just wanted to look at him for another month and they agreed but they had a couple of bad injuries on the Saturday, so on the Sunday morning I got a call from Dave Bassett saying that they would like him back the following day and I had no option but to agree with that.

I had put Keith Hill on the transfer list, and said it was better for him that he found another club but Hodgson going back gave him another chance in the side. Martin Barlow hadn't impressed me in the reserve games, but I only had Cardiff asking after him and he actually went up and spoke to them but wasn't really impressed about moving.

His attitude wasn't very good in training and I decided to pull him aside and said to him that people hadn't been rushing in to sign him and I felt that he would be better saying to himself every morning when he came in for training, that he was going to show me that he was better than what I'd got and that he deserved a game – whether it's running or shooting, he should set his stall out to be the best in the training session. If he did that then, if he changed his attitude, I would consider him.

He agreed because I think he was disappointed that nobody had come in for him. His attitude changed and I think from that time on I decided to consider him for selection, although he didn't get in straight away.

We then had a Tuesday game against Doncaster, a team who had only conceded two goals away from home all season until the previous Saturday. We didn't know how they played, so we got the team-sheet and thought they would play with the back-five, including a sweeper, and it turned out they did just that.

I gave our instructions to the front three – Chris Billy, Micky Evans and Adrian Littlejohn – to go all over the show and be thorns in the side and enjoy it. We ended up winning 3-1 but it was the way we won that pleased me. It was also very pleasing that the last goal was a well-worked set-piece which we had worked on in training. It was great to see that go in.

The crowd was good that night. It was a great night for football – greasy on top from the dew. I always think the crowd look great at Home Park when it is a night match.

Then we went to Barnet the following week. Another great following – the London Branch were out in force. It absolutely bucketed down, and when we did the warm-up before the game the lightning was the worst I have known. We were warming up on the pitch and I was afraid for the players, thinking back to my days when John White got struck by lightning, so I took them off after two or three minutes.

Our supporters stood out there with the rain absolutely bucketing down on them and they never shut up from start to finish. They were marvellous.

We scored first from a penalty when Chris Billy got pulled down with 20 minutes to go, then we gave an equaliser away almost immediately. Micky Heathcote left his man and Mark Patterson let a man get a cross in and before we knew where we were, it was one each.

Instead of going back in our shells, we went forward and attacked and did our best to get back in. We were rewarded by Adrian Littlejohn, seizing on to great ball from Micky Evans late on, and ended up winning 2-1 which was a great result for us.

We went over to the supporters at the end of the game. They were absolutely drenched and I made sure that the lads went right back over. The supporters were marvellous and I am convinced that they were one of the reasons why we got the winning goal after Barnet equalised. I knew that it was important after the Doncaster game to get maximum points, so that we didn't get too far adrift.

Then we went up to Wigan and it was there that we had a bit of good fortune, although I felt we deserved to win. We missed chances and they never really had a shot in 90 minutes but, with about 15 minutes to go, they had what I thought was a certain penalty.

Wigan's two Spaniards had been diving about all afternoon and whether the referee had had enough of it, I don't know, but one got pulled down by Mark Patterson in the box and it did look a certain penalty from where I was. Then we had a cracking move with about seven or eight minutes to go. Micky Evans turned tremendously in the box, good shot, good save.

Our most pleasing goal so far was finished by Adrian Littlejohn being there to clip it over the 'keeper for the rebound which gave us three valuable points.

Argyle's next match was a home Auto Windscreens Shield preliminary round group match against Second Division Peterborough, which was lost 3-0. A measure of how seriously Warnock treated the competition can be gleaned from the team he put out – James Dungey, Paul Wotton, Dominic Richardson, Micky Ross, Simon Dawe and Chris Twiddy all made rare first-team appearances – and the fact that he spent the night away from Home Park running the rule over Bristol City striker Ian Baird.

A combination of miserable weather, the attractions of Liverpool and Manchester United on television, and the sheer unattractiveness of a competition sponsored by manufacturers of spare parts for cars, proved enough to keep fans away in their thousands.

The 1,682 who braved pneumonia saw Argyle put up a good performance but they were ultimately outclassed by the higher division team. Victory over Northampton in their other group match would still see them qualify for the second stage of the competition. The question was: did they really want to?

Warnock, it seemed was more concerned with his players' hairstyles than the possibility of adding to a crammed fixture list by being successful in the Auto Windscreens Shield. In his next popular *Warnock's World* weekly column for Plymouth's evening newspaper, the *Herald*, he revealed – wait for it – that Chris Twiddy had joined the shaven-locked brigade.

Inspecting Chris Twiddy's new haircut

"It brings back memories of my mum getting the basin out of the bottom cupboard," he wrote, in a revelation that would have had psychologists nodding sagely. "The only problem with our basin was that it had a chip in it – I used to lose a bit of hair in certain places I didn't want to."

There was rather more important news than Twiddy's crop in that edition of the paper, however. Not only was Twiddy's hair gone, so, too, was forward Kevin Nugent, who had moved to Bristol City in exchange for £75,000 and the services of Ian Baird, whom Warnock had watched in preference to the midweek defeat by Peterborough.

Nugent, who was Peter Shilton's first Argyle signing at the end of the 1991/92 season, when he paid Leyton Orient £200,000 for his services, had not played for Argyle since the fourth game of the season, after which he had been unable to displace a resurgent Michael Evans.

Baird, a 31-year-old whose experience with the likes of Southampton, Leeds, Newcastle, Portsmouth, Middlesbrough and Hearts allowed journalists to religiously use the words "veteran striker" before his name, had also enjoyed a less-than-auspicious start to the season. Bristol City manager Joe Jordan had transfer-listed him after he responded to crowd barracking during a pre-season friendly against Chelsea by flicking the Vs at Ashton Gate supporters.

Baird was joined in the home dressing-room by Kevin Magee, a Scottish winger who had been released by Preston North End after failing to win a new contract. Magee had taken apart Mark Patterson when the Lilywhites had whitewashed Argyle earlier in the season, which Warnock had obviously remembered, although subsequent displays by both players indicated this was probably due more to poor form on Patterson's part than good form by Magee.

Baird made an immediate impact as Argyle ended September as they had begun it, with a thumping no-nonsense victory. Bottom-of-the-table Lincoln City proved no match for the back-to-strength Pilgrims, who raced into a 3-0 lead within 19 minutes of the kick-off and held that score-line until the end of the game.

Former Exeter City defender Jason Minett set them on their way with a powerfully headed own goal from Michael Evans' cross. Minett, wary of debutant Baird stealing in behind him, attempted to clear the measured delivery but succeeded only in scoring one of the best headed goals at Home Park all season.

Within two minutes, Evans doubled the lead, racing on to Mick Heathcote's headed clearance from deep inside his own half, holding off the impish attentions of a visiting defender, and striking a sweet shot past goalkeeper Andy Leaning.

Opposition manager Steve Wicks greeted the goal the same way as Argyle supporters, by leaping off his seat, but, while the home fans were acclaiming the goal, Wicks was raging at the referee for allowing it to stand. Adrian Littlejohn had been clearly offside when Evans took Heathcote's pass, but, since he was returning from a previous run, he was deemed to be a "non-active" participant in proceedings.

Littlejohn was entirely active for the third goal, finishing off an intricate passing move at which Baird was at the centre to curl a sweet left-foot shot past a falling Leaning and into the far corner of the goal.

A more purposeful second-half performance from Lincoln and some fine goalkeeping by Leaning ensured the score-line remained respectable.

Magee made his Pilgrims debut with two minutes to play when he came on as substitute for surprise inclusion Martin Barlow. Barlow, who had been unable to claim a place in the very much second-string Pilgrims side which had lost to Peterborough in midweek, had rejected a move to Cardiff despite Warnock hinting strongly that he had no future at Home Park. The popular theory behind his shock inclusion in the first team was that another club was interested in signing him and wanted to see him in league action.

NW: *I could see Micky Evans was enjoying himself so much and in training his finishing was super. However, I needed to look around for cover when we got an injury to Chris Billy, Evans or Littlejohn but I didn't see much about, if I'm honest.*

We looked at Andy Mutch and I think if I could have found a Ronnie Jepson it would have been ideal. Kevin Nugent had told me that Bristol City manager Joe Jordan was the only manager that had rung him in the summer asking about him. I had noticed that he had been trying to sign one or two strikers to no avail, so I rang Joe and asked him about Nugent and said that we were looking to change things. They were struggling as well, so I asked him about Ian Baird, who I knew had a problem with the crowd there and who I thought was a good professional.

Joe thought he was a good professional but he had no future at the club because he had gesticulated rudely to the crowd and they were on his back. With them being interested in Kevin Nugent and struggling, I thought there could possibly be a deal there so I went to watch him play for Bristol City's reserves at Clevedon one night with Sharon. After about five minutes, I turned to Sharon and said "That's enough for me, I've seen enough but we'll hang on and go at half-time to make it look as though we are not interested" and that was exactly what we did.

I saw enough in the first five minutes to know that Baird could do for me what Ronnie Jepson did for me at Huddersfield. I needed an old head to talk to referees, etc. I think also the way that Ian is, he gets two or three defenders aware of him all the time which I don't think is a bad thing. It takes pressure off the other lads.

We did go at half-time and yes, they did ring us and said to us: "You went early, you obviously didn't really like what you saw." I said: "No, he didn't do very well, if I'm honest, but we will see how things go and if we can do some sort of deal."

They paid £300,000 for him and they valued him at around £125,000. We wanted £75,000 and Baird for Nugent. They said that was a bit too much but, needless to say, they came back and then did the deal within a space of about a week.

I also missed out the Auto Windscreens Shield in which we played Peterborough at home before we visited Northampton away in November. In our situation and the division we were in, we were not going to win the Autoglass so I decided to try to give a game to four or five lads who hadn't had previously had one.

I decided to play Martin Barlow, who hadn't had a game, and see how he went but he picked up 'flu so he didn't play anyhow and we ended up losing 3-0. I must say I didn't even watch the game. I went up to watch Ian Baird play at Oxford and what a terrible place to park it was. It was bucketing down with rain. It was a 7.45 p.m. kick-off and we got there at 7.50 p.m. and had to walk about a mile and a half to get in because we couldn't get a car park pass.

We got in the ground eventually, having gone to three different ticket-offices, and there is terracing at the back of the goal as you walk in at Oxford. So Sharon and I stood with the supporters in the first half. As we walked up the stairs there was a big roar and, of course, Oxford had scored. We'd missed a goal. So I said to a chap: "1-0, eh?" He said: "No pal, 3-0." I said: "You what?" We had missed three goals in 12 minutes. Poor old Bairdy – he never had a look-in. In fact, if you looked at him play in that game, you wouldn't have touched him. Having said that, to be fair, you wouldn't have touched anybody in that game.

I still decided to get on with it and, if anything, that helped me clinch the deal, because I think Ian Baird knew that he had to get away from them and I think that they knew that they wanted a new player, a new face, in Kevin. So it worked both ways.

I thought we needed experience and I thought "Well he is the right one for me." By all accounts his attitude was good. All right, he had got a bit of a reputation on the pitch but I quite liked the idea of that because I think we had got too many nice lads and if anything I thought he would be just what we needed.

I telephoned Joe Jordan back and tried to get the deal going again and he agreed to get Ian Baird down to speak to us on the Tuesday.

I told him that I felt at his age, and with him not having to move house, that it was an ideal move for him and also we had got a lot of young lads with good legs who would complement him. I think he was quite excited at the prospect but his terms at Bristol were a lot more than we were prepared to pay. I think Ian realised that it was important for him to play first-team games, which he wasn't doing at Bristol, and that he knew about me and my teams and I got him interested in wanting to play for us.

Ian said "Yes" to me, and took a drop in wages and then it was down to Kevin. It didn't take long, although Kevin took a bit of persuading, and we ended up doing the deal just before lunchtime on the Friday – £75,000 for him and Kevin Nugent went the other way.

Training was good that week. I kept it short and sharp because the lads were putting so much into the games together that I had to make them hungry for Saturday.

If I had let them train every day of the week, they would have done. They were putting that much in, so I had to restrict training and at one stage we were just training on Tuesdays, Thursdays and Fridays before a game, but the quality of training was unbelievable at the early stage of the season.

That Saturday, we played Lincoln and beat them 3-0 at home. I had asked Micky Evans, who had done well up front, to play a wider role but, having said that, they came with five defenders at the back so I told Micky to go all over the show after a couple of minutes.

It was marvellous because we were three up after 20 minutes, some good goals, a well-worked free-kick again and cracking goals, and it was nice to relax just knowing that the points were in the bag. But you get greedy as a manager and I wanted more goals. To be fair to the lads, they did try. They weren't being selfish and shooting when they should have been passing – it was obvious to me that they all wanted to score more goals. The goalkeeper pulled off some brilliant saves; we hit the bar; we missed a few good chances; but we couldn't add to the score.

We'd have settled for 3-0 before the game, and I don't like bottom-of-the-league games because you can't really gain anything. Everybody expects you to win and I knew they were going through a dramatic time, but on the day, we more than deserved the victory. I think we could have got 10 that day. I thought the players were quite superb.

The Pilgrims proved they were now on an irresistible roll the following week, when they rolled over Fulham with utter disdain at Home Park. The score was again 3-0 and Warnock proved what astute business the Baird-for-Nugent transfer deal had been as his new striker scored twice: how he managed to acquire a better player and £75,000 in exchange for Nugent, only he will know.

Warnock's transfer dealings were the subject of Fulham manager Ian Branfoot's post-match Press conference, in which he confessed he had been dreading facing Argyle. He might have been speaking for all his Endsleigh Third Division peers.

Branfoot was sarcastically of the opinion that Warnock's achievement in taking Argyle from 24th in the division to fourth within seven games was largely attributable to chairman Dan McCauley's undeniably generous backing.

His envious remarks did not bear close scrutiny. For a start, however much money a manager has available, he has to have the sense and ability to spend it wisely. Supporters of Liverpool, Wolverhampton Wanderers and Derby County – to name three clubs which have heavily backed managers with large pots of cash in recent seasons – know that money alone does not guarantee success, otherwise Graeme Souness, Graham Taylor and Roy McFarland would have been successful Premiership managers.

Secondly, of the 14 players on first-team duty against Fulham, three were free transfers (Kevin Blackwell, Chris Leadbitter and Gary Clayton); three were products of the Pilgrims' youth set-up (Martin Barlow, Michael Evans and Chris Twiddy); two were at the club before he arrived (Mark Patterson and Keith Hill); and one was on trial (Kevin Magee).

Moreover, with Wayne Burnett set to end his schizophrenic existence as both a North West Premiership reserve and South West Endsleigh League first-teamer by signing for Bolton, Warnock was still ahead of the market in terms of transfer fees. Although, in fairness to Branfoot – and McCauley – much of his £1/2m paper profit was likely to be used up in signing-on fees and higher-than-average Third Division wages.

"People should not think we have £500,000 to spend," said Warnock. "If we did have that sort of money we wouldn't be in the situation we are in, i.e. financially dependent on the

chairman. We are losing a lot of money each week. When I came down here, the chairman and his directors agreed to let me have a wage-budget. At the moment, I am probably £70,000 to £90,000 over it for this season. At a time when most relegated clubs would be cutting their wage bills, credit must go to the chairman and directors for allowing me to carry on as we are.

"I would not have come to Argyle unless I thought we had a good chance of attracting good players. Those we have brought to

Making a point to the referee, against Fulham

the club are not just short-term buys to get us out of the Third Division. Most of them could hold their own in a higher division. That is an added bonus. I don't think we have thrown money away stupidly."

Warnock's most expensive signing, £200,000 Adrian Littlejohn opened proceedings against empty Fulham with a carbon-copy of the training-ground rehearsed goal he scored in the dying moments of the home match with Doncaster Rovers.

He won a 20th-minute free-kick just outside the penalty area which Keith Hill shaped to thump over a defensive wall that included interloper Littlejohn. Instead, Chris Leadbitter played a diagonal pass to Michael Evans, who knocked it into the path of his strike-partner as he span out of a wall cowering in expectation of Hill's blast. Presumably Fulham's relative poverty precluded the employment of scouts to watch their forthcoming opponents.

Ian Baird added the second three minutes later, receiving Mark Patterson's pass after the full-back had torn apart the cover with a 50-yard run. Baird obeyed the striker's maxim of "one-touch to control, two to shoot" and Fulham goalkeeper Tony Lange was powerless to prevent his debut goal. Baird's second was altogether less complicated, a sweetly struck direct 77th-minute free-kick which fizzed past Lange and riffled the back of the netting while the goalkeeper was still in mid-air.

"I have been looking for someone like him for a long time," said Warnock, of veteran striker Baird, "and I think he needed us as much as we need him, if I'm honest. His career was going nowhere and I think it might have been over for him at the end of the season. Now he has got something to lift him."

And he had lifted the Pilgrims to within a point of second-placed Chester and five points of surprise early-season leaders Gillingham. If it was difficult to see where the Pilgrims' first victory was coming from six weeks previously, it was now impossible not to imagine them winning promotion – at the rate they were accumulating points, probably by mid-March.

Delighted with the win over Fulham, Warnock told his players when they racked up for training the following Monday that he would select the same side for the following Saturday's visit to Mansfield.

"I've never done that at such an early stage before," he admitted, "but there is no point in changing things just for the sake of it."

His contentment with the settled squad allowed him to look at off-loading players. Goalkeeper Nicky Hammond, the man most likely to win Argyle promotion whom Warnock would not swap for anyone a few weeks earlier, was made available on loan, and Sam Shilton, son of former manager Peter, was the subject of transfer talks with Coventry City, where his old man was on short-term contract and where Shilton junior had spent two weeks on trial.

Meanwhile, former Argyle goalkeeper Alan Nicholls signed for the Pilgrims' Third Division promotion rivals Gillingham after a successful trial. Argyle, who had cancelled Nicholls' contract but kept his registration, covered themselves by agreeing to the transfer on condition they would receive 20 per cent of any future transfer fee.

The mood of optimism surrounding Home Park transferred itself to the junior sides, with the reserves becoming the first team to stiff Bournemouth and the youths trouncing Bristol City 9-1, and the general feeling was the team which represented the biggest threat to the Pilgrims carrying off the Third Division title was not Gillingham or Preston, but Argyle themselves.

Having disposed of Lincoln and Fulham with an assuredness that made shelling peas appear a complex task by comparison, the danger they now faced was tripping up on the cloak of confidence in which they were swathed. However, Warnock realised the line between arrogance and confidence is a slender one and urged caution from players and supporters alike on the eve of their Stag hunt.

"We are sometimes not going to play at our best and will have to scratch around for points," he said. "That will show what sort of a side we are. Mansfield are not a soft touch. To be honest, I would settle for a point, although we will be going all out to win."

Warnock's sensible pre-match philosophy was rewarded as the Argyle manager and his merry men left the forest of Nottingham with a point hewn from the face of rock-hard opposition still on a high after their 6-2 demolition of Wigan a week earlier.

Argyle took the lead through Mick Heathcote in the ninth minute but were pegged back by Simon Ireland's short-range header on the half-hour and although both sides traded blows throughout an exciting second half, 1-1 was how it ended.

Martin Barlow, still being trailed by an unnamed club from a higher division (Oxford and Charlton were media favourites), provided the delivery for Heathcote's opener, floating over a free-kick which picked out the Argyle club captain's unmarked run into the penalty area. Heathcote used the time and space accorded him by Mansfield's defence to bat his header past a despairing Ian Bowling.

Warnock admitted after such a positive start that he was "a little disappointed we didn't go on and win it" and certainly Argyle did appear to call off the hounds, allowing the Stags to draw second breath. Twenty minutes later, Argyle's defence let them down for the first time in nearly five hours of league football, losing concentration at the vital time to allow Ireland to convert a cross by Manchester City loan-signing David Kerr.

Either side might have won the match in an even second-half. Argyle's best chance came from a 72nd-minute penalty appeal after Michael Evans was treated to a five-second bear-hug by Bowling which referee Kevin Lynch interpreted as a show of affection, while, at the other end, Paul Williams and Mark Patterson headed goal-bound shots off the line.

Argyle had duly scratched out a point, and remained fourth in the table, behind, in ascending order, Preston, Chester and Gillingham.

NW: *Fulham was an even game for 10 or 15 minutes. We attacked, with them playing an extra defender again against us, and then we scored two in about a minute. They were cracking goals and the lads were full of themselves. They were enjoying it, so were the crowd, and they were doing everything I had asked of them. We ended up winning 3-0.*

I was disappointed after the game when I went into the Press conference to hear that Ian Branfoot, who is a mate of mine from the past, said that if he had got the money I had had, he would be top of the league. It's all right saying that but I have always generated profits at clubs I've been at regarding transfer fees, I was £400,000 up at that time with the possible £100,000 for Wayne Burnett to come in on my dealings so far and I had got lads who I thought were worth a lot more money than we had paid for.

I thought I had looked after the club both ways, and that it was a case of sour grapes from Ian, something he shouldn't have said about another manager. I don't think so anyhow.

The other point is, it's all right having money, but spending it is not always easy and you don't always spend it on the right players. I was very pleased with the players I'd got, because most of the players I got I would have tried to sign at Huddersfield if I had stayed there, and they were in the First Division.

I had been told Plymouth was a very difficult place to get players to come and although it was, I think it was nice that the players who I would have signed at Huddersfield, came to listen to what I had to say and decided to throw their lot in with me.

I don't think there was a player I really wanted that I didn't get and when it came down to it, the chairman was super, irrespective of odd stories that were flaring up in the papers about wage-bills. Behind the scenes, he was brilliant with me.

All right, we had little hiccups, but with two personalities like Dan and myself, you are going to get that in any healthy situation. The way we are both made, we are going to have disagreements. But, within a matter of hours of any disagreements that we had, we both washed our anger away and the next day we were all right again.

Then we went up to Mansfield. We knew that was going to be hard because I know Mansfield inside out. We started off the best we had ever played. The first 15 or 20 minutes was unbelievable. We went 1-0 up with a free-kick again, but then we allowed them back in through a bit of sloppy defending. In the second half, we could have won the game but then we hung on for the last 20 minutes. We had to defend, probably the best defensive 20 minutes we had ever had – on a par with Birmingham. Everybody defended well and we managed to keep our unbeaten run going.

Against Mansfield, Martin Barlow had just come back into the side and was playing too many short passes and they were getting cut off and I went to the lad and I said to him jokingly: "Martin, I don't want you playing too much football like that – you'll get me a bad reputation."

The hotel we stopped at up at Mansfield was red-hot all though the night. I felt terrible on the Saturday. I didn't want to give the players an excuse, but it's not a hotel we would be stopping at again.

One of my old players, Tommy Johnson, who I sold to Derby for £1.35m had moved to Aston Villa, and he popped in at the hotel on Friday to see Mark Patterson, his old team-mate, and we had a laugh because Mark had said to Dan McCauley before I was appointed, if Warnock came as manager he would have to go from what he had heard about him.

I ribbed Tommy Johnson, because it must have been him that told Mark those things but, it was all light-hearted.

"THAT'S WHAT MANAGERS DO AT NIGHT TIME, WATCH CORONATION STREET"

IF a point had been acceptable to Warnock against Mansfield, he knew that nothing less than three points would satisfy Argyle's Green Army from their subsequent game the following Saturday – the first of the season's four Devon derbies, against Torquay United.

Before taking on Torquay, both manager and chairman had to take care of other business. Warnock agreed to sell Sam Shilton to Coventry for a fee which could rise as high as £300,000 in the unlikely event of the teenage midfielder following in his dad's stud-marks and playing for England. The initial fee was a more realistic £12,500.

Meanwhile, Dan McCauley was in dispute with fellow director Denis Angilley. McCauley claimed Angilley, a board member for four years, had resigned by taking back a £50,000 guarantee he made when appointed: Angilley insisted he had not sought the return of the interest-free guarantee.

"He has resigned," said McCauley. "If he hasn't, I will sack him anyway because he's taken his money out of the club."

Angilley retorted: "I have not resigned. Sackings and resignations are matters for the board. I, and other directors, have been trying to meet with the chairman since July but, despite repeated requests, I keep getting stonewalled. The chairman obviously hasn't had my most recent correspondence in which I was begging him for a meeting – anytime, anywhere."

McCauley said Angilley had told him eight weeks previously "he felt he should have his money back" and, consequently "as he has no money in the club, he has relinquished his position as a director."

The Argyle chairman also revealed he was annoyed with his other fellow directors. "I just don't feel they are doing enough work or putting enough money into the club as compensation for the work they are not doing," he said. "I think a directorship of the club is worth more than a £50,000 guarantee."

He estimated that the £50,000 deposit would accrue around £40 a week interest if invested in a bank. "That is what they are losing each week for their investment in the club" said McCauley, "but in return they are getting a place on the board; four seats in the directors' box; food before and after the game; and the possibility of away travel.

"The benefits they derive far exceed their investments and I don't see why directors' positions on the board should be subsidised by the club."

As it turned out, both McCauley and Angilley took their seats at Home Park for the South Devon Derby (although McCauley did express the opinion "How he has got the gall to appear when he has got no money in the club, I don't know") in which Warnock was prepared to stick the knife into a club which had provided him with one of his sweetest memories of the Beautiful Game.

Warnock had worked at Plainmoor at the end of the 1992/93 season. Although he was officially "consultant" to the Gulls' inexperienced manager Paul Compton, Torquay's future – indeed, their whole viability as a professional league club – rested entirely with the former Scarborough and Notts County manager during the last three months of the campaign.

A victory at faraway Carlisle in United's penultimate game ensured they avoided relegation to the GM Vauxhall Conference and probable extinction. The success had Warnock reaching for the *Kleenex*.

"I cried," he admitted. "I mean tears, proper tears. The kids gave everything for me. I am convinced they would have gone out of the league if I wasn't there. That's how bad it was. Torquay gave me a big lift when I needed it. I was disillusioned after leaving Notts County and to get a response from lads on £100 a week, as opposed to £100,000 a year, was great. It helped me in my own personal battle. It was a marvellous three months, probably one of the happiest parts of my career. The supporters were brilliant: the commitment from the players was superb; everything was great."

Warnock recommended Don O'Riordan to Torquay chairman Mike Bateson as his successor and departed to Huddersfield content that he had left the club in safe hands. However, Torquay were struggling again, second from bottom of the Third Division, with the Conference trap-door beginning to creak ominously again.

Conversely, Argyle were now unbeaten in eight league matches – surely an enviable position for Warnock to be approaching his first West Country Derby from?

Well, no actually. "If I had a choice, I'd be going into this game – just this game – in Don's boots," said Warnock on the eve of the match. "No-one fancies them; they got beat 4-0 last week, while we got a good draw; their position in the league, our position in the league; they're away, we're at home – everything is in our favour, but I've been in the game long enough to know that when everything's supposed to go as it does, it doesn't.

"More than ever, my build-up has centred on the pitfalls of playing in a Derby. Derbies are a huge leveller. They are twice as hard physically and mentally as any other game. Everyone will be giving their all."

And how. For once, the actuality matched – no, bettered – the hype and anticipation. The October 21 West Country Derby was the the one which nearly appeared as a story-line in *Roy of the Rovers* but was rejected as being too implausible: a hat-trick; seven goals; nine bookings; a sending-off; incident from the eighth minute to the 88th, all played out under the most perfect azure sky.

True to Warnock's pre-match prediction, the form-book followed its usual pre-Derby journey on a parabolic arc out of the window and the 11,695 who packed into Home Park witnessed a match between two sides made equal by their determination to prevail.

Argyle won the game in the final five minutes when Adrian Littlejohn completed a hat-trick of left-foot strikes to give the Pilgrims a 4-3 win which kept their promotion drive in top gear. However, Torquay did their best to try and remove the wheels and Warnock would have been happy to discover that his players had the stamp of a side seemingly destined to win promotion – they could triumph in games in which they were palpably second-best.

Littlejohn's match-clincher came six minutes after Ronnie Maugé had levelled the score for the third time in a game of wildly fluctuating fortunes, but Torquay's tremendous support will still tell you the game was effectively up in the 64th minute, when their captain Ian Gore was sent off.

His two-booking dismissal would have been fairly run-of-the-mill for any referee – foot-up on Argyle goalkeeper Kevin Blackwell, who made an unnecessary meal of the challenge, and a tackle from behind on Littlejohn – and he stood no chance of leniency from Oxford official Bob Harris, who took another eight names including O'Riordan's for "waving an

Mark Patterson and Scott Partridge

imaginary flag" at a linesman who did not even see his impromptu semaphore.

Torquay were 3-2 in front at the time and for the next 15 minutes it was impossible to tell at a glance which side was playing a man short. As it seemed the Gulls would hold on, Argyle's spirit and greater numbers told. Substitute Kevin Magee smacked a cross to the far post, from where Maugé cracked a downward volley past goalkeeper Ashley Bayes.

Warnock's touch-line urgings immediately cranked the Green machine into overdrive. He implored Blackwell to put it in the mixer and the goalkeeper obliged with an upfield punt that Ian Baird and Maugé helped into the path of Littlejohn, whose blinding pace left Lee Barrow standing and whose rapier thrust had precisely the same effect on Bayes.

Even after the goal, Torquay might have snatched some consolation when Blackwell, who was beaten as many times in the first 45 minutes as he had been in the previous six matches, made a hash of Chris Curran's corner. However, no-one was on hand to convert the opportunity.

Earlier, the Gulls had refused to flap after Littlejohn had booted Argyle into an eighth-minute lead when he finished off a five-man move ("Careful, lads, you'll give me a bad name," joked 'long-ball merchant' Warnock afterwards) and within 15 minutes they had taken the lead through two goals from Jamie Ndah.

Littlejohn levelled within a quarter of an hour after Chris Leadbitter played an unintended one-two with himself, notching his ninth goal in nine games and reaching double-figures for the season, but Torquay were back in front by the half-time interval.

The Gulls' third goalscorer was Scott Partridge, who converted Rodney Jack's cross with such ferocity that, although Blackwell got a full hand to the ball, he could not deflect it from its path. Although Torquay did not score again, the strike was not to be Partridge's last goal at Home Park.

Torquay could rightly claim they deserved to win a throbbing game but Warnock knew that you did not always get what you deserve in football. You often get what you work for, though, and Argyle worked for the points, which satisfied him.

"It's a team game and we won as a team," he enthused afterwards, an observation backed up by hat-trick hero Littlejohn.

"We weren't on our game today," said the striker, "but we battled through it. That's what it's all about at the end of the day – helping each other out."

His assistance to the common cause was a stunning hat-trick which he made sound simpler than winning a gold medal at the Log-Falling-Off World Championships.

Adrian Littlejohn celebrates his hat-trick against Torquay

"The first one, I'm not sure how the ball popped up to me. I felt the geezer [Barrow] pulling at my shirt and I just struck it to the far post. The second one, Chris [Leadbitter] was running through and juggled it between his legs. I took it off him and just struck it. The third one, Ronnie [Maugé] did great for me. He flicked it into my stride and I just hit it."

NW: *I had had a couple of triallists down, Kevin Magee, who had ripped Mark Patterson to pieces for Preston against us in the first home match, came down on a month's trial and did well. The lad's a diabetic and had to inject himself with insulin every day, and his attitude was spot on. You have got to admire players like that.*

Young Dominic Richardson had started to come through from the juniors, scoring six goals in one game, so I had had a chat with him and told him that he should be pushing for the first-team before the end of the season. I also decided then that Rossy [Micky Ross], who was a credit and a super example as a professional, could go out on loan, which would let him have some first-team games, and young Dominic needed to play in the Reserves.

At that stage Sam Shilton had gone. It had taken two weeks' negotiations with Big Ron [Atkinson] at Coventry, to do that. They wanted him for nothing and we weren't prepared to do that. In the end, we got £12,500 cash up front and then a deal which could net £300,000 depending on appearances. Which really is all you can expect for a young lad.

We had offered him a two-year contract because I think he will make a good living out of the game, but obviously for personal reasons and with his father being up there as well, I think it was best all round for the lad and the club that he moved on. What a nice lad, as well. He was a credit. Well mannered, super lad.

Big Ron must have fancied him really, even though he said he didn't to get the price down. He rang me twice one night, once when the television was on. I remembering saying to him, had he any idea when he rang me? "Do you know that Coronation Street *is on, Ron?" He said: "Oh, don't worry about it, she is leaving the pub this week."*

He obviously knew the story-line and he was watching it himself. So that's what managers do at night time, watch Coronation Street.

I had made a couple of enquiries, because we were desperate for cover for Micky Heathcote. We had got Heathcote and Keith Hill at centre-back and nobody at all if either of them got injured. At half-time against Fulham, Micky said he had got this hamstring injury and might have to come off but it turned out to be his back and we got him through it because we realised then that we had got two forwards and Gary Clayton on the bench.

We hadn't really got any cover whatsoever for the defenders or centre-halves, so I made some more enquiries. I had been after Chris Curran at Torquay and Richard Logan, a player who also played in midfield for me at Huddersfield. Dougie Hodgson, who had gone back to Sheffield, was now available again and he spoke to me as well.

I was hoping to tie a deal up, but decided to leave the Curran deal until after we played Torquay. Mick went to watch them against Swindon in the midweek Autoglass, and they did ever so well. He told me it would be a hard game.

I knew Derbies are levellers. I had got to get over to the lads how important it was and how we hadn't got to worry about positions in the league. To be fair, I hadn't got many lads that I had to worry about week in, week out. I had tried since I started in management to have as many lads out of the 11 that I put out that I could rely on 100 per cent and if they had a bad game, it's not much of a bad game and it's on the ball, rather than off it.

At that stage, I had got nine lads out of the 11 who I knew what they were going to do, which wasn't bad really. I was quite pleased with that. The thing about the other two was usually they were the ones that would win the games!

After the Mansfield game, I gave the lads the Monday off and when I came in on Tuesday I was told that Micky Heathcote had needed a wisdom tooth out on the Monday and wasn't coming in. I didn't think anything of it.

I knew that, with the players that Torquay had got coming back for the weekend, it would be a difficult game so, I stressed to the players as early as Tuesday, what was going to be needed to get the points. We did all the set-pieces with young Paul Wotton at centre-half.

The week went smoothly and I was able to name an unchanged side the only problem being on the Thursday when we came in for training, Heathcote had reported that his mouth was very, very sore and he was going back to the dentist. He hadn't been able to sleep for more than one hour at night and went back to his dentist, who gave him some strong painkillers and told him to see how it went on Friday.

I still didn't think anything about it, because with Micky Heathcote being like he is, you know that he will play with a broken leg. It would have to be something serious. On the Friday morning I telephoned him at 9.30 a.m. and he had had a dreadful night again. He said that he felt at that moment in time, he couldn't play. He was that bad.

He rang the dentist to see if he could go and have his stitches out. He was supposed to have them out later but he thought the stitches were too tight which was causing all the hassle. We found out afterwards he had actually split the tooth in three places when the dentist took it out.

Mick was going to have a walk on the Friday afternoon and a couple of hours kip after having the stitches out, just see how he went. I told him I wanted him to come into the ground because I knew that if he came to the ground and saw a few faces going out on the pitch, he might just forget about it a little bit and he might get himself through it.

Anyhow this he did. He had a bit of a session at the ground with Mick Jones and he decided that if everything was all right the following day, he would give it a go. Little did I know then that he was to have his worst night of the week on the Friday. He had had no sleep all week, no training. You couldn't have had a worse preparation than that.

I knew it would be a big crowd for the Torquay game and was privately optimistic it might be more than the 10,000 being forecast. As it turned out 11,600 people turned up, which was tremendous. I also found out that on the Endsleigh League Extra highlights programme, they covered one particular club each week and they were coming to film the game and interview us. They wanted to film me before the game but I refused because I am a bit superstitious with my preparation and I didn't want it to affect anything, regarding mistakes or blame. But I agreed to talk to them after the game.

I knew it sounds daft but when we scored very early on I remember thinking to myself "I hope that's not too early" because almost immediately after that, we got a bit lax at the back. There just seemed to be one mistake after another at the back, and within a couple of minutes of equalising, Torquay had taken the lead – bad defensive play from my point of view; good goals from Torquay's point of view.

The pleasing thing was we were still creating chances and we popped up with an equaliser before half-time and I just thought to myself "I wish we could just go in at 2-2, I wish the referee would blow the whistle now" so I could sort it out, but I just had a feeling, I could sense trouble. Lo and behold right on half-time, we gave them their third chance of the game and they took it. [Scott] Partridge cut across Patterson and whacked the ball in.

We went in 3-2 down. Martin Barlow had got a knock which solved a problem, as I wanted Gary Clayton on because there was nobody actually getting tight in midfield. I also wanted to bring Magee on because they were playing five at the back, with Chris Curran at right-back, and I wanted a winger to have a go at him rather than a midfield player in Leadbitter.

Leadbitter was unlucky because he had done quite well, but I still wanted to bring on Magee as we had nothing to lose. So we put them both on at half-time.

I stressed it could be 90 minutes before we equalised and it might just be the one point that we needed at the end of the season and to be professional. We attacked for most of the second half, and then their centre-half got booked again. He'd been booked in the first half, did a stupid tackle on Adrian Littlejohn from behind with 25 minutes to go, and got himself sent off which allowed me to change the formation again, putting Mark Patterson into midfield with Gary Clayton, and letting Ronnie Maugé have a free role behind the front lads.

We sustained the pressure and then Magee popped up on the right, put a great cross

Gary Clayton

in at the back post and Ronnie Maugé equalised. Then, with five minutes to go, we played another ball through from Ian Baird to Ronnie Maugé. He flicked it through to Adrian Littlejohn, who rounded off a great afternoon with the winning goal in a 4-3 victory which was harsh on Torquay, but you are not going to turn any points down like that. We deserved the odd chances but you just had to feel for them in their position.

It was also ironic that on the Friday, Ronnie Maugé came to me and wanted to know if I knew why he wasn't scoring that many goals. I said to him he must be patient and the chances would come and if he didn't go looking for them, half-chances would arise. His was the most crucial goal of the afternoon and it was good for him because a few weeks beforehand we had had a session on crosses to the far post and finishing and this was ideal. Ronnie had done what he did in training and finished it off well.

Magee had been out most of that week as well, with sickness and diarrhoea, and, being a diabetic, he had to be careful. He wasn't fit to play in the reserves but I wanted his pace on the bench.

The referee had a poor game. He booked four of ours and five of theirs. I shouted over to Ian Baird during the game and said to him that he had got to be careful because this guy would use any excuse to send him off after he had been booked. He acknowledged that. He sent off their centre-half within five minutes of me shouting to Ian Baird.

I think the occasion just got to him and anybody could have been booked if he had been consistent with some if his bookings.

After the game, I was out within 10 minutes and [Torquay manager] Don O'Riordan was just coming out of the referee's room. I went and popped my head around the door and he went "Oh no, I've just had the other manager for eight minutes." I said "Ref, I don't want you for that, I have only got one quick comment to say." He said: "Will you make it quick?" and I said "Yes. All I want to say to you, is be careful driving home tonight, the kind of afternoon you've had today, you've got to be careful. Owt could happen."

It brought a wide smile to his face because I think he was quite drained, and his linesmen smiled and laughed and off I went.

The size of the crowd showed to me that we were on the way to a full-house before the end of the season. I know it was asking a lot in the division we were in, but I still thought we could get a bigger crowd before the end of the season.

I managed to keep all the hype with the local Derby all finished by Thursday so at least the lads only had to concentrate on the game ahead, and I also made sure at the warm-up on the pitch that their minds were right on the game.

They were not doing badly. I knew the defence gave opportunities against Torquay, but they didn't have that many chances other than the three chances they took, and Micky Heathcote not training all week might have had something to do with that. He was a credit but I think it must have affected the other lads.

It was lovely to see Adrian Littlejohn gain a hat-trick. I am a big believer that this lad can do the works. I fancied him at Huddersfield and although he had taken a bit of settling in – we helped him and his wife get a cottage near us towards Callington – he finally moved his family down before the Torquay game. I think being settled brings the best out of him because he is a lad who thinks the world of his kids.

I had to go and find him the match-ball and present it to him after the game. All the lads signed it. He was telling me that this was the first hat-trick he had ever got, although he had scored quite a few twos, and I said I hoped that it was the first of many.

Although we beat Torquay, we didn't move up a place in the table. We were still fourth, with Gillingham still four points ahead of us, and Preston and Chester only one point ahead. When you looked at the table, it just made you realise how we wasted the first four games, getting no points at all.

Plans regarding youth development by the Plymouth Argyle Trust were very exciting. After the first three meetings, we came up with a sponsored car for Kevin Blackwell and were looking into buying a hostel. We needed to raise £100,000 for the purchase of this hostel and the overheads for the youth policy for the first 12 months.

There were lot of positive vibes and a lot of experience in the trust committee. They are really organised and I was really looking forward to trying to raise the £100,000 with them. Obviously, I would oversee it with Kevin Blackwell and Martin Hodge, but it will have a separate identity from the football club so funds won't get diverted as they do in a lot of clubs. If it is a charitable trust – a non-profit making organisation – it will be eligible for certain grants.

All the supporters' branches were kept informed and seemed to take it under their wings to try to help. After all, as I said to them all, it will be like the cornerstone – the concrete foundations – of the long-term success of the club. They all seemed to take it on board with a lot of enthusiasm.

I thought the hostel was a cracking idea. I actually bought one myself at Scarborough for the YTS lads and it can pay for itself. We also had one at Notts County which paid for itself.

There were a couple of schoolboys who moved in the week the Trust had its meeting, 15-year-olds from Cornwall who went to Everton and Norwich. We wanted to stop this happening in coming years. I know most managers don't look to the future regarding youth policy, but I didn't see why I shouldn't. After all, I could be at Plymouth for 10 years, who knows?"

"I WOULDN'T LIKE TO PLAY BADLY REGULARLY WITH SUPPORTERS LIKE THAT"

THE excitement of the Derby victory was still in the air over Home Park the following day when the draw for the first round of the FA Cup was made, when for the fourth successive season, the wooden balls and velvet bag conspired to give Argyle an away tie against non-league opposition.

After victories against Dorking, Marlow and Kettering, the Pilgrims were paired with GM Vauxhall Conference side Slough Town, whose players included two former Pilgrims from the days of David Kemp's management reign at Home Park – Mark Fiore and Andy Clement.

NW: *When we drew Slough in the FA Cup, Harry Redknapp said it would be "a tough one for Plymouth, I saw them play last week, they are a very, very good team. Big, tall, strong, good front lads, they will do well to come out with anything." I thought if our lads needed any incentive it would have been listening to him. Obviously you would like a home tie, but there was a lot worse than Slough. We just had to get on with it.*

After the draw, I was asked once again how could I think about coming down to Plymouth having got promotion with Huddersfield, and why I turned down the Chelsea job when it was offered me a while back. It seemed like nobody could understand the reason for coming to Plymouth. As I said to them, I always do my own thing and had no regrets whatsoever.

Argyle had three league matches and an Auto Windscreens Shield tie to play before making their Cup journey to Berkshire and little could they have known in the aftermath of the victory over Torquay, they would face Slough on the back of a four-game winless streak.

Richard Logan

Before the opening of the pre-Cup-tie quartet, against opponents who were later to become all-too-familiar, Warnock spent more of his chairman's generous supply of money.

Richard Logan, a utility player adept at playing in defence or midfield, became the sixth member of the previous season's Second Division promotion-winning Huddersfield Town squad to de-camp to Home Park when he signed for Argyle for £20,000.

The 6ft 2in former Gainsborough non-leaguer joined former Terriers manager Warnock, his assistant Mick Jones, and ex-team-mates Kevin Blackwell, Gary Clayton and Chris Billy on the Argyle pay-roll and went straight into the squad of 16 which travelled north for an away double-header against Darlington and Scarborough.

Neither Warnock nor Jones could be accused of overselling Logan to the fans. Warnock said: "Some people might be thinking we've got a Rolls Royce but I would say we've got something more like a Ford Popular with a wooden floor," and Jones warned: "He won't be the most talented player at the club, that's a certainty."

However, both agreed that the former bricklayer's presence was essential to their squad-building plans. Jones qualified his assessment of the new boy by adding "… but there won't be a bigger winner, either" to his remarks about Logan's relative lack of talent, and Warnock said: "Richard can provide a lot of the things we need and he will make a tremendous contribution to the squad. He is a genuine hard-working player, although his style might not be easy on the eyes of the fans."

Never mind the fans being worried about Logan's style, Logan must have been worried about the style of the team he had just joined as his arrival coincided with a down-turn in the Pilgrims' fortune.

After sailing through nine games unbeaten, the good ship Pilgrim came aground at Feethams, when they lost in only their second visit to the North Easterners' ground.

There were no early warnings of impending disappointment as Argyle carried on where they had left off against Torquay, enjoying the upper hand throughout a first-half in which Darlington struggled to come to terms with their direct approach.

The Quakers stood firm in the face of the onslaught, their deep-lying five-man defence soaking up the pressure exerted by their similarly religiously nicknamed visitors, and it was Plymouth's brethren who found themselves without a prayer of victory once Gary Himsworth opened the scoring in the 53rd minute.

Logan made his debut as a second-half substitute and came closest to levelling the scores when goalkeeper Mike Pollitt was forced into a brave save at his feet. However, the Pilgrims were caught out in the last five minutes as they continued to push forward in search of the equaliser.

Robbie Painter burst clear from defence and even though goalkeeper Kevin Blackwell charged down his shot, Glenn Naylor was on hand to collect the rebound and sidefoot the match-clinching goal into an unguarded net.

Warnock was hypercritical of his side's efforts. "It was so easy in the first half that some of our players just thought they had to come back out to win the game," he said, "but the most reliable players usually – Keith Hill and Mick Heathcote – let us down. The forwards didn't score the goals and the two centre-backs didn't do very well. I couldn't fault the players for effort. We are better than most sides but we have got to earn the right to win at places like Darlington. They are an average side who worked very hard and kept going right to the end, but they were terrified of us for the first hour."

Warnock and his players stayed in the North East in preparation for a midweek trip to his former club, Scarborough, whom he famously guided to the Football League after the first season in which automatic promotion from the Conference was introduced nine years previously.

It was the first time the Argyle manager had taken a side back to play his former club in a league match and, with former Boro goalkeeper Kevin Blackwell in tow, Scarborough were expecting a large crowd, i. e. around the 2,000 mark.

Ford Popular, aka Richard Logan, made his debut in place of Mick Heathcote, whose let-down performance against Darlington was partially explained by the discovery he was carrying a virus, the after-effects of having his wisdom teeth removed the previous week.

Healthy mind, healthy body is part of the Warnock creed, and to relieve boredom and while away an hour before dinner on the eve of the game, he designed a football quiz to keep his players entertained.

"The answers are all Football League clubs," he explained, "so here's clue for you: what club is a heavyweight toilet?

"The answer's Luton – Loo-Ton, get it?"

The Argyle players seemed sure to have an extra spring in their step as they left the dressing-room to take on Warnock's former club ("deface a district?" – "Scar-Borough"?), even if it was because they would be escaping their manager's dreadful puns for 90 minutes.

The prospects of putting the defeat at Darlington (or, as Warnock might have it "a heavyweight sweetheart") behind them seemed assured after two minutes of the second half, by which time Chris Leadbitter and Adrian Littlejohn had put Argyle two goals up.

However, when the chips were down at the McCain Stadium, Argyle were found wanting and Scarborough took full advantage of the six minutes of injury-time added by referee Neale Barry to pull them back for a 2-2 draw.

Leadbitter swept the Pilgrims into a 16th-minute lead when he took full advantage of a poor defensive header from Jason Rockett, and Littlejohn doubled the lead in the 47th minute when he seized on a rebound from Logan's blocked shot to drive past goalkeeper Ian Ironside.

Midway through the second half, substitute Andy Ritchie set up Steve Charles for a shot which beat Kevin Blackwell from the edge of the penalty area, and Argyle were further thrown when Logan limped out of the middle of the defence to be replaced by rookie Paul Wotton. The Pilgrims' youth-team captain had been whisked up to the North East when Heathcote had failed to pass muster after the Darlington match.

Wotton proved an able deputy, after a nervous start, and when he hacked a goal-bound shot off the line in injury-time, he must have thought he had helped Argyle to a valuable three points. However, injury-time went on and on. Scarborough striker David D'Auria had a goal disallowed for a foul on Blackwell and still it seemed Argyle would hang on.

Then Darren Knowles pumped in a last cross and Neil Trebble's shot was deflected past a helpless Blackwell to claim an unlikely point for the home side and leave Warnock in a reflective mood, which once again demonstrated his almost extra-sensory feel for how the season was developing.

"Points will prove to be vital by the end of the season," he said, "and we may look back at games like the one at Scarborough and say 'if only.' Our biggest problem comes when we think we are a good side and start cruising. Whenever that happens, we become complacent and certain players start doing things that reduce part of the overall team-strength we require. Consequently, we end up with seven or eight players trying to do the team-work for 11 – and that gives the opposition a chance. Darlington and Scarborough both cashed in when we dropped a gear."

NW: *The Sunday morning after the Torquay game I went off early to Manchester, where I received an award from the Northern Sports Writers at the* Portland Thistle Hotel. *It is always an achievement to receive an award, especially from sports writers, because they don't give them away willy-nilly.*

The only thing is when you are in Plymouth it's not a two-minute job just to pop up to Manchester and back, which I noticed especially in the week before what I knew would be a very, very hard weekend, Darlington and Scarborough away in four days.

Fortunately the chairman let us stop up there with the players. We stopped in a guest-house on Saturday night after the Darlington game, and then got down to the preparation again for the Tuesday and the Scarborough game.

We asked to play the game on the Monday, which originally Scarborough agreed, but then they changed their minds. I would imagine that they thought we would go back down and then come back up which would be to their advantage. So I hoped that it would backfire on them with us staying up.

We took Darlington on after their best run of the season, with them having beaten leaders Gillingham in their previous home match to make it three wins on the trot. They were on a bit of a run and Scarborough, too, were doing quite well. I would have settled for three points from the two games.

I worked hard to try to get Richard Logan. I agreed £15,000 with Huddersfield and £5,000 at the end of the season and got him down with his missus, Adèle, who wanted to see the place. We had him at our house on the Wednesday night and talked for two or three hours. I said signing for Plymouth would be an opportunity for him. He knows me inside out – I took him from non-league – so I would have been disappointed if he didn't join us. Obviously he wanted time to think about it overnight and I said I would speak to him at 9.30 in the morning.

When I spoke to him in the morning, he said he would join us so everything was signed and we picked him up at a motorway services on the way up to Darlington. When I arrived at the hotel in my car at around 4.00 p.m., it was getting dark so I tried to get a gymnasium with lights or an outdoor pitch in order for us to practice our set-pieces, which had to be done, but to no avail – nobody had got one near the hotel. It was half-term week, so all the kids had booked things.

I kept ringing the team-bus to find out where it was and it turned out to be stuck in a jam on the M1. In the end, the players got to the hotel at 4.50 p.m. and we went straight into our warm-up. By the time we had done 15 minutes, it was pitch black. We ended up walking through set-pieces. It was farcical, really. We had set off at 9.00 a.m. Eight hours travelling. We needed to think about alternative travel arrangements, especially with the new laws governing coaches' speeds due to come into force after Christmas. With the busses only able to travel at 60 mph, Plymouth to Hartlepool would be a nightmare journey.

I decided to leave Richard on the bench against Darlington and I dropped Martin Barlow and brought Gary Clayton back in. I told Martin I thought he was a little bit off at Mansfield, and in the first half against Torquay and he accepted it all right.

The hotel at Darlington was red-hot. We seemed to be getting every hotel with traffic making a noise or heat you couldn't turn off.

We arrived at the ground and found out there were no tickets for the players, so we couldn't give any relatives and guests tickets. Micky Heathcote had six members of his family up there and Chris Leadbitter had about five, so they had to go and buy tickets.

My old kit man from Huddersfield – John Credland – had come to see us and I couldn't even give him a ticket, so I got him on the bus outside the ground and let him help us take the kit in. I wasn't going to have him pay to go in.

The referee was a young chap called Mike Riley, who I feared the worst from the time when we had an unbeaten run at Huddersfield. We went 12 games, and then we had Mike Riley at York City in a local Derby. We got a man sent off early on and we got beaten 2-0 and my report on him was, well, put it this way, it wasn't complimentary.

Obviously, my feelings on seeing this guy on the pitch before the game, having gone nine games undefeated, weren't exactly those of confidence. I was prepared to give him the benefit of the doubt, but I could tell throughout the 90 minutes that nothing had changed from the previous season.

We looked so dominant in the first half. They were so frightened of us. They had nine men back and didn't even look to try and get forward apart from the full-backs. But we couldn't score when we should have done and then after half-time Micky Heathcote went to pieces for some reason. We found out 24 hours later that he had a temperature of 100 degrees which went up to 102, but obviously I didn't know that at the time.

He had 10 minutes of complete suicide and I think it rubbed off on Keith Hill then. We gifted them a goal and never really looked like getting back in although we should have taken the lead just after half-time with a corner. But Adrian Littlejohn got in Ronnie Maugé's way.

So we lost that game 2-0 and Ian Baird got booked again. I could see we were going to have a problem with his bookings. It was not as if he was getting booked for anything, it was just continual fouling. Ian Baird does get booked because of the way he is, it's just him.

We went over to Scarborough on the Saturday night, and the lads had a good night out. They actually paid for themselves that night. I said to the chairman it was going to be an awful expense for the club if he let us stop up there from the Saturday to the Tuesday so we would pay for ourselves on Saturday night. When he agreed that, I booked us into a guest-house, which we had all to ourselves.

It was run by a former YTS lad at Scarborough and his mum and dad and they booked us all in at £13 a night. All the lads forked it out themselves, Ian Baird collected it. Bed and breakfast, although I'm not so sure everybody had breakfast.

We trained on the Sunday afternoon because I wanted to give them a little bit of a run to *try and get rid of the night out and I thought it would break the day up as well. There was a match on Sky as well, and we trained Monday morning at a college and that's when we found out that Heathcote wasn't well at all.*

He couldn't train and had be confined to bed. Norman took him to see a doctor who thought he would struggle against Scarborough and gave him some antibiotics. He said he thought it was a culmination of losing his wisdom teeth, being run down, and playing when he shouldn't have played. He looked dreadful.

So we had to send for young [Paul] Wotton. We telephoned his dad down in Plymouth to ask him if he could pop him up and we arranged to meet him at Doncaster at nine o'clock on the morning of the match.

We had a five-a-side on the Monday morning up there, but were one man short, so I played. I picked my team and scored a cracking goal. We won 5-2 against Ronnie Maugé's side and to say that I was the best forward really spoke volumes for what Ronnie's side was. I think Adrian Littlejohn was on his side, with Mark Patterson, Ian Baird, and Micky Evans.

The chairman came to watch us train and I think he was impressed. He thought it might save him money on a new striker because I looked that sharp.

On Tuesday morning, Norman said Micky Heathcote had no chance. I was disappointed because with a strong centre-half I thought we could beat anybody. I wanted Micky Heathcote for Scarborough because I knew we would need him.

I decided to play Richard Logan back there. I was originally going to play Logan in midfield but I thought I would go for him because he had a bit more experience than young Paul Wotton. I left Gary Clayton, who had done well at Darlington, in midfield, and I wanted to put Logan in midfield with Ronnie Maugé.

I also decided to play Micky Evans up the middle with Adrian Littlejohn and bring Martin Barlow in, in place of Ian Baird. I knew Bairdy was going to be suspended from the following Saturday for three games, and I just thought that Evans and Littlejohn could cause the two centre-halves a few problems with the movement.

I went up to the ground in the afternoon to get some tickets and had a walk on the pitch. It brought back a few memories of 1986/87, when I won the championship. I looked around and just thought about one or two of the games when we had some special times while I was there but I really wanted to win that night.

We got to the ground and there were quite a few of our supporters outside the gates which was quite surprising. I went back to give a couple of tickets out, one to Noddy, our friendly town-crier supporter, and one of the guys at the side of him shouted to me "Come on, make sure they do better than Saturday, that was garbage. We came all this way." He was a big bloke and I wasn't going to argue with him. I said to him, "You're dead right, pal" and went back in and told the lads what he had said. It was a good job there was a gate between us – I wouldn't like to play badly regularly with supporters like that.

The preparation was good. I didn't go and socialise with anybody apart from when I presented them with a signed shirt of Stuart Mell, the top scorer in the 1986/87 championship side, before the game. I said to Mick it might make the crowd more appreciative and a bit quieter and not give me so much stick, but we didn't need it.

We started off the game in total control and played some good stuff. Leadbitter scored a good goal, then just after half-time we scored another one. However, I just had that feeling while I was sat on the bench that something had to go wrong – we were so much in control. Then Richard Logan hurt his foot in the second half and hobbled about, and if Logan is injured, he is injured. I know for a fact that he never, ever comes off the pitch if he can stop on.

Within a couple of minutes we realised that he couldn't continue and I had to send young Paul Wotton on. It gave Scarborough that little bit more, because Logan had been doing well, not only with the defensive duties but with taking long throws and slowing it down a little bit, and we threw it away with 20 minutes to go.

How we didn't score three or four goals I don't know, but we didn't and they got a goal back which lifted them. Then they just threw everything into the box. We gave away stupid free-kicks, one at the end of the game in their own half from which they put another ball right into our box for a scrambled equaliser, well into injury-time. I would say two or three minutes into injury-time.

The referee said they played about four and a half minutes, but we timed it about seven minutes. I'm afraid you are going to get that when you go up North, but I was absolutely gutted. Not just because it was my old club but the two points we had thrown away was not down to the ability of our opponents – it was our own fault. It felt like losing,

I was livid. I couldn't contain myself. I remonstrated with two or three players and was annoyed for giving the free-kick away in the last minute. I was annoyed that we crossed balls that we should have kept in corners – it was so unprofessional – and when I got back in the dressing-room I went absolutely loopy. I threw tea all over, told Chris Billy, who wasn't playing, to get out of the room while I said what I wanted and I just laid into the players. I told them I was disgusted with them. I just couldn't figure out how they could give two goals away like they did, 2-0 and cruising and then give two goals away when were were so much in charge. I knew how hard it was to get these points in the bag.

You always think about these points thrown away later on in the season and these were definitely two vital points thrown away. I kept finishing having a go at one player and then starting up again. All the lads were just sat there, hiding behind their hands. I went and got a shower and came back in and started all over again while I was drying off. The players still hadn't moved.

It just felt like you'd bloody lost. That's the worse thing about management, I think. When you're down and you have to go and make sure the Press don't realise that you're rock bottom or you're really low. The same with the visiting directors and your own directors. When you go into the boardroom and you say niceties, like "Well done, it was a good point for you in the end" and I'm thinking to myself "How can they get a point off us?"

They were smashing people and they looked after us well. I couldn't sleep that night, tossing and turning I just couldn't understand how we could have been so unprofessional, especially when we learned that Preston scored at the same time that we conceded a goal. They scored a winning goal, so instead of being level on points with Preston, we ended up being four points behind them – all in a space of a minute.

With Chester winning again, it put us four points behind the top three. So overall, it was the most disappointing weekend for at least six weeks.

I didn't really want Micky Heathcote going back on the bus with the lads, carrying his virus, so I asked Graham Hambly, who came up with the Evening Herald, *if he would mind putting him in the back seat on the way down to Plymouth, and he agreed to that. So at least it got Micky away from the bus.*

After their short Northern tour, Argyle entered November by returning to Home Park to face Cardiff City, and it soon became evident that the double away trip had left them jaded. For the first time since Warnock's arrival in the South West, Argyle supporters were treated to the dubious joys of a goalless draw.

"It was probably the worst game I have seen for two or three seasons," admitted Warnock candidly afterwards. "There's no point in being anything but honest about that. You have just got to say to supporters 'We apologise' but you get these games now and again. To be fair, it doesn't happen very often but I expect even our supporters have bad days at work. I'm just glad it's out of the way and we got a point out of it because every point will count at the end of the season. We just had too many players not on their game."

Opposition manager Kenny Hibbitt had designed a game-plan to frustrate Argyle, which largely involved getting eight men behind the ball at all times and not giving Adrian Littlejohn the opportunity to turn defenders and run away from them.

"Our central defenders were told not to get too tight to him," said Hibbitt, who should have known all about Littlejohn's pace after giving him a free transfer when he was in charge of Walsall. "If you get too close, he'll spin you round and get behind you."

With their cutting-edge thus blunted, Argyle looked less like Third Division championship favourites and more like the Rose and Crown Fourth XI after a night on the ale.

Two points from three games left Argyle in sixth place in the Third Division table – behind Colchester, Rochdale, Gillingham, Chester and new leaders Preston. Three wins from their previous three games, which was not beyond their capabilities, would have seen them top the table by a point.

The only consolation for Argyle from their stalest of stalemates against Cardiff was that the watching officials from Slough, whom the Pilgrims faced the following week in the FA Cup, would have learnt nothing of value.

"They'll be laughing," suggested Warnock. "They'll have gone away asking who they will get in the next round."

Argyle's preparation for their visit to Berkshire was riddled with problems, both on and off the pitch. On the same day – Tuesday November 7 – as they were knocked out of the Auto Windscreens Shield competition, director Ivor Jones resigned from the board.

Jones had taken umbrage with chairman Dan McCauley's assertion that the club was subsidising its directors, which came after several months in which, he claimed, he was not being consulted or asked for advice on the running of the club.

"I took great exception to those remarks and expressed it strongly at a board meeting," he said. "We had a full and frank discussion and the chairman invited me to resign if I felt that strongly. I was upset because what he had said was a slur on my character and my wife's character. He accused us of being subsidised by the club, which I took exception to. It's not just about that, though. In fairness to the chairman, he puts the money in and he should have the final say, but the board should be part of the decision-making process. He has three very good directors [Denis Angilley, whose future on the board was still unresolved, Peter Bloom and Graham Jasper] who have a wealth of experience, and he should use them. They are successful businessmen, and know a lot about the game and the area. He should start consulting them. After all, at the end of the day, he's still got the vote.

"I would just like him to get together with the other three and realise they are not his enemies. They are his friends."

It is doubtful whether Angilley still thought of himself as McCauley's friend. The Cornish-based property developer was predicting that the club's forthcoming AGM would turn into a direct confrontation between McCauley and himself, and he was welcoming the chance to tell all about the boardroom bust-up.

"I think the fans and the shareholders should know what has been going on," said Angilley. "It would be in the best interests of the club for everyone to know the facts."

Whether McCauley agreed with Angilley or what he thought about Jones's resignation, it was impossible to tell. The Argyle chairman was in France on a business trip and unavailable for comment.

Not so Neil Warnock, who had plenty to say after the Pilgrims limped out of the Auto Windscreens Shield with a 1-0 defeat at Northampton. Once again, he rested a number of regular first-teamers for Argyle's first ever visit to Northampton's plush £5m community stadium at Sixfields, although this time he did at least make the effort to be at the game.

He made his presence count, too. After making Keith Hill captain for the night in the absence of Ronnie Maugé and Mick Heathcote, he promptly substituted his acting skipper in the 26th minute, seven minutes after Hill had given away a penalty which Chris Burns converted for the game's only goal.

"I thought he started slowly and I did not feel he was helping young Paul Wotton [Hill's centre-back partner]," said Warnock. "Obviously his mind was not on the game, so it was pointless him carrying on. I was extremely disappointed with his performance, especially with a young lad playing alongside him."

Hill was not the only Argyle defender to suffer at Sixfields. Richard Logan was sent off, on the word of a linesman, following a second-half off-the-ball incident with Northampton's Christian Lee. An undisciplined moment in a meaningless match would cost the Pilgrims the services of Logan for the much more important forthcoming home league game against Rochdale.

Nevertheless, Warnock was not too disappointed at being knocked out of the Auto Windscreens Shield. "Apologies to anyone who wants us to get to Wembley," he said, "but this is not the right time for that with the numbers we have in our squad. These games are more trouble than they're worth."

However, having seen the Pilgrims' progress to Wembley halted once in a week, Argyle's worldly-wise manager was anxious that his team's FA Cup campaign did not end in a slough of despond in Berkshire.

He did not regard defeat by Northampton at Sixfields as a visit to the valley of humiliation, although a similar result against GM Vauxhall Conference Slough would bring about giant despair.

"Pride-wise defeat would hurt, especially with *Match of the Day* cameras there," said Warnock, a qualified chiropodist more *au fait* with bunions than Bunyan. "It gives us an opportunity to show everyone where the club is going. We have got to show everyone in the country we mean business. Some of the Slough lads will play as if they are Third Division players, some may even play as if they are Second Division players – we've got to make sure we put up with that."

At least two of them used to play in the First Division – with Argyle, too. Mark Fiore, an outrageously gifted but terminally under-confident midfielder, and Andy Clement, confident but terminally ungifted, represented the Pilgrims in the cash-strapped era of David Kemp's management and had followed their former gaffer to his post-Argyle posting of Slough.

Mick Heathcote, still suffering from the after effects of the virus which had kept him out of the Pilgrims' side since their defeat at Darlington, returned to duty at the heart of the defence and proved the inspiration behind a 2-0 victory that was not always as comfortable as the scoreline might suggest.

Argyle did not drop any bombs on Slough but did enough to ensure that Des Lynam did not have a first-round shock from Wexham Park to report to late-night football

Mark Patterson tussles with Slough's former Pilgrim, Mark Fiore

fans. The Pilgrims took the lead in the 61st minute, when Lee Harvey bulleted an own goal past goalkeeper Delroy Preddie, and Heathcote wrapped up matters with 13 minutes to go when he headed in Chris Leadbitter's free-kick.

"Mick Heathcote was inspirational and typified the whole club's attitude today," said Warnock afterwards. "I can't speak too highly of him. He missed his lunch to warm up in the gym – that's the sort of guy he is."

NW: *Micky Evans and Ronnie Maugé had colds which seemed to be clearing up, although Ronnie was complaining of his knee. He said it restricted him at Darlington. I gave him the benefit of the doubt because I thought he was poor at Darlington. It might have been his knee.*

It was disappointing that Micky Heathcote had no chance of recovery for the Cardiff game. Richard Logan said he would play despite his injured foot, and I knew we needed him because Cardiff had a big lad up front.

I decided to stick with two wide midfield players, Chris Leadbitter and Martin Barlow, against Cardiff even though Chris Billy passed a fitness test. He hadn't had a game since his cartilage operation and I didn't really want to risk him, if I'm honest. I thought we should get by without him, but I realised that we might not.

Mick [Jones] said to me before they went out that he thought the dressing-room was a little bit low. I tried to get them going, but I got that feeling that they weren't really clued in. You don't get that feeling very often.

It was the worst game since I'd been at Plymouth. Probably one of the worst games I had been involved with for a couple of years. Cardiff had two or three young lads in and they played eight behind the ball. They defended very deep so we couldn't get Adrian Littlejohn or Micky Evans in behind. I think if we'd got one goal, we would have got an avalanche. But we couldn't get that one goal.

The longer the game went on, the more I became glad we got a point – it was that bad a game, I could see us losing it. Afterwards, the players all sat down with their head in their hands waiting for a bollocking, and I just said "Well done lads, what a great point. If we can play as bad as that and get a point, it can't be bad" and really just laughed it off. There are so many lads off their game, I couldn't really do anything else.

I stopped in the bath afterwards and was last out for a change because there was no rush; we were having to stay until eight o'clock for a firework-display which the club was putting on. As I came off the pitch, three or four guys were screaming at me: "Warnock, you're useless, we paid good money for this." I just turned around and said: "Don't you realise I watched that game too? You don't have to tell me."

The disappointment was that we had gone six points behind the leaders, five points behind the play-off place. We needed to install a bit more ruthlessness and we missed Micky Heathcote without a shadow of a doubt. I think if Micky Heathcote had played at Scarborough and against Cardiff, we would have got five more points. All because a bloody dentist left a bit of tooth in when he had his wisdoms out – we had been told that he had to have a second opinion from the hospital, because he had it X-rayed and a piece of tooth still there.

The chairman, directors, myself and Steve Birley were invited on a full day's course at Hewlett Packard in Reading and were asked about our plans for the next five years. To which I said, "New stadium, pushing for a Premier League position from the First Division, in the black. Let's see how far we can go, why not?"

For the second game in the Auto Windscreens Shield at Northampton, I decided to play young Paul Wotton at centre-half to see how he went with Keith Hill, because we had no real cover for Hilly other than Logan. I played Barlow and Logan in midfield and gave Chris Billy his first game since his cartilage operation. I wanted to rest Ronnie Maugé because he had lost some of his sparkle. Magee had his first start and Micky Ross and Micky Evans played up front. I also played Nicky Hammond in his first game since I dropped him from the team earlier.

I decided to watch the game up in the stand and I think I lasted 20 minutes before I came down. Although we lost 1-0, it wasn't until the last 10 or 15 minutes that they had a lot of chances. We had a few chances and I was pleased to see Micky Evans hit the bar. I thought how good it was that he was back on song again. Although he had been quiet, I thought he was having a tremendous season.

The only doubt after the Northampton game was Richard Logan who got sent off for stamping on somebody – so the linesman said – but the referee issued a yellow card, then a red card. When I saw him after, he said it was for violent conduct, I said to him "Well, you did show a second yellow card?" and he said that it was his second bookable offence. I was thankful with that because it meant that he would only miss one game and not three.

Then we went on to Slough, whose manager had been saying that he thought they might beat us. We had had them watched a few times and knew they were lively up front.

Micky Heathcote hadn't played since the Darlington match and although he had actually been training that week, we didn't risk him at Northampton in the Auto Windscreens.

He got stronger and stronger during the week and I said I would leave it up to him and he said he wanted to play. We set off on Saturday morning on the coach, having decided to travel on the same day to see how it went, stopping off at Newbury for a pre-match lunch.

It was the first time the chairman had come on the bus and while we all went in for our pre-match meal, Micky Heathcote picked his kit-bag up and went off to the gym. He didn't like travelling long distances on the day of the match and went to the gym to loosen his back. I thought "What a good professional!"

When I got to Slough and I saw Brian Barwick the chief of Match of the Day, *I said to him before the game "You've got some big guns out here – Barry Davies, for instance – you must be expecting a mishap, a giant-killing." He just smiled at me and said it was just goals they were expecting but I could tell we were one of the giant-killing matches that they were expecting, so it made it even better knowing that they were all there waiting.*

We stressed that we had to try and perform together and that there would be only one loser and that was going to be us. I think the comment I made – "Tonight we either get no mentions on Match of the Day *whatsoever or we get tomorrow's headlines for the wrong reasons" – put the point over.*

The first half was a bit dull, but I never thought we were in any trouble. One or two people said to me afterwards that we didn't play well but I don't believe you ever play well in FA Cup ties, especially the early rounds. FA Cup ties are all about getting through and I have always been a believer in that.

At half-time I thought four or five lads were below the level of what I expected of them and although we were playing within ourselves, I just felt we were content to do that.

I had to stress to three or four players – Chris Billy in particular – that I wanted more out of them. I think Chris did more in the first 10 minutes of the second half than he had done in the entire first half. He went around his full-back with a super dribble and put in a great cross and we were 1-0 up. It was an own goal, but we didn't know at the time. It was just such a great cross from Chris, it was just invited to be put into the net.

Then a Chris Leadbitter free-kick and Micky Heathcote rose above the goalkeeper and we were 2-0 up and home and dry. I thought it was a professional second half. The only disappointment again was Mark Patterson's booking which put him one more booking away from a suspension. It was so unprofessional, his booking. He had had three or four bookings which were really amateurish. I tried to stress this to him but only time would tell whether he could eliminate this. He is keen, he is so keen.

Keith Hill got booked in the first minutes of the game, for a reckless challenge on the halfway line and could have even gone later on for another foul. Paul Durkin was the referee, a Premier League referee and a bit more understanding. I think some of the first-year referees would have had him off.

The second-round draw sent Argyle on their travels again, this time to ICIS League Kingstonian, a match which *Sky Sports* deemed worthy of live coverage which meant a Sunday, December 3 early afternoon kick-off and a £60,000 guaranteed television coverage fee in the bank.

Argyle could certainly have done with the financial boost. On the same day that Sky came over the horizon, the club had announced they made a loss of more than £1/2m during the previous relegation season.

The expected deficit left them with liabilities of around £2.5m, which were covered by directors' loans of £200,000; a bank overdraft of £635,000; and, illustrating just how much the club was indebted to chairman Dan McCauley's personal generosity, a sum of nearly £1.5m owed to the chairman's *Rotolok* company.

McCauley saw the alarming financial downturn as an inescapable consequence of the disastrous relegation season. "Attendances were down, there was no play-off pool [as there had been the previous season] and commercial income fell," he said. "The wages bill alone was 30 per cent higher than the turnstile income.

"Ultimately, we must rely on selling players to cover this shortfall or alternatively look to *Rotolok* to inject yet more money."

Of course, promotion would help offset some of the club's financial shortfall, but to achieve that Argyle needed to find a significant improvement on their league form, although a defeat and two draws since the stunning victory over Torquay hardly rated in the South Sea Bubble category of collapses.

The Pilgrims' search to rediscover the winning formula once again took them north to another of Neil Warnock's former clubs, this time to Hartlepool, where he had once plied his trade as "a brainless winger."

Just as they had done at Scarborough, Argyle contrived to snatch a 2-2 draw from the jaws of victory after going 2-0 up.

Although the match never looked like being a repeat of the 8-1 humiliation Argyle had inflicted on Hartlepool when the two teams met in Division Two at the end of the 1993/94 season, Argyle were in control from the start, when home goalkeeper Brian Horne scrambled a save from Gary Clayton.

The Pilgrims took the lead from the penalty spot in the 13th minute, when Michael Evans converted from 12 yards after Chris Billy had been fouled by Tony Canham, and Hartlepool's weaknesses at the back were further exposed 22 minutes later when Ronnie Maugé made it 2-0.

Maugé, who had retained the captaincy despite Argyle's defeat at Darlington and Mick Heathcote's return to fitness, used his spring-heeledness to jump into Mark Patterson's long free-kick from inside his own half and loop a header out of Horne's reach.

Hartlepool were jeered off at half-time and the home fans called for player-manager Keith Houchen's dismissal. Maybe this derision galvanised Pool, because it was a completely different team which emerged from the dressing-room after the interval.

Houchen put himself out of earshot of disgruntled supporters by coming on as a half-time substitute but it was another replacement, Steve Howard, who launched the fightback when he drove in a powerful 48th-minute shot which goalkeeper Kevin Blackwell could only parry. Danny Ingram hacked the loose ball over the line for his first-ever league goal.

Thirteen minutes later, Howard equalised with a long-range shot that left Blackwell flat-footed and furious with his defence for allowing the Pool man time and space to fire home his sixth goal of the season.

Argyle rallied in the final quarter of the game and came close to covering up their embarrassment in the final minute of the game when Heathcote met Chris Leadbitter's corner with a header that required an athletic full-length dive from Horne to keep the ball out.

The long coach journey from the North East back to the South West must have seemed even longer than usual for Argyle's players if their manager's sullen mood after the game was anything to go by.

"We should have done a lot better than this," he said. "We expect to win against the likes of Scarborough and Hartlepool but we have failed to do so. We should be winning these games and to say I am not happy is an understatement. I will have to do something to make sure we get better results in games like these. I can't fault the effort but we have got to defend better. We worked hard and dominated the game for long spells and then ended up scrapping for a point."

The point they scrapped for still kept the Pilgrims in a play-off position – sixth – but, significantly, they were now at least two victories out of the top three places in which they needed to finish to obtain automatic promotion at the end of the season.

NW: *On the Sunday night, we were drawn against Kingstonian away. My first reaction was disappointment that we were not drawn at home but when I looked at the draw, we could have gone to Swindon or Oxford. At least we had a chance of getting through easily, it would be in our own hands.*

When the draw was announced on Sky, Harry Redknapp said exactly the same as he did for the first game. "That will not be an easy one for Plymouth," he said.

During the week, I popped out with one of the YTS lads down to a company called Remploy, where a lot of disabled people work, including one of our biggest fans Michael Parsons, who has supported us through thick and thin. He goes everywhere. He went up to Darlington and came back the same day then went up to Scarborough. He takes his holidays to watch Argyle and then if he hasn't got any leave left, he has time off without pay.

He has to sit down every week and itemise everything to the penny – how much he has got for the coach journey, etc. It just shows you how keen some people are. I think that showed in the crowd at Slough.

I told Micky Ross that he could have a free transfer because I really wanted to play one or two of the other lads and some of the youngsters and really he is stopping somebody from coming through now. So I would like to get him away if I could.

On the Tuesday before the Hartlepool game, I wanted to do some training, some technical play, and had planned everything in my mind. Then I got a telephone call from Adrian Littlejohn who was stuck in Sheffield. He had a leak in his house and he was waiting for the plumber. So I had to disband everything I was going to do.

I thought I would do it again on the Thursday morning after the warm-up. The players were an absolute disgrace so I called them in and I said they needed to give me quarter of an hour of quality or we would forget about it.

We set off again. I gave them another five minutes and I just blew the whistle and shouted to Mick Jones, "Jonah, take over because I don't want to train with this rabble this morning – it will depress me." And I walked off the training ground. They were that bad.

On Friday we travelled up to Doncaster, where we had decided to stop for a couple of hours because we could do some afternoon training before it got dark. We trained at a local school and then went up to Hartlepool.

We went 2-0 up in the first half an hour and we could have got more. They had already made one substitution and then we knew they would bring on Keith Houchen, the manager, at half-time. We talked about being tight, what I wanted to do, and then went out and within a minute and a half we conceded a goal.

Paul Williams should have cleared it or left it for Kevin Blackwell and

Paul Williams

Hartlepool had a scramble and ended up scoring a goal. It was the magic lift that they had wanted and they bombarded us after that.

They got a lucky deflection from which they equalised. Then we hung on for five minutes and in the last 25 minutes we came back in and attacked. We should have scored with a great shot from Adrian Littlejohn and then Evans missed an opportunity to sneak the win right at the death. It was so disappointing.

I went into the boardroom quickly afterwards, and, because I played there one of the Press guys asked me how it felt to come back to the club. I said "It's great. I am glad I can look after Hartlepool, having played for them." I won the player of the year award there in 1972, even thought I didn't get it presented to me until 1990.

But deep down I was seething again. Even more so than Scarborough because we really had some great chances, even when they got back in again at 2-2. But, it wasn't to be.

I was talking to a guy before the game who said to me "Come on Neil, let's make sure we have a win today." I asked where he came from and he said Penzance – 97 miles before he gets to Plymouth and he had come up on the Saturday morning to Hartlepool. I thought "What kind of supporters have we got here?"

So in the space of four games we had been to Scarborough and been 2-0 up and Hartlepool and been 2-0 up and had thrown four points away. All the top teams had won and we got back on the bus six points adrift of the automatic promotion placings. I couldn't stop thinking "How the hell did we throw two points away?"

"YOU HAVEN'T DONE ANYTHING AT ALL, SO HOW CAN I CRITICISE YOU?"

"IT'S time to put our house in order," said Warnock, as his team prepared to entertain Rochdale by enjoying a morning in front of the telly and good chat – which might have seemed a trifle too relaxed an approach for a side which had disturbed its supporters by failing to win its last three league games.

However, the essential viewing for Warnock's men was not Richard and Judy's makeovers or the tepid topical debate of *Kilroy*, but, rather, a video-screening of the previous week's pre-Christmas giveaway at Hartlepool.

"I wanted to ask each player what they felt about their own performance; where they could have done better; and where they thought the team could have been better," said old dog Warnock, who admitted to having learnt a few new tricks. There'll always be some lads who sit on the fence or tell you what you want to hear," he said, "but there were four or five who made constructive comments which I thought were quite legitimate and which I've taken on board."

If Warnock's description of the affair makes it sound like a vicar's morning tea-party, be assured that it was not. Politicians would have described the meeting as a "full and frank discussion", which is the polite form of saying "Cards on the tables lads, and don't hold back."

The management-by-committee approach was something Warnock had tried only rarely before. "I've run out of ideas," he joked. "No, not really. It's just that sometimes you are so involved, you overlook the obvious."

What was obvious was that Argyle needed to lose to Rochdale like the Princess of Wales needed another member of the tabloid *paparazzi* following her. The Dale had climbed to fourth place in the Third Division table, three points ahead of Argyle, on the back of an impressive away record.

"I bet it's a long time since Argyle have been underdogs against Rochdale at home," said Warnock shuffling his psychological deck of cards. "If we perform like we did at Hartlepool, Rochdale will score four or five."

Argyle did not play like they did at Hartlepool and, consequently, Rochdale did not score four, or five. In fact, they did not score any at all, which meant that second-half goals from Adrian Littlejohn and Michael Evans were enough to give the Pilgrims a 2-0 victory which moved them to fifth place, behind Rochdale, Preston, Gillingham and Chester.

Littlejohn's 12th strike of the campaign in the 48th minute maintained his record of never scoring a dull, simple goal. Nothing seemed to be on for him when he chased down a seemingly lost cause – Evans' wildly misplaced channel-ball – and arrived at the same time as opposition defender Peter Butler, who had been odds-on to win the race to the ball.

Then he stole the ball off Butler with a perfectly-timed toe-poke tackle, and followed that with a trademark spin that left his marker trailing in his wake. What Butler then saw was Littlejohn sprinting away from him in the general direction of the goal, his tight control depriving the opponents converging on him from all angles of a chance to tackle. Argyle's number nine kept his head to place the ball, rather than blast it aimlessly, past goalkeeper Ian Gray. Genius.

Littlejohn's masterclass in the art of scoring injected some life into a previously dead game and Argyle proved well worth the three points which Evans' 86th-minute conversion of Littlejohn's cross sealed.

"I didn't think Adie contributed in the first half and I asked for more from him," admitted Warnock afterwards. "The goal was his answer. We needed that little bit of spark, and Adie answered me very early on. His goal was as good as any you will see at this level."

Littlejohn was more blunt regarding his manager's half-time dressing-room dressing down. "He kicked me up the bottom," he admitted, coyly.

An indication as to the resolution that emerged from the Argyle committee which had met in midweek to thrash out differences of opinion between management and players was the relatively large amount of time the ball remained in close proximity to the grass. The manager, tarred with the long-ball brush throughout his career, was as delighted as the supporters with this subtle change in style.

"I think that players read the papers and start whacking the ball everywhere," he said. "There have been times when Ronnie Maugé's been in 25 yards of space and he's started ale-housing it because no-one's told him to bring it down and play.

"It's a fallacy about the long-ball game. We're better on the floor than people think."

NW: *We tried to have a week doing a bit of short stuff in the gym because the weather had been terrible over the previous couple of weeks and the players had been a bit heavy-legged. Then on Tuesday after training, we had a meeting and showed the highlights of the game. Everyone had a point of view and it was good.*

It wasn't all what I wanted to hear. Some of the things were facts and lads disagreed with other lads and we talked about how we could become a bit more professional when we went in front instead of going out trying to get a third goal. Let's make sure we defended, because we were just flying forward and weren't defending in numbers. Quite a lot came out of that meeting.

I also had a chat to the lads about looking after themselves during Christmas and making sure they are professional.

I had another meeting with the Plymouth Argyle Supporters Trust regarding the youth system, and that was all systems go. Trevor and Chris Heayns were masterminding it and everybody was so confident that it would begin to pay dividends within 5 or 10 years.

The main decision before the Rochdale game was whether to bring Ian Baird back in because Chris Billy still wasn't back to his best, but having looked at Rochdale's team, I have decided to go with the same team and leave Chris on the right wing, hoping he could get at their left-back, which we felt we could get some joy out of.

I had my first taste of real Devon and Cornwall weather, non-stop rain for a week. I went out on Friday morning to do the set-pieces and it was absolutely sodden. We had to go into a gymnasium. I'd also got damp and condensation in two of our bedrooms and when I asked the surveyor he said that it was a Cornish problem, Welcome to Cornwall.

I went to Dingles *the previous night, where some of the staff had dressed up as Plymouth Argyle supporters for their late-night shopping. I asked three or four of the lads – Gary Clayton, Micky Evans and Kevin Blackwell – and Mick Jones to come with me. It was funny to see Gary Clayton in the boardroom where their chief executive, the manager of the store was there with his personal assistant, and Clayts address the PA in his broad Sheffield accent, "All right luv?" One thing about Gary is he will not change who he is for anyone, whether it is royalty or a drop-out.*

Before the Rochdale game, we told the players to get the ball in to Adrian's feet, having decided to leave Bairdy on the bench because we knew that Rochdale played deep to stop Adrian. In the first half, I must have put my head in my hands 10 times. The ball was a red-hot potato. They were whacking it everywhere. I thought it was no wonder people said we were long-ball merchants, it wasn't constructive at all. I was glad when the half-time whistle went.

I had a chat with Mick at half-time to gather my thoughts and we both decided that I had to lace into one or two people. I lifted the roof a bit with Adrian. I made comments to all the midfield, Leadbitter, Clayton, Maugé. Hardly a tackle had been made in midfield and I said

Ian Baird

Rochdale must be laughing their heads off.

They had come to be beaten, that's what I thought, and I said that if they didn't change it in 10 minutes' time, I'd put Ian Baird on and have another go. We had only been sat down for four minutes, and Adie scored a brilliant individual goal. I could see him looking towards me at the bench as he was coming back with his celebrations. No doubt he would have loved to have come over to me but it just showed you, we decided that we would give him 10 minutes or we would pull him off. He just scored the goal and from then on he was dangerous every time he got the ball. I thought we did well in the second half and ran out easy winners even though only Michael Evans scored with five or six minutes to go.

It was interesting when I saw the interview with Adrian on the television the next day. He said that the gaffer had given everyone a few choice words at half-time and kicked everyone up the... I think he was going to say arse but changed it at the last minute and he said bottom! "Give us a kick up the bottom." I thought "How very articulate."

The Monday morning back-page headlines trumpeting Argyle's return to some sort of promotion form were overshadowed by tragic news on the front page: Alan Nicholls, the young goalkeeper sacked by Argyle only weeks earlier, had been killed in a motorcycle accident on Saturday evening.

Nicholls, who was just 22, was the pillion passenger on a bike which crashed on the A1 near Peterborough. He perished instantly, and the 24-year-old driver of the machine, Matthew Lindsey, died later in hospital.

Hours earlier, Nicholls had made his debut for GM Vauxhall Conference side Stalybridge Celtic in a 3-1 victory at Dover. He had just left Gillingham, after finding his first-team opportunities blocked by in-form Jim Stannard.

Lindsey was the elder brother of Scott Lindsey, who had also been released by Gillingham and had been playing for Dover on the fateful afternoon. According to police, he lost control of the bike for reasons which were not immediately clear and the machine left the road at a place called Norman's Cross.

Nicholls had only got on the bike at Stilton – about a mile from the crash scene – after swapping places with the Lindseys' father, Keith. Mr Lindsey then travelled on in a car driven by Scott, their destination being the Lindsey family home near Scunthorpe.

Sometime after realising the motorcycle was no longer following them, Keith and Scott turned back and, tragically, came across the accident scene with the police already in attendance.

The shockwaves generated by the nature and sheer suddenness of Nicholls' death rippled across the West Country. Nicholls had been no angel, either on or off the field of play, but his loss was keenly felt.

Peter Shilton, who had signed Nicholls for Argyle from non-league Cheltenham two and a half years previously and coached him to a place in the England under-21 set-up within seven months, said:

Alan Nicholls

"Alan did exceptionally well for me as a player, particularly during his first season. I know he was a little wayward but I liked him as a lad, even though he did lose his way a bit."

Shilton's former assistant John McGovern said he remembered Nicholls "for his extravagant character and tremendous ability. To play for England under-21s after his first season in league football was something quite remarkable."

Argyle chairman Dan McCauley called Nicholls "a wonderful talent whose death is a sad loss for football. I know he had his troubles but he treated me and my wife with respect. I always found him to be a gentleman."

Former Home Park director Ivor Jones revealed that he had pleaded with other clubs to give Nicholls a chance because he felt a change of environment from one where his bad reputation preceded him would make all the difference.

"There was light at the end of the tunnel – a real chance there," said Jones, "but sometimes fate can play nasty tricks in life."

Nicholls was always popular with the Green Armada which travelled to Argyle's away matches, and they staged their own tribute to the late wayward talent from the terraces of Kingsmeadow the following Sunday. If any of Alan Nicholls' relatives were tuned into *Sky Sports* to watch the FA Cup second-round tie between Kingstonian and Argyle on December 3, they would have been proud to hear the chant of "There's Only One Alan Nicholls."

The general consensus being that there would be a green moon over Plymouth before Neil Warnock was out-verballed meant that astronomers had been eagerly scanning the heavens in the week leading up to the televised match.

Shy and retiring Warnock ain't, but compared to Chris Kelly, chief executive of ICIS League Kingstonian, the Argyle manager appeared positively Garbo-esque. The Leatherhead Lip, who enjoyed his 15 minutes of fame when the Surrey non-leaguers dumped professional opposition out of the Cup with admirable regularity two decades previously, had not become less vociferously opinionated with the passing of time.

"He's done all the talking," admitted Warnock, "saying how they don't expect to get beaten; how we might get a draw if we're lucky. We don't have to do any spouting off. I think we'll do our talking on the pitch."

Nevertheless, Warnock was aware that Sky's decision to televise the match live had not been made purely on the Pilgrims' pulling power.

"They've picked us because they feel there's a chance of an upset," he agreed. "So we've got to make sure there isn't an upset. The tie is in our hands. Put it this way: where would you rather go – Swindon away or Kingstonian away?"

There was, however, no upset and not much for Chris Kelly to talk about afterwards, except for another run-of-the-mill spectacular Adrian Littlejohn goal which settled the tie 2-1 in Argyle's favour six minutes from time.

Standing with his back to the goal, Littlejohn flicked the ball over his head and then past the startled Kingstonian goalkeeper, Dave Root by name and rooted by nature, to memorably end an unmemorable match.

"The goal would have graced the Premiership," said Warnock afterwards, "but I was relieved when it went in because we didn't play well."

Well enough to feature in the FA's new high-tech draw at Lancaster Gate the following night, however.

Chris Leadbitter gave the Greens a Sunday lunchtime lead when he seized on a poor eighth-minute clearance to sweetly half-volley the ball back with interest from the edge of the area.

Chris Leadbitter celebrates his goal against Kingstonian

However, after the bright start, Argyle went to pieces, arguing amongst themselves, panicking at regular intervals, booting the ball aimlessly in the air, and generally defending too deep. Kingstonian took advantage of the general malaise to equalise just before half-time, political graduate Eddie Akuamoah finding Jon Warden parked at the far post for a routine header.

Argyle played much better in the second half and avoided the need for a replay when Littlejohn pounced on Gary Clayton's cross with five minutes remaining.

Pilgrims' supporters and players could now enjoy a day of sweet anticipation, dreaming of the visit of Manchester United or Liverpool; directors could spend the time calculating how much revenue that sort of draw would generate. Small matter that Argyle tended to have the same attraction for the likes of Cinderford and Woking as cow pats do for flies.

Not for Warnock was the stock anyone-as-long-as-it's-at-home approach when questioned on who he fancied being paired with in the third round. A life-long Sheffield United supporter, he wanted a crack at the Steel City's other club, Wednesday.

With equal honesty, he admitted: "The third round is glamorous for little clubs unless you get Oldham away or Stockport away. It's not so good then."

England coach Terry Venables and former Scotland international Denis Law made the draw and managed to avoid sending Argyle to Greater Manchester. Instead, the Pilgrims were drawn at home to FA Carling Premiership strugglers Coventry.

"It's a cracking draw," said Warnock, who had watched Ron Atkinson's Sky Blues lose to Sheffield Wednesday on Sky earlier in the evening. "We couldn't have asked for much more. We have nothing to lose and I'm sure we can give them a good game." The question was: could Coventry give Argyle a good game? Bottom of the table, with a single win from 16 Premiership games, Pilgrims' supporters were already using the words "cup" and "upset" in the same sentence. The more realistic members of the board preferred "sell" and "out".

The prospect of a positive boost to Argyle's negative bank account was followed by the generation of further income with the completion, after trials and a two-month loan, of Wayne Burnett's move to Bolton Wanderers. The fee of £100,000 represented a depreciation in value on Burnett's behalf of some 30% in the two years since he had joined Argyle from Blackburn Rovers reserves.

While he was in a give-away mood, Warnock also let Kevin Magee join the Pilgrims' Third Division rivals Scarborough in a move designed to give him first-team football. Magee had made four league appearances as substitute since being released by Preston in September.

NW: *"I organised a golfing event for the Tuesday before the FA Cup-tie at Kingstonian. The lads hadn't had a game of golf since the start of the season, so I took them to St Mellion just to give the TV cameras some coverage. I thought we would get rid of all the rigmarole early on in the week so the players' minds would be focused on the match. They are all supporters at St Mellion. Even the owners, the Bond brothers. They can't really do enough for you.*

The weather was absolutely terrible – lightning, thunder, all sorts – all morning and then we came out for 10.20 a.m. tee-offs. Two minutes before the first tee-off, it stopped, and it was brilliant right to the end. Then it poured down again. I think it must have been some divine intervention!

It was funny when we were being interviewed by the BBC. The camera guy went back up on the bank to get a good shot of us with the commentator and he slipped right down and there was a big bang. His trousers were absolutely covered in mud. Of course, the other cameraman turned around and filmed him. He said "That will be a good shot for Christmas."

Every manager fears non-league teams in the FA Cup but you know whether you win those games or lose them lies in your own dressing-room. We knew it would be a harder game than Slough, especially with Sky's cameras being there but it was a great opportunity to project the club nationally.

They asked us if the 1.30 p.m. kick-off on the Sunday would upset us. I said for £60,000 we would kick off at midnight. It was super for us to get that sort of income from a match like that and obviously great for Kingstonian.

Baird had a little practice match on the Wednesday and had to come off. His groin was still not right so I decided to leave it alone on the Sunday.

I had also spoken to Roy McFarland at Bolton and basically agreed about Wayne Burnett. We had kept it out of the newspapers because he had been involved in trouble with Arsenal's David Hillier. Bolton were going to sign him early on, but decided to wait and see what developed in that particular case.

I also agreed with Scarborough that Kevin Magee could go up there after the weekend's game. He hadn't had a proper full game with us and I felt sorry for him. He was a smashing lad. We hadn't had that many injuries and with him only playing wide left, I decided I'd try and get him a few games up there.

We went up to London on the Saturday. What a difference travelling on a Saturday made. Super traffic-wise, a lot better. Got up to the hotel about 40 minutes from Kingston and trained in good facilities. Everything was right.

I knew, having talked to Rob Hawthorne from Sky on the Friday, who had come down to look at all the players because he was doing the commentary, they were expecting an upset

Wayne Burnett

and I suppose it just made me a little bit more nervous. I think also, with me being at Plymouth as well, it was like being two-in-one, to see me lose to a non-league team would probably have been a plus.

Everything went well preparation-wise and we went out with a positive attitude and took the lead within seven minutes, a cracking goal by Leadbitter. Then the front three stopped completely and gradually we were pinned back, simply because the front three weren't working. I couldn't wait for half-time, but just seconds before half-time Kingstonian snatched an equaliser and I knew that their tails were up.

I went in the shower at half-time, which I always do and Mick Jones came in to talk to me. I was furious with the front three and he agreed. While we were there, we could hear the Kingstonian dressing room, which was absolutely bubbling. It sounded as if there was 100 people in there. Because they had equalised, they were all shouting, "We can do them now, they are nothing" and I said to Mick "To be fair, having watched us play in the first half, we were nothing."

I then went back in and criticised Micky Evans for his contribution. He was trying to do too much, to beat everybody when he could lay the ball off. I criticised Chris Billy for certain things he did and then I turned away and came back and said to Adrian Littlejohn: "You haven't done anything at all, so how can I criticise you?"

That was all that was said. The second half started and the front three could have had two or three goals in the first five minutes. Adrian made some super moves and in the end, with five minutes to go, he hit a quality goal, a Premier League goal. I was pleased for Adrian. He ran towards me and I jumped off the bench – I don't do that very often – and gave him a slap.

The FA Cup is a lovely competition and it was nice to travel back having won. I think that's when you don't mind being in Plymouth and having to travel a few hours back because, after games like that, everyone is satisfied. It's a nice situation to be in on the coach. There is nothing quite like being on the coach travelling back with a good result.

With the adrenalin, you are definitely on a high, although within two hours of the end of the game I am always shattered. It must take a lot out of you but you don't realise it because you don't do any running. I was quite tired a couple of hours down the motorway although Sky gave me a copy of the video of the game and we watched it on the way back.

It was nice to see the commentators at half-time saying "This could be a big upset." It was good to prove them wrong.

We had to wait until the Monday night for the draw. Sharon and I were hoping that we would get a good tie. We watched it on television and the main thing was if we didn't get a great tie, to make sure we were at home, because we had covered some miles travelling.

When 64 came out, we knew we were at home and we both cheered. To get Coventry was *just brilliant, we had just been watching them on the television – Coventry against Sheffield Wednesday – and we knew Big Ron would be a big pull because he has got some good players. We would probably get almost a full house. It was a great draw for us. We couldn't lose.*

We went into training on the Tuesday and all the lads were talking about it, Paul Williams in particular. I said that when we came in on the Thursday, all we would talk about was Wigan. Looking ahead, we had got some tough games, three out of the following four were top-form teams, so we knew what was at stake now.

I finalised the Burnett deal and we agreed £100,000 with Bolton on the Monday. I was pleased for Wayne. He is a smashing lad and I know he was in a bit of trouble but I was sure everything would work out all right, because I had no trouble with him at all.

We'd had quite a few groin injuries. Adrian Littlejohn did his groin again in a training session and Ian Baird had this stomach-pull. Ronnie Maugé had hurt the back of his knee, so he was doubtful. Mentally, I think he knew that he had got something wrong with the back of his knee and I didn't think he wanted to play against Wigan.

I also didn't think Chris Billy was 100 per cent right since his cartilage operation and I was tempted to play Ian Baird up front and Micky Evans back on the right. Also, Martin Barlow had done well again. He had been to see me, which was understandable, and I told him he was still part of my plans. And I was tempted to fling him in against Wigan.

Snow had hit the country. We spent Thursday in the gym because it had been freezing, minus three or four down our way, but the rest of the country was covered in snow and the forecast was quite good for the weekend. I must admit, winter is the time of year when people in Plymouth are lucky, being out on a limb.

While Argyle readied themselves for one showdown, another took place in the Vice-Presidents' club at Home Park on the evening of December 8 – McCauley v Angilley at the annual meeting of the Pilgrims' shareholders.

Angilley was duly voted off the board, although it required the full weight of the chairman's massive share-holding in Argyle to remove his fellow director from office. When the resolution to remove Truro-based property developer Angilley from the board was put to the packed meeting, not one shareholder approved the motion on a show of hands.

However, McCauley, who owns 75 per cent of the the club's share-holding through his *Rotolok* engineering company, immediately called for a card-vote and the motion was carried by 45,637 votes to 736 – a whopping 98.4 per cent majority.

Angilley and McCauley had been at loggerheads over the former's role at the club since before the start of the season, when McCauley had accused some directors of deriving benefits from Argyle "which far exceeded their investments" and called into question the efforts they put into the running of the club.

McCauley, who had underwritten Argyle to the tune of £1.6m since becoming chairman in October, 1990, had then returned Angilley's £50,000 interest-free deposit he placed with the club upon joining the board four years previously, claiming Angilley's acceptance of the money represented his resignation.

Angilley, who had always insisted he did not resign, told the meeting: "Let me make it quite clear – I did not seek the return of my capital. On the contrary, I have written to the club several times, reiterating my willingness to put more money into the club.

"I didn't want that back. I have been supporting the club for 40 years. I have got green blood. The chairman has given me no justifiable reason for seeking my resignation."

Neither was he about to. "Whatever I am doing is for the benefit of the club," he told the shareholders. "That's a fact, whether you like it or not. If Denis had been doing so much for the club, I would not be seeking his resignation. I am not prepared to give my reasons. I don't want to cause too much trouble. Whatever I am doing is not detrimental to the club. It might be in your eyes, but it's not in mine."

When Angilley tried to speak again, McCauley refused to let him, saying: "You have had your say, Denis."

"I think that's entirely unfair and unjust," replied Angilley before the fatal vote was taken.

"I am disgusted by the manner in which this club is being run," Angilley told the waiting Press. "It is totally autocratic."

Earlier, former Argyle director Ivor Jones had asked McCauley for an apology over the chairman's "offensive" remarks that the club was "subsidising" its directors, the issue upon which he had resigned the previous month. McCauley declined, saying: "At the present time and at present rates of interest, I am not prepared to make an apology. I think a directorship of this club is worth far more than £50,000 in a guaranteed deposit."

Before the vote on Angilley, McCauley had been re-elected as a director – his position coming up for review by rotation – on a simple show of hands. Director Graham Jasper was similarly re-elected and although admitting he did not support the demand for Angilley's resignation, paid tribute to McCauley for bringing Neil Warnock to the club.

"I think we are on the verge of something great," he said. "For the good of Plymouth Argyle, I would like us to work together to win promotion this year and probably next."

Warnock had attended the meeting, though for the most part he looked as though he would rather be watching Exeter City beat Argyle 5-0, and it was relief to him and most supporters when the focus of the club returned to attempting to win the promotion which Jasper wanted.

The next match posed a real threat to their ambitions. Wigan had been unbeaten in eight matches since John Deehan took over as manager from Graham Barrow – who had been sacked in the wake of Argyle's earlier victory at Springfield Park – and their Spanish contingent of Isidro Diaz, Roberto Martinez and Jesus Seba were helping to mount a promotion charge of their own.

However, Wigan's vaunted Spanish contingent had about as much joy as the last of their ilk to head for the South West intent on making off with the spoils.

The name of Adrian Littlejohn was fast becoming as associated with the City of Plymouth as that of Sir Francis Drake and, like Tavistock's famous salty-dog, the Pilgrims' striker left it late before seeing off the challenge of Argyle's Iberian-boosted visitors.

By the time Littlejohn sealed the victory with yet another quality strike from his seemingly endless repertoire of virtuoso goals, the Latics' Three Amigos had been reduced to a sad lone *hombre*: Seba did not even make the bench; Diaz was dragged after being shepherded up a blind alley by Paul Williams all afternoon; and Martinez had been rendered ineffective by the omnipresence in his vicinity of Gary Clayton.

Littlejohn was by now worth big money. Only three other players had scored more league goals than his 14 and two of them were vying for the England number nine shirt. Argyle's lethal left-footer might not have been able to command the sort of fee that would have tempted Newcastle and Blackburn to part company with Les Ferdinand and Alan Shearer, but he had certainly become more valuable than the £200,000 Warnock had paid for him in the summer after twisting chairman McCauley's arm up his back.

Not that Warnock would be likely to consider any offers. "Littlejohn will be here as long as I'm here," said the Argyle manager. "Well, no, he might not – he's only got three years. He'll be here for three years, whether he likes it or not. It's not all Littlejohn – it's a team game. The team actually makes Littlejohn what he is. All right, he can get us out of prison but I thought today his contribution in general play was more than it has been for some time – the best it has been in his career."

Argyle, who went into the match with their Wigan peers having registered one victory from five previous attempts, were locked into another missed opportunity when Littlejohn burrowed an escape to a 3-1 victory.

With 15 minutes of the game left, he gave the Pilgrims a 2-1 lead from granny-scoring range after Mark Patterson and Michael Evans had one-twoed their way out of some nervous defending on the edge of their own area to the opposition danger-zone in a sweeping move which spoke eloquently of Argyle's power and stamina.

Then, in the 89th minute, he span off his marker on the left-hand touchline to latch onto Martin Barlow's accurate pass down the channel and, with the entire Wigan half at his sole disposal, danced up to goalkeeper Simon Farnworth and side-footed nonchalantly home.

If his celebrations of such a fine goal appeared somewhat muted, it might have been that he was getting into the habit of making the extraordinary look mundane or it might have been that he had been booked for celebrating with the Lyndhurst Road side after his previous strike.

Whatever, it was impossible to disagree with Wigan manager Deehan's observation that "any centre-half in the land would have struggled to cope with his pace. The boy is a big threat at this level."

To complete a fine afternoon's work, Littlejohn also set up Barlow for Argyle's eighth-minute opener with a low, driven cross that progressed to the recalled midfielder by way of Chris Leadbitter's involuntary air-shot. Wigan equalised through Andy Farrell five minutes later and for more than an hour, the visitors weathered not so much an Argyle storm, more a squally shower.

Nevertheless, Deehan was impressed. "They are the best team we have played," he said. "Physically and organisation-wise, they are above anything else we've played."

"I think John Deehan's a sensible bloke," joked Warnock, who had now steered the good ship Pilgrim to fourth place in the Third Division, behind Gillingham, Preston and Chester.

NW: *I went to the AGM. The first question was "Do you think that somebody who doesn't have any shares should be allowed to be in the meeting?" Everybody said "Who do you mean?" And they said "The manager." I thought "Well, I am off to a good start here." It was 7.30 p.m. and I thought to myself, I wish they would second him or vote on it and I could go home, but I wasn't that lucky. It was quite a heated meeting, I must admit, and at the end of the day the chairman had his way.*

I was asked questions and gave a question-answer session. I thought everybody cared – you could tell that by listening to the crowd – and I said to myself "Here we are in the Third Division and nobody wants to be here." I just hoped I could do my job and get them promotion, although we were six points behind the top three at the time.

Mick Jones finally moved house and Richard Logan moved down as well, so nearly everyone was settled just before Christmas. It just showed how long it had taken to get people to move down. It hadn't been easy, with nine new players.

I had a chat on Friday morning with Ronnie Maugé and I could tell his leg was not right. We managed to get him booked in for a scan and there was no serious damage there, so at least he knew that, but he was not himself, so I decided to play Martin Barlow against Wigan.

Martin has looked ever so sharp in training and I just thought it was the right time to bring him in. I told Ronnie to get himself right, even if it took him a couple of weeks, just get ready for Christmas. I needed to have him right, to have him sharp, and he was not sharp.

We had our Christmas dinner on the Tuesday. Ian Baird had told me he didn't think he could go to it so I said to him: "Bairdy, can you go on Tuesday? because if you can't, it affects my selection tomorrow against Wigan." He said: "It can't do, gaffer." I said: "It does. If you can go on Tuesday, you can play tomorrow. If you can't go to the dinner on Tuesday, you can't play." And we both burst out laughing.

We won the game, 3-1, two great last goals from Adrian and our best performance I felt. Before the game, I made Adrian Littlejohn captain. I didn't want to make Micky Heathcote captain because we seemed to lose every game with him as captain and I am so superstitious.

So I got 11 pieces of paper, put a cross on one and said "Come on lads, £2 each. Whoever draws the cross out is captain." So they all laughed, although Gary Clayton said he thought he should be captain, being the oldest.

They all started pulling the paper out, but nobody pulled the cross out. There was only one left and Blackie hadn't pulled one so we threw it in the bin. Adie said he wanted to be captain, and Paul Williams said: "He can't be captain boss." I said: "I can do anything, Charlie. Right Adie, you're captain." So his eyes lit up, and down the tunnel we went.

Martin Barlow scored the first goal from an Adrian Littlejohn cross. Legsy missed it and Martin was there. We started off quite well, but then we let them get back in it. They played passing football. I was disappointed with the equaliser for numerous reasons.

It started up front, where Adrian let the full-back go, and when they crossed it, the centre-halves were behind the striker. And Blackie could have saved it, I thought. Anyhow, we were 1-1 and we were against the wind for the second half. It was freezing cold but I had never heard anything like the fans that afternoon – 5,900 and it was the best I had ever heard them shout, even when there was 7,000 or 8,000 here.

They willed us to win in the second half. Their 'keeper pulled off some great saves from Leadbitter, but we kept driving on and then we got the break, a tap-in at the far post from Adrian. I was really pleased because it was a move right from our own box. And then the last goal was brilliant.

I was obviously delighted and John Deehan said some kind things. He said we were the best side he had seen since he had been at the club. Well-organised, disciplined. At the Press conference they asked me what I thought about John Deehan's comments. And I said, he obviously knew what he was talking about and smiled.

Obviously I was pleased because I knew we looked a solid outfit on the day and I thought we were going to cause a lot of people problems.

Warnock's mood had changed sharply a week later. On the morning of the match against lowly Lincoln City at Sincil Bank, the *Western Morning News* carried an exclusive story headlined "Warnock 'will quit Argyle.'" Once again, the behind-the-scenes events at Home Park threatened to overshadow efforts being made on it.

"IF HE SELLS THE CLUB, I WILL GO"

NEIL Warnock's promise to walk out on the club he had been at for just five and a half months was spurred by sacked director Denis Angilley's threat to oust Dan McCauley as chairman. Angilley said he would launch a hostile bid for McCauley's 75 per cent share-holding in the club if the chairman did not sell him the shares willingly.

Warnock said: "As far as I am concerned, if he [McCauley] sells the club, I will go. I have had a chat with the chairman and he is adamant he won't even consider selling the club. He's perfectly happy with the management side of things and I am perfectly happy with him. We are working together. Let us get on with it. The club is not for sale."

Angilley, who had kept his powder dry since being muscled off the board the previous Thursday had called for a meeting with McCauley "to discuss whether he is prepared to sell the club and for how much."

He further hinted he would make a hostile bid for the shares should Tiverton-based millionaire McCauley refuse to sell. In a long statement, Angilley said he had been approached by businessmen who wanted to invest in Argyle; that he wanted to form a "democratic" board with no one person holding a majority of shares; and that he supported Warnock "wholeheartedly."

The object of his wholehearted support was, however, less than enamoured with the backing. "If these people are supporters of Plymouth Argyle, they should get behind us and let us get on with it," said Warnock. "Dan and myself both want to win, to get success for Plymouth Argyle, and we're well on our way to doing that. I think there has been enough said about Plymouth off the the field. I wish people would just let us get on with it."

McCauley, too, was dismissive of Angilley. "I am disappointed at the timing of the statement, with the side in with a real chance in the promotion battle and seemingly going in the right direction," he said. "We can do without these sort of distractions right now. I am surprised Mr Angilley has taken a week to think all this out. It should only take you a few minutes to decide you want to buy a football club – that's all it took me. As for the financial position of the club, it's not worrying me and I'm the one with the money in the club."

The off-field head-to-head diverted Warnock's attentions from the match against Lincoln, who had changed managers since losing 3-0 at Home Park earlier in the season. John Beck's success at stopping the rot he had inherited from Steve Wicks had resulted in him winning the Third Division manager of the month award for November.

Beck's Imps included only two players – Udo Onwere and Matt Carbon – who had lined up at Home Park at the end of September and the new players showed more fortitude than their predecessors in holding Argyle to a goal-less draw at Sincil Bank.

Once again, Adrian Littlejohn – captain in the absence of Ronnie Maugé – carried the Pilgrims' greatest threat and the closest Argyle came to scoring was two minutes into the second half, when he robbed Alan Johnson on the bye-line and cut in to send a ferocious drive just over the bar.

"I knew what we would be up against and I thought the commitment of our lads was great," said Warnock. "If you don't show that sort of passion, you will go under. I am sure Lincoln will do us a few favours over the next few months."

The week before Christmas brought some tidings of comfort and joy for Argyle supporters. Firstly, Denis Angilley drew back from his attempts to oust chairman Dan McCauley.

"We have four important games over the holiday period and it is vitally important that we win them and get to the top of the Third Division table as quickly as possible," he said. "The other reason I do not intend to keep the disagreement raging is that this is the season of goodwill and I do not believe anyone wants to read about hostile bids during the Christmas and New Year period."

The former director said that his main reason for making public his willingness to buy out McCauley was to dispel the fears of some supporters that Argyle would face a massive cash crisis if McCauley withdrew his considerable financial backing and demonstrate that there was an alternative.

"When we lost the first six games of the season, the chairman said he would consider resigning. I would like to think his commitment to the club is reliable and solid," he said. "It is important for the club to have security and stability."

The second seasonal surprise was the signing of Torquay United defender Chris Curran on the eve of the home match against Cambridge United two days before Christmas.

Curran swapped the threat of impending relegation for the prospect of possible promotion, moving 20 places up the Endsleigh Third Division and 35 miles down the A38 for an undisclosed fee.

"I am delighted to have got him," said Warnock, who had kept tabs on the Birmingham-born defender since his three-month caretaker stint at Plainmoor. "He'll bring a bit of additional strength to the squad because we are short of both centre-backs and full-backs and he can play in either position. I think he's been at Torquay a bit too long. He responded to me when I was down there and I hope I can give his career a lift."

With Argyle facing four games in 10 days, the arrival of Curran could not have come at a better time.

"Points will come from places that we least expect them," said Warnock, "but I am hoping we will not be too far adrift from the top after the four games. We don't want to be six or nine points behind the leaders. We want to be three or four points behind, at most."

The first three points, which left Argyle two points behind new table-toppers Preston (who had overtaken long-time front-runners Chester by virtue of having scored more goals), came from a 1-0 home win against Cambridge.

The only goal of a match which was far from the Christmas cracker Warnock had prophesised it would be came from midfielder Ronnie Maugé in the 75th minute. Maugé, who had missed Argyle's previous two matches with a knee injury, had been a surprise inclusion in the Pilgrims' line-up.

Warnock was encouraged to plunge the golden-toothed Londoner back into action after he came through a training session on the Friday before the game. "We knew he would not last the game, but he was looking sharp and we decided to give him a go," said Warnock. "In fact, we were just asking him to give us another five minutes when he scored the winner. No goalkeeper in the country would have saved it."

The goal, a vicious dipping drive from outside the penalty area, would not be the last vital scoring contribution Maugé would make to Argyle's season.

NW: *I spoke to Dan and he had no intentions of selling the club. He was perfectly happy that I was down at Plymouth and I was happy with him. We both needed to make a statement to counteract all the other statements that were going around about takeovers. I would say that I was happy as long as he was in charge. And he would say the same about me. I thought it would be wrong not to show my loyalties.*

There had been a slight hitch in the Burnett deal even though it had gone through. It could be a little while before it was finalised because of a blood disorder he had. They were doing further tests on this.

We couldn't get in our favoured hotel at Lincoln so we went back up to Rotherham, even though it was a bit further it was where we stayed when we played Hartlepool. We knew the training facilities were good and the hotel was nice.

I decided to put Richard Logan in and leave Martin Barlow out, even though he had scored in the previous game, because I just knew what John Beck would do and I thought we would need another big lad, especially with Logan's throw.

True to form, you could see that the pitch had been narrowed three yards and plenty of sand had been put in the corners to help hold up the ball.

I was worried about the tactical switch, because Martin Barlow had played well against Wigan but I knew in my heart of hearts that I had to have Richard Logan in the team and I did need him. He did well defensively and nearly scored a goal, had a header cleared off the line by the defender with the goalie beaten.

I would say the game was probably the worst type of game I have ever played in. I couldn't remember Cambridge being as direct as Lincoln were but Gary Clayton and Micky Heathcote assured me they were. You have to give John Beck credit even though I wouldn't like to play like that. He had got them off the bottom when they were fighting for their lives. Good luck to them.

We could only draw 0-0 and it was down to us to score but we couldn't manage to get a goal. There again, Gillingham lost and the other two drew so we were still only three or five points behind the top three.

Mick Jones moved house at last and I gave the other lads in Sheffield a few days off until Tuesday after the Lincoln game so they could go back and see their families. I made it a condition that they did that as long as they went to the London Supporters' do after the game with Lincoln, which they did.

The kids beat Eastleigh in the Youth Cup, which meant that we had a home game against Tottenham Hotspur which was a tremendous game for us.

I asked for peace off the field so I could get on now that Dan was not selling and I was definitely happy. Let's just get everybody behind the team and get on with it.

Once again we didn't have Ian Baird or Adrian all week. Adie trained on the Tuesday but he never came with us for the rest of the week because it was so wet and he didn't want to go in the gymnasium. Bairdy had 'flu earlier on in the week but Ronnie Maugé started training and he looked quite sharp.

On Friday morning we were doing set pieces and had no Adrian Littlejohn, He had telephoned Mick to say his house had been flooded in the evening and he had not had any sleep. They slept downstairs and all the downstairs had been flooded, and he had to move all the beds upstairs with the kids. I told him to get himself off home to try and get some shut-eye and just report for the game.

Burnett's deal was still on hold as Bolton were waiting for the test results. His blood showed signs of jaundice, which he had when he was a child. The Bolton doctors were in agreement that it should be all right but obviously they wanted to wait and see.

I spoke all week with Mike Bateson at Torquay about Chris Curran. I wanted to get him in the squad as quickly as possible. I said to them a couple of weeks previously, that I would leave it until they were out of the Cup and just give Eddie May a chance to line up one or two players.

But I telephoned Mike and he agreed to the deal which had already been discussed and Chris came over and we put it through on the Friday morning.

It was marvellous how it brought the best out of the lads during the training session to see a new face and I hope it has the desired effects on the Saturday. Chris could push both centre-halves

Chris Curran

and full-backs, so I thought he was a good addition to the squad.

I had a chat with Ronnie Maugé and he assured me that he did feel back to normal, so I put him back in. Martin Barlow would be the odd one out, although he hadn't done anything wrong. I told him that and that I wanted him to keep his head up.

Ronnie scored a cracking goal with 15 minutes to go just when I was contemplating bringing him off because his legs were going, and he had already asked about the substitute. We defended well, although Bairdy was put through and a lad pulled him down and should have got sent off.

The referee was Rodger Gifford, who was in his last season. I spoke to him after the game and asked him why he had not sent the player off and he said for the first time in his career he had listened to a player. Ian Baird, our centre-forward, had pleaded with him to leave the player on.

It was ironic at nearly the end of the game, they nearly equalised with a long throw-in from the player who would have been sent off. All right, it's professional to try and stop your man being sent off, but there is nobody in the country who would have done it for Ian Baird. If it had been Ian Baird committing that offence, he would have been off, make no mistake.

Boxing Day dawned bright and early for the loyal Argyle supporters who had determined to follow their team from one side of the country to the other for the most ludicrous of Bank Holiday fixtures. Even accepting objections by the police to local Derbies at holiday times, there were surely few less appropriate matches the Football League fixtures computer could have programmed to spew out than a visit to Gillingham.

The long trip would be physically and financially wearing for the Pilgrims and their most loyal of supporters as the winding road to Kent had been the most difficult in the country for clubs to negotiate.

Priestfield, the rock on which the resurgent Gills had been building their promotion campaign, was a miserable place to visit because in 13 Endsleigh League hours played there, only twice had the ball ended up in the home side's net. Indeed, in their 20 league matches, Gillingham had conceded only a miserly seven goals. Their defence, which included former Pilgrim Dominic Naylor, made Scrooge look like a paragon of generosity.

There was precious little goodwill between the two sides, either during or after the post Christmas clash, which Gillingham won 1-0 through an 83rd-minute penalty from striker Steve Butler. Butler, making his home debut after signing for the Gills for £100,000 from Cambridge United, converted the spot-kick after Gary Clayton had handled Leo Fortune-West's header off the line.

Clayton was sent off by referee Graham Pooley, who, along with his linesmen, was the subject of Argyle manager Neil Warnock's ire after the game. Warnock was convinced goalkeeper Kevin Blackwell had been impeded in the build-up to the incident and made his point forcibly after the Pilgrims' first defeat in eight games.

"I thought we were playing against 14 men for the whole game," he said. "I don't think the penalty would have been given if it had been at the other end."

Not even Warnock could have argued against a first-minute booking for Chris Leadbitter, following a foul on Richard Green which set the tone for a fiercely competitive 90 minutes that often threatened to get out of hand.

Pooley also yellow-carded Mark Patterson for throwing away the ball after conceding a free-kick – an impetuous act which would cost the defender his place in the FA Cup tie against Coventry – and Ronnie Maugé, for dissent.

Maugé's dissent might have been provoked by racial abuse which Warnock alleged his midfielder had been receiving from one of the Gillingham players. He threatened to report the player, who denied the suggestions, to the Professional Footballers' Association.

"I was a bit disappointed with the sort of racial abuse I heard him shouting on the pitch," said Warnock. "I don't think they were called for at all. I wonder what some of his own players, like Dennis Bailey [a black player and a Born Again Christian], think about those comments?"

All in all, Warnock had a Boxing Day to forget. The defeat at Gillingham was followed by a minor car crash on black ice as he and his partner Sharon – who had been running a temperature of 103 during the day – returned to their Cornwall home.

The third of Argyle's holiday games, against Northampton, scheduled for Saturday, December 29, was called off after Sixfields became Sixdegreesunderfields and the frost-bound pitch failed a morning inspection.

NW: *We travelled up to Gillingham on Christmas Day evening, and Micky Heathcote wanted to use the gym at the Posthouse in Chatham. This guy from the Posthouse gymnasium looked like a right poseur and said he couldn't use it because it was closed at 8 p.m. As if Micky Heathcote was a rebel – I nearly lost my temper, but I didn't.*

Boxing Day probably started off the worst day I had had for many years. In the night Sharon wasn't very well with a temperature and I had to telephone the doctor. So I had to leave her in bed all day while we were at Gillingham.

Mick [Jones] went to the ground while we went training and said the ground was hard but he thought the referee would play it and we proceeded to have an afternoon when we were really up against it but we played ever so well. We showed such a lot of commitment and I think we were the better side in the first half. They got more pressure in the second half but we didn't have any help whatsoever from the officials.

The opposition were standing in front of Kevin Blackwell at corners and obstructing him every time. Apart from once, when Blackwell ended up on the floor and the referee had to blow, he never gave us a thing in that situation.

We lost to a foul on the goalie from a corner, from which they headed the ball on and Gary Clayton was sent off for handling on the line. If the referee had been anywhere near the situation, it would have been a foul, but his positioning was a disgrace. The referee must have had a good Christmas, I think.

The thing that bugged me that day was one of their lads asked one of our lads before the game if there were any coloured lads playing. He then proceeded to give Ronnie Maugé so much verbal racial abuse, it was untrue.

Three or four lads complained. We told the referee about it and he just sniggered while the player kept smiling away. The referee just smiled when we told him on the pitch and our physio went and told him as well, while he was treating a player.

I find it ironic that a Gillingham side with coloured lads in Fortune-West and Bailey complained about verbal abuse at Hartlepool and Darlington earlier in the season. Here was their team-mate giving it more about racial abuse than anyone else. I ask you: is there a need for this sort of hatred?

I had a word with Butler, who scored the winner, after the game and just said to him: "You want to tell your team-mate there has got to be more to his game than that, if that is the only way he can get players going."

We got back to the hotel after the game and took the doctor back to see Sharon, and he gave her some antibiotics.

We set off on the way back and she was terrible. We had to stop the car. She obviously had a temperature of about 103 degrees and we got back in freezing conditions. It was minus seven as we got into Cornwall and half a mile from our house, I was going down a little hill on the approach where we live, and there was one sheet of ice 50 to 60 yards long, which I didn't realise.

I was only doing 20 m.p.h. and touched the brakes. They just locked completely and the car went off on this skid. I could see a telegraph pole in front and I had about 50 yards to find out what I should do, I took the foot straight off the brakes. I knew we were going to hit the pole, but it would just lessen the impact from where we were sitting in the front. As we got there, I just steered the car gently to the side, and it hit the telegraph pole and dented the back door and made a mess of the back panel. Apparently the ice was caused by a burst water-main.

We limped back home and I got Sharon straight into bed. During the night, I had to get the doctor out again because she was still running a temperature. I think it was 104 degrees at one stage, which is really dangerous, and that was the end of what you would call a bleak day.

The following day I had to try and get the car sorted out, but I also had to appear on a radio show at Radio Devon. They had suggested a Christmas programme with prizes etc., but I must admit it took some doing to get in there.

I remember after the game, even though we were disappointed, I just said "I can't believe how much effort you put in lads, for nothing" and Mick Jones said that would win the league. We were four points behind Gillingham once again, but we had been 12 points behind after four games.

I thought our run-in was pretty good. We had only got one more away game against the leaders – at Preston – and the rest had got to come to us.

I went to see the referee after the Press conference, which was over very quickly, and he had scarpered. I knew exactly why he had disappeared, because he must have known. I can't believe it. The Gillingham guy at the Press conference said "He's usually bad against us" and I said "Well he has made up for it today, pal."

At least I could have my hair cut now because it has been looking a mess. I don't usually have it cut until we lose. So I could have a trim at last.

I will remember Boxing Day, 1995.

I watched the goal on television the day after. Bailey made no attempt when the corner came up, just blatantly stopped Blackie coming out, but what chance have you got? All I can do is write my comments on the referee's report.

We had about 70 calls in the space of 45 minutes on the radio show. Everybody was so enthusiastic about the club. There was the odd critic but on the whole, it was really good.

I'm not sure whether people enjoyed all my music, but that's tough. I picked a record out for the chairman and myself called That's What Friends are For. *I said that that was what both of us needed. I thought that was quite appropriate.*

We had one day's preparation before the Northampton game and I had made up my mind beforehand I wanted to use the squad even though Mick was against it. I just felt it would give us a good chance to have a look at Chris Curran before Mark Patterson was suspended and probably give Bairdy a rest because I think the way Ian Baird played against Gillingham, if he played like that on Saturday, he would be gone for the Exeter game on New Year's Day and I wanted him to be ready for Exeter.

So I told the lads the team. I was going to play Mark Saunders instead of Gary Clayton; Chris Billy instead of Ian Baird; and Chris Curran instead of Keith Hill. I just felt that we had to use the squad.

The game at Northampton was called off and to say that I was not too disappointed was an understatement. I had definitely got something like the 'flu and at least we would be able to go into the Exeter game with the same team that played at Gillingham. I gave the lads Saturday off and told them to report on Sunday morning.

The Gillingham player I had a go at came back at me in the Press and completely denied his racial abuse and tried to pass the buck to me. So although we were going to let it rest, I think Ronnie Maugé was that annoyed at him saying things about me as well and was willing to write a letter to the PFA. As I said to Ronnie, if it deters him for doing it again, then there has got to be some good coming out of it.

The enforced break at least gave Warnock a couple more days to attend to some minor injuries as the Pilgrims prepared to celebrate the arrival of 1996 with the New Year's Day visit of the more bitter of their Devon rivals, Exeter City.

"It has been said to me that beating Exeter is more important than winning promotion," said Warnock. "That is ridiculous, but it shows just how important this match is to the supporters. This is the game of the season as far as both sets of supporters are concerned and the one that everyone has been looking forward to since the fixtures came out last summer."

Following the game, Warnock was ashen-faced (though predictably far from tight-lipped) after watching his Pilgrims bounce back from 2-0 down to escape with a point from the 47th meeting between the two sides.

Stricken by 'flu, Warnock declared he would not have got out of bed for any other fixture and 10 minutes after the kick-off he must he wished he had stayed tucked up with the *Lemsip* and a hot-water bottle. By then, Exeter were a goal to the good and could have scored twice more to kill off a game they deserved to win from first kick to last.

However, it said much for Argyle's sheer stamina and physical commitment that the Pilgrims brushed off an early battering and the potential knife-through-the-heart blow of conceding a second goal in first-half injury-time to level a Derby low on quality but high on passion.

Warnock, after delivering his verdict on the match ("it could be the point that wins us promotion") said he was going back to bed and not moving, in which case he would have been doing a fairly passable impersonation of his defence when Grecians' captain Mark Came scored the first goal in professional football of 1996 after 94 seconds of the morning kick-off. Came conquered after Darren Hughes' corner fell to him and he stabbed the ball home from two yards. It proved to be a long-range thunderbolt compared with the three goals that followed.

Paul Buckle's tap-in further undid Argyle after Paul Williams and goalkeeper Kevin Blackwell watched Mark Gavin's pass slither across the face of the goal, before Argyle's players were able to retreat to the sanctuary of their dressing-room. Sanctuary? More like purgatory.

"I asked them to be professional and stressed to them the importance of the match to our fans," croaked Warnock, sanitising his own remarks. "It was a terrible first half. Our commitment was absolutely nil. I could have done more with a temperature of 102 than seven or eight of them. I could only count Chris Leadbitter who won a tackle or a header in the first half. In the second half, they did tremendously well. We won tackles and headers in the second half that we never got anywhere near in the first. You have got to give the players credit – it was a tremendous fightback. I think the standard we set ourselves for 1996 has got to be the way we played in the second half."

Ronnie Maugé began the fightback in front of the Third Division's largest crowd of the season just before an hour's play. Keith Hill sent a Hail Mary free-kick into the opposition penalty area which Mick Heathcote headed on and Ian Baird returned across the face of the goal for Maugé to finish off the four-man move.

The lackadaisical Hill was substituted, followed shortly by Leadbitter and Gary Clayton, who were given a dressing down on the way to the dressing-room by assistant manager Mick Jones after becoming involved in a full and frank discussion with supporters about the merits of tactical substitutions.

The changes worked as Baird finally levelled the score with 10 minutes to go when he converted another headed assist from Heathcote, falling over the goal-line as he notched his first goal since the pair against Fulham.

So Argyle ended their Christmas and New Year programme with a complete set – a win; a defeat; a weathered-off game; and a draw – at the end of which they were six points behind leaders Gillingham and four behind Preston, who occupied the third of the the three automatic promotion places. Colchester were three points behind them and Darlington a further point adrift, having played two games fewer. The midway point of the season had been reached.

NW: *I had been struggling with terrible 'flu, worse 'flu symptoms than Sharon had had even though I had the 'flu jab. But I had to go to the Exeter game, even if I didn't feel like it.*

I said to the players before the game that the way I felt, I would like them to be professional and do a job without me having to raise my voice. It's strange when you don't feel well and you are giving your team talk.

We went out and we were absolutely abysmal in the first 45 minutes. We were lucky to be 2-0 down. I thought we might get away with 1-0 but they scored in the last minute, but really should have been two, three or four-nil. I couldn't believe some of the players. I went and had a cup of tea in the shower room with Mick Jones at half-time. I said "Mick, I know I don't feel too well, but I have got to say a few things." And Mick said "I don't blame you."

So I went in and let rip. I explained that 12,500 fans expected better than that from a set of professional footballers against their local rivals. And then I mentioned individuals. In fact, I said it was only Leadbitter who got a tackle in in the first 45 minutes.

To be fair, in the second half we went about it in the right way. We were a lot better and we pulled it back to 2-2. In the end you had to say it was a good point but I know that if we had been right from the start, it would have been our game. It just showed me that I couldn't really leave them and had to be behind them all the time.

Having played difficult matches against the Third Division leaders and their Devon neighbours in previous weeks, Warnock genuinely looked upon Argyle's FA Cup third-round tie against Coventry on Saturday, January 6 as a welcome break from the pressure of their promotion campaign.

Despite the Pilgrims' home advantage and Coventry's poor form in the first half of the season, Argyle were very much underdogs to win the tie and that came as rare relief in a season where every other club was gunning for the big spenders from the West Country.

"We've got half a season of very tough games ahead of us," said Warnock. "Now is a good time to relax, switch off, enjoy ourselves under no pressure, and do our best. We can't lose."

His priority remained, not the transient glory of an FA Cup surprise, but the indelible stamp of winning promotion at the end of the season. "If you could guarantee we'd get thrashed 7-1 by Coventry but beat Preston 2-1 next weekend, I'd snap your hand off. I'd be embarrassed but it would only be pride because I don't send sides out to get thrashed by anyone, whether it's Manchester United, Coventry or Doncaster Pork Butchers."

Nevertheless, Coventry manager Ron Atkinson was wary of his side becoming fall-guys. "This club certainly knows about clubs in lower divisions beating bigger clubs – they won the Cup and then got knocked out by a non-league side the next year."

Atkinson's relish for the game, and the individuals encountered along the way, remained as sharp as ever. Those individuals included plenty of opponents lining up against his side in green and white. His brief second spell at West Bromwich Albion allowed him a glimpse of a teenager called Littlejohn – "always a good little player, always bright and lively" – and he had sold Paul Williams to Argyle the previous summer – "he needed the change and it could turn out to be a great move."

While turning out for Cambridge's reserves at the end of his playing days, Atkinson even played in front of a noisy young chap called Blackwell. "Young lad, blond hair, shouting away," he mused. He will have been glad to have discovered nothing had changed.

Three-hundred and twenty-five seconds – about as long as it takes to boil a kettle – was all it needed for Argyle's dreams of an upset to evaporate into thin air as Coventry escaped from Home Park with a 3-1 victory.

The platform of genuine hope which had been built upon a passionate first-half display and topped out by Ian Baird's 20th-minute free-kick strike was ripped from under their feet at the start of the second half as Coventry quickly, efficiently and devastatingly turned round the third-round tie.

The Premiership side, which had been reduced to 10 men following the dismissal of defender David Busst, scored three times between the 53rd and 58th minutes to take the wind from the sails of the good ship Pilgrim and leave it foundering.

A goal pregnant with controversy and fluke levelled the scores. Paul Telfer appeared to receive Dion Dublin's pass in an offside position and Ally Pickering's shot from Telfer's cut-back which lolloped over Blackwell was certainly intended as a hanging cross.

There followed what Warnock correctly identified as the game's crucial minute. Argyle striker Michael Evans carved a huge hole in the Coventry midfield, skipping round three markers, before bearing down freely on the opposition goal. However, he sliced his shot wide and Coventry cruelly countered within seconds as John Salako showed the young Plymothian how to finish from such a position.

Salako, the only visitor to display genuine Premiership quality, then set up the sucker punch, taking possession from Mick Heathcote on the left flank and crossing for Dublin to deliver the ball into the path of Telfer, whose searing shot zipped across Blackwell into the far corner.

A near full-house for the visit of Coventry

Salako said afterwards that he felt sorry for Argyle, that they did deserve better – which they sort of did and sort of did not. There was little excuse for such naïve defending but, the mad five minutes apart, Argyle were a credit to their manager and the city.

Not for one moment did there appear to be three divisions difference between the two sides, and the best kick-back from the defeat would be for Argyle to ensure that the following season there would not be.

Anyway, Neil Warnock was delighted with the afternoon's work. "We have had a great result. Preston lost and Chester only drew," he said, of his team's two Third Division rivals, who had been in league action. "We have got nothing to be ashamed about. I said after we beat Kingstonian [in the second round] 'Let's draw a Premier League side, get a good pay-day and get knocked out.' And we've got no injuries. All my wishes have come true."

Earlier, Warnock had shown by the team he had chosen that his priorities clearly lay with the Pilgrims' league campaign. He had dropped Mark Patterson and Gary Clayton, who were available but under suspension for the following week's league match with Preston at Deepdale, partly to teach them a lesson for getting needlessly banned and partly to get replacements Chris Billy and Richard Logan up to match speed. One can only imagine how Patterson and Clayton must have felt in being omitted from such a big match but there is no "I" in the word "team" and it takes more than 11 men to win promotion.

For his wholehearted endeavour, Logan narrowly shaded Evans as man of the match and he was instrumental in setting up the Pilgrims' goal, which came after 20 minutes of intense pressure.

Logan headed an attempted Coventry clearance into the path of Evans, who was clearly fouled by Busst as he made for goal. Referee Gary Willard had no option but to dismiss the indiscreet Busst, whose season was later to end so horrendously at Old Trafford, and Baird exacted maximum punishment by driving in a 20-yard free-kick that was lifted over goalkeeper Steve Ogrizovic after clipping Dublin's shoulder in the wall.

NW: *I made up my mind to to try one or two things against Coventry, because the most important game for me was the week afterwards, against Preston, where we were going to be missing Mark Patterson and Gary Clayton. I thought I might as well experiment against Coventry, even though it was an FA Cup tie.*

I wanted to play Chris Billy at right-back and ask him to mark John Salako. Chris Curran was cup-tied so I had to leave Keith Hill in the team. I thought it would have been time to leave Hill out after his abysmal performance against Exeter, which was the worst I had seen him play. I thought he could have stopped both goals. I also wanted to play Richard Logan to start with and keep Mark Saunders up my sleeve.

I also fined Mark Patterson for his suspension for the unprofessional way he picked up his last booking. Even one or two of his previous ones weren't the best, so I fined him a week's wages which was later reduced when Mark appealed. I also fined Gary Clayton £100 because when he came off the pitch after being substituted against Exeter he showed dissent to me and that was not the first time. It was about time that he learned to shut up. I was not having that any more. I actually thought he was the best midfield player on the pitch against Exeter but I wanted to chuck two players on to get an equaliser back, and it proved right in the end as it was Chris Billy's cross that got us the equaliser.

Playing Billy instead of Patterson was designed to show Patterson how professional he has got to be. He might have missed out on a bit of a star Match of the Day *job against Coventry, but I was not bothered about that. It might have taught him a lesson.*

We got confirmation through that Bolton had actually signed Wayne Burnett, and we were going to get the money. We had been concerned about his blood test. Everybody thought the deal had gone through, but it hadn't. We had to keep it quiet for obvious reasons and just cross our fingers for the lad.

The same night as I had been told it was a definite starter, Roy McFarland got the sack so we had still to wait to see if the signing would go through.

Physio Norman Medhurst tends to Mark Patterson

I thought about going ahead with James Dungey in goal so I could have a look at him. He wouldn't have a bigger test than Coventry and we had got Preston to come. Having thought about it, I decided to go with Kevin Blackwell in goal because of the two other changes. I thought the three would be too much and I didn't think that would be fair on the other lads.

At least I was recovering. It was probably the worst week's 'flu I had ever had.

As we got off the A38 at 1.40 p.m., it was absolutely chock-a-block. To see the car-parks full as we pulled up – they were actually turning everybody away, it was completely full – created a marvellous atmosphere.

The game started in horrible conditions – gale force winds and driving rain – but we had 17,700 supporters behind us, which was fantastic.

We took the lead, they had a man sent off and it looked good. It was funny, at half-time I was talking to Mick Jones in the shower room and we were saying that we knew how Coventry would come at us even though they were against the wind and how they had to go deep. We were discussing things and all of a sudden I got wet through and had to run out of the way. I had leant back and hit one of the shower handles and it absolutely soaked me right through. Mick had to go and get me a towel. It was a good job the video cameras weren't around, because it would have been one for Beadle's About.

In the second half we conceded three sloppy goals in the space of five minutes, which was like shooting ourselves in the foot. But instead of going under – it looked like we had collapsed completely – we came back strongly and in the end we had two or three good chances.

It was a marvellous day for the city. One or two people said to me after that the crowd reminded them of Leeds United's crowd, who contested every decision, and I thought that was the most vociferous they had ever been. It just whetted my appetite for what we had got to try and get to come in the next few years.

It was back to business for Warnock the following week. He sold Nicky Hammond to Reading, recouping the £40,000 he paid to Swindon for the unfortunate goalkeeper. Hammond appeared just seven times for the Pilgrims (four in the league), made almost as many crucial errors, and never enjoyed helping the Pilgrims to a draw, never mind a win.

After three games on loan at Reading, the Elm Park joint-management team of Jimmy Quinn and Mick Gooding were impressed enough with Hammond's performances to snap him up. "He's done brilliantly for us since he's been here," said Gooding, "and we are delighted to have got him." Despite Gooding's happiness, many at Home Park thought the money-back transfer represented an even better piece of business by Warnock than the Nugent-for-Baird-plus-£75,000 deal he had done with Bristol City.

However, Warnock remained keen to sign another goalkeeper as cover for Kevin Blackwell, who had been unexpectedly propelled into the first-team because of Hammond's loss of form. The Argyle manager did not fancy having to promote James Dungey into the Pilgrims' promotion campaign, preferring to monitor the youngster's development carefully.

Before Argyle's visit to Deepdale for their promotion battle with Preston, Warnock had noted that the top three – Gillingham, Preston and Chester – were beginning to put clear blue water between themselves and the Greens. Preston were three points above the Pilgrims. "We have got to make sure Preston don't open a seven-point gap over us," he said. "It would be nice to win and be a point behind them."

Nice, but not to be. Preston completed the double over their rivals for promotion with a 3-2 victory in which just about everything that could go wrong for Argyle, did. Adrian Littlejohn was sent off for mouthing something unpleasant in the direction of an incompetent and over-sensitive linesman, and his strike partner Michael Evans missed a penalty.

The game started reasonably brightly for the Pilgrims, with Mick Heathcote giving them a 22-minute lead after controversial referee Neale Barry saw nothing wrong with his somewhat robust challenge on opposition goalkeeper John Vaughan.

However, with Chris Curran having an unconvincing debut in the heart of defence and neither full-back able to fully contain the menace provided by Preston's wide men, the equaliser, from North End captain Ian Bryson, was not long in coming.

The home side then took the lead before half-time when Simon Davey headed home a cross by Graeme Atkinson which Kevin Blackwell badly misjudged, underlining that Warnock's desire for fresh hands between the posts was not misplaced.

Adrian Littlejohn, about to be sent off at Preston

Preston increased their lead five minutes after the break when right-winger Lee Cartwright caught the Argyle defence flat-footed before shooting crisply under Blackwell's body. Ten minutes afterwards, Littlejohn was red-carded, and five minutes later Evans knocked his spot-kick too close to Vaughan's body after the goalkeeper had upended Chris Billy, who seemed to have developed a happy knack of being fouled in the penalty area.

Argyle pulled a goal back at the death when the hard-working Richard Logan nodded Williams' cross back in front of goal for Mark Saunders to head home his first goal in league football. Preston, though, had two 'goals' disallowed and two penalty appeals turned down. If fortune had smiled kindly on them, and on leading scorer Andy Saville in particular, they could easily have doubled their margin of victory.

"We made it hard for ourselves, having established a one-goal lead," said Warnock. "It was a terrible time to concede two goals, just before half-time, although I still thought we would obtain something from the game We then had a crazy few minutes when Preston scored and Adie got his marching orders, which meant a reshuffle of our team. That left us with a mountain to climb, but we still played well and the goal near the end was what we deserved. It was a pity we couldn't have scored earlier because I felt we might have snatched a draw if there had been more time."

Warnock remained encouraged by the fact that Argyle had now played most of the Third Division's top teams away from home. "We have now got Gillingham and Chester from the top three at home, along with most of the other leading sides," he said. "It's in our own hands now. We have got to crack it at home."

NW: *When I got in on the Monday morning, I had a telephone call from Reading. Micky Gooding was on the phone telling me they would buy Nicky Hammond. I had put it into their minds to buy him, and it had come off. I managed to get £40,000 for him, which, obviously, I was delighted with.*

Having sold Hammond, I decided to go and get a goalkeeper and the first two or three people came to mind. I telephoned my old 'keeper Steve Cherry, and asked him to come down but he had hurt his shoulder and would be out for three weeks.

Mark Saunders

We also decided, Ronnie Maugé and myself, to actually write a letter to the PFA regarding the racial abuse at Gillingham even though the player concerned had completely denied it. We just felt a letter might just put him off from doing it again, without making a song and dance about it.

I thought they were in the right frame of mind before the game at Preston. We got off to a good start, we played well and then we scored a goal. Then, once again, we were so unprofessional five minutes before half-time, giving them two goals.

Patterson had been suspended for stupidly kicking the ball away on top of two other bookings which were a joke – deliberately tripping people after they had gone past – so I went with Mark Saunders at right-back. Unfortunately it was his man that scored. He got on the blind side of Mark, but he shouldn't have even been able to cross.

Gary Peters had a slanging match with the official after they had won. He said it was the worst display he had ever seen and he was telling him to his face. And I felt, "My God, and they won." The official just had one of those games where he was nowhere near anybody.

Although we started well, it was disappointing. I felt they were a better side than us, although I couldn't say that publicly. I made up my mind that we needed a lot of work doing and we weren't playing as much as we should do from midfield.

I decided to try and involve Steve McCall after the Preston game. I went in on the Tuesday morning for a practice match with a view to Colchester on the Saturday and I was told by Norman Medhurst that Steve had got a calf strain and he couldn't play in the practice match or the reserve match.

I had tried to involve him but I think he had been fit for two reserve matches in seven months, so I would just have to forget about him, which was disappointing.

The youth team played against Tottenham. We had moved the game to the Saltash ground and I got there with 10 minutes to go for a 7.30 p.m. kick-off. The queues were hundreds of yards around the ground and we couldn't get parked anywhere. I got inside and watched it from the terracing.

It was a tremendous atmosphere and we were 1-0 down in the first couple of minutes, but we fought back to equalise before half-time and scored the second goal in the second half to win the game. It was was probably the best Youth Cup result in the club's history. Tottenham got to the final the previous year and we were in the Third Division. It was incredible. It just showed what could be achieved.

Colchester United, the team against whom Argyle had begun their 1995/96 campaign, would provide the first test of Warnock's resolve to crack it at Home Park. Although the expectations of some Pilgrims' supporters had changed since the last time the two teams met, Warnock's priorities remained precisely the same as they had done on August 12.

Defeat then by Colchester and three subsequent league losses, followed by a worrying inability to kick into a gallop when they finally did discover their stride, had convinced Argyle supporters that a play-off position would be the best position their side could attain by May. Indeed, there was a school of thought which reckoned three-times post-season specialist Warnock actually fancied going up the long way.

"It's ridiculous to say we are concentrating on the play-offs," Warnock insisted, after strengthening his promotion hand by signing Charlton Athletic goalkeeper Andy Petterson on a month's loan. "I'm still looking to win the league. I don't think of defeatist things like the play-offs. I can assure everyone that, while the play-offs are lovely when they are finished and you've won and are sitting in the Wembley bath, they are hard work."

The arrival of Petterson, an Australian who arrived at Home Park by way of Luton and loan spells at Swindon, Ipswich and Bradford, was designed to breathe new life

Andy Petterson

into a team which had looked jaded since Christmas – and it also promised to provide some potentially hilarious team line-up announcements over the PA system when Mark Patterson returned from his suspension.

Petterson replaced Kevin Blackwell, allowing him to step out of the breach which he filled when Nicky Hammond did not pass muster and return to his duties with the youth team. "We owe Kevin," said Warnock, "but he was brought here to coach the youngsters and I never expected him to play as many first-team games."

Petterson made an immediate impression on the Home Park crowd, giving away and then saving a penalty, and making two other splendid saves which should have ensured a clean-sheet and – with Ian Baird scoring another of his deflected free-kick specialities in the 31st minute – a home win.

However, rather that cracking it at home, Argyle cracked late on in the game, Mark Kinsella taking advantage of too much time and space afforded him by Paul Williams and Mark Saunders to cross for David Greene to power home an 88th-minute equaliser.

Warnock afterwards greeted the assembled media with the request: "Let's try and get through this Press conference without the F-word, eh lads?" referring to his own fondness for the Anglo-Saxon expletive – rather than the media's. His determination to curb his sometimes colourful tongue spoke as forcibly as any swear word about the frustration at seeing Argyle throw away two valuable points.

True to his intention, the subsequent conversation would not have caused his maiden aunt to raise an eyebrow, but it was not long before he introduced another F-word to explain his side's inability to kill off Colchester.

"There's a fear-factor here which has crept in over the last two games and I don't know why," he mused. "They have got to have more confidence in themselves. If you lose your confidence, you don't play football. The lads want to do so well for the crowd, but it's as if every time people expect something of them, some of them are getting over-anxious. We've got to get together and work out why it's happening."

There seemed no fear when Petterson saved Simon Betts' weakly-struck penalty although his concession of the spot-kick – for hauling down Paul Abrahams – was not entirely his own fault, Mick Heathcote having tested his Ocker mettle with a distinctively iffy back pass.

Neither was it without dispute. "The linesman ran straight round for a corner and the ref was 50 yards from the incident," said Warnock, still commendably restraining his language. "How could he give a penalty from there?"

It was not to be the last time Warnock was to be heard questioning an official's judgement at Home Park, neither was it to be the last time during the promotion campaign that Argyle would face Colchester, who had now opened a four-point gap over the Pilgrims.

With 25 games gone, and 21 to go, Argyle had slipped to seventh in the Third Division table – behind, in ascending order, Darlington, Colchester, Doncaster, Chester, Preston and Gillingham. It was their lowest league position for 16 weeks but they had an early opportunity to reassert their promotion credentials with the visit of Scunthorpe United three days later.

It was an opportunity they spurned in spades redoubled. The lowest Home Park crowd of the season – 4,712 – appropriately witnessed the Pilgrims hit their season's low with a 3-1 defeat in which they looked anything but play-off candidates, never mind automatic promotion hopefuls.

Richard Logan scored Argyle's lone goal, from Martin Barlow's inswinging left-sided corner – two substitutes combining – in the 89th minute, by which time the game was well and truly up: the Irons had already pressed home their superiority with goals from Chris Hope, in the 20th minute, Lee Turnbull, in the 35th, and Andy McFarlane, in the 81st.

Perhaps Argyle officials should have been wary when the opposition asked to borrow the Pilgrims' second-choice yellow shirts, after mistakenly assuming their own all-white tops would not clash with the Pilgrims' colours. The previous season, when they rolled up to Deepdale having left two shirts in the wash, they had borrowed Preston's yellow tops and inflicted a 1-0 defeat on the home side.

The defeat prompted Warnock into some straight-talking. After the game he gathered his players together and told them: "I am determined to get us promotion, hopefully this season, and if you want to join me, fair enough. But if you want to perform like you did today then obviously you will be on your bike. I'm not bothered who you are."

It must have been a strange introduction to Argyle for Scott Partridge, the Bristol City striker who had scored for Torquay against Argyle at Home Park earlier in the season while on loan at Plainmoor, and whom Warnock had now borrowed from Ashton Gate. Partridge had played the previous 45 minutes after coming on as substitute.

"I knew when I got out of the bath that this was the start of a new period in my reign as Argyle manager," admitted Warnock after his dressing-room dressing down. "This is when you earn your money. Any manager can cope when you are winning games, when confidence is high."

NW: *I chased a 'keeper. I went and watched Andrew Petterson at Charlton and had him down for a couple of days before deciding to give him a shot. It gave us a chance to have some competition with Kevin Blackwell, and the breathing space to have a look at one or two other 'keepers.*

We were very disappointing against Colchester, we didn't play well at all. I didn't really want to go into the Press conference, because I knew we hadn't played well and yet I knew that I couldn't criticise the players too much because they were just getting a little bit anxious and a little bit frightened to play and express themselves. I think everyone was expecting that much and I think it got to one or two lads.

Andy Petterson played well. He saved a penalty, but the way we conceded the goal was just absolutely untrue. That's six points we had thrown away in the last few minutes of games.

We needed to try and pass the play and play more from midfield. I was thinking of pairing Mark Saunders with Ronnie Maugé and playing two wide in Billy and Evans, especially with Patterson coming back. It would mean leaving Richard Logan out, unfortunately. Richard had played ever so well, but it was one of those things I needed to do.

Maugé went to have an X-ray and they discovered he had broken his toe. He had been playing with a broken toe for three weeks and I didn't know anything about it until two days before the Colchester match.

It was ironic to read in the newspapers that Steve McCall was saying he had wasted a year. I had to respond to that because I would have played him the previous week, but how could I play somebody if they were not fit? I would have liked to have said a lot more, but I suppose you have just got to keep things to yourself.

I had another chat with Steve McCall to put my point of view forward and said to him not to let any other concerns worry him, but if he got himself fit, I still thought he could do a job. I was still not sure whether he would get his fitness. If he had been watching us in the first half against Scunthorpe, he would probably not have wanted to rush back.

I took Scott Partridge on loan at the last minute on the Monday morning because I really hadn't got a clue about Adrian Littlejohn. He was looking sharp in training and yet he had this stomach problem which could have been a hernia and he was due to see a specialist.

I played Adie because of who he is against Scunthorpe but it backfired on me. He didn't contribute anything, and didn't make any effort to work hard. It disappointed me so I substituted him after about 35 minutes. We were 2-0 down, and I was so disappointed with four or five in that first 45 minutes.

I changed it at half-time, bringing Martin Barlow and Partridge on for Chris Billy and Ronnie Maugé and we did battle better in the second half but we had no chance of winning the game.

I went straight into the shower and didn't say a word after the game and then I came back and as I was drying off I just said to them: "Well lads, I am determined to get this club promoted and if some of you want to join me, then you are quite welcome, but if you haven't got the bottle to get a club like Plymouth promoted then you are going to be on your bike. It's entirely up to you, because I am not going to tolerate another 45 minutes like that again."

I couldn't knock the crowd behind the tunnel for having a go at me. I know you get yobbos and foul-mouthed people, but you have to accept that. In fact, when I watched the video afterwards in the early hours of the morning, I thought the fans behind the goal at the Devonport End were absolutely tremendous. Instead of chanting horrible slogans, they were chanting "Warnock, Sort It Out" and it only made me more determined to sort it out.

Obviously I had a bit of thinking to do as we had two tough away matches and I really had got to play the people who I wanted alongside me in the trenches.

I found after the Colchester game Micky Heathcote had been complaining that his back had been killing him since Coventry, which I didn't know anything about. He went up to Cambridge to see a specialist but I kept it out of the papers.

"FOOTBALL IS VERY CRUEL"

WITH four of Argyle's next five matches away from Home Park – and the fifth at home to Chester – the Pilgrims' chances of winning automatic promotion were looking increasingly dire.

They looked even worse a week later. The day after the defeat by Scunthorpe, leading scorer Adrian Littlejohn had undergone a hernia operation, recuperation from which would, it was estimated, put him out of the Pilgrims' promotion picture for up to five weeks.

It was small consolation that he was due to miss Argyle's next two matches through suspension in any case but there was some relief that his failure to score in Argyle's previous seven matches could now be put down to a lack of full fitness caused by carrying the injury.

Argyle's next scheduled game, at Hereford, was postponed because of a snow-bound pitch and moved back to later in the season, when the opposition would be in a better run of form. Argyle took the opportunity of a Saturday away from action to work out at the College of St Mark and St John in preparation for a midweek trip to Northampton.

The breathing space also afforded defender Mark Patterson the opportunity to recover from an ad-hoc operation by Warnock, who used his other professional expertise as a chiropodist to dispose of a problematic toe-nail. "There was blood everywhere," confessed Warnock. "He would have been struggling for the Hereford game."

The Pilgrims' miserable January came to an appropriately miserable conclusion at Sixfields, where the home side won 1-0 despite Warnock's satisfaction with the general performance.

"It's probably the best we have played since December and the most we have ever dominated a game. Northampton were more concerned about not conceding a goal, rather than scoring one. I even thought about taking the goalkeeper off for the last 10 minutes."

Nevertheless, Northampton cobbled together a victory, courtesy of Ian Sampson's 16th-minute shot which deflected past goalkeeper Andy Petterson off Micky Heathcote's heel, giving Argyle a return of two points from their last six league matches. Including the FA Cup defeat by Coventry, their January record read: Played 6, Won 0, Drawn 2, Lost 4.

In that light, it was amazing that Warnock should stick his neck out by insisting: "We have turned the corner. You could see the confidence was back and everybody wanted the ball. The only thing missing was the players believing in themselves and taking the gamble to get in positions in front of goal."

NW: *We thought the Hereford game would be on on the Friday, and they didn't even put that there was a pitch-inspection on* Teletext *and yet nine o'clock on Saturday morning, we heard that the game was off. The pitch apparently had some snow on it.*

Mark Patterson would have struggled. He had a problem with his big toe and I had to do an operation on it. Good job I am a chiropodist. It took me a couple of hours on the Thursday to remove a nail which was actually implanted into the surface of the skin below his big toe. It was a bit messy and although he was sore, we would have had him injected so he could play. With the game being off, it gave Mark a couple of days to recover.

Ironically, Adrian Littlejohn went down with 'flu. I think he decided to get everything out of the way at once.

We were told the Tuesday night game at Northampton was doubtful so we sent Kevin Blackwell up and he reported in on the Monday night that he thought it would be playable.

I had encouraged the players all week to pass the ball. I was fed up with the criticism they were getting. Anybody would think that I told them to whack everything long and it is not something that I had done. From the halfway line onwards, I wanted them to pass the ball but we had got to move and we had to have confidence. We worked on that and the mood in the camp was quite good.

I didn't really want the game off because I wanted a game before we came up against Chester on the Saturday. We lost 1-0 at Northampton but it was probably the best we had played away from home. We passed the ball around all night and created chances. They scored after 20 minutes through a deflected goal off Micky Heathcote's foot and for the last 70 minutes we absolutely paralysed them.

We knocked the ball about, and all they could do was whack it long. We played some cracking stuff and we had enough chances. Yet Mike Sampson reported in the Western Morning News *the next day that we lacked creativity in midfield, which I thought was a load of bullshit! For me, if he was watching that game he should have talked about all the plusses in the game.*

He obviously didn't see himself that once they went 1-0 up, they had eight men behind the ball and I don't think Ruud Gullit could have got through eight defenders with inch-perfect passes.

I thought we were patient, we got around the back and had enough chances. I don't think our goalie, Andy Petterson had a shot to save other than the goal when he collided with striker Jason White. It was an obvious foul on the goalkeeper, later confirmed when the ref saw the video, unfortunately too late to change the result. Petterson had to have stitches at half time.

I think it was a super performance and when you come up against a team like that, playing at home with so many men behind the ball, it is up to you to break them down. But I think the yard missing in the six-yard box was just because we had had a bad run and I think if we had been top of the league and playing with some confidence, we would have converted some of the chances that we had got.

I was ever so pleased with them, for everything, not just the effort but the way we played football. I thought it was superb and we had got to just keep going forward now. I thought it would be interesting to see if they had the guts to do the same at home against Chester on the Saturday.

Kevin Ratcliffe was at Northampton, watching us. I don't know what he must have thought. We paralysed Chester at Chester's first game and lost 3-1 and we had 80 minutes out of 90 at Northampton and lost 1-0.

January ended and I sent a letter to the Footballers Manager's Association saying that I believed we should have a month's rest in January. After January 1, we should have a month's shutdown. It is obvious to me that it would benefit me because we hadn't got a win under our belt in January.

Football is very cruel and when lads give their all like that and play some cracking stuff and come away with nothing, it could actually destroy you. I needed to really make sure that I spent time encouraging them to pass. We had to go for that even if it took three or four games to get it right.

To get us back on the road we needed a little bit of luck, something like Northampton had, when a shot going nowhere deflected from Micky Heathcote.

We actually ate on the bus going up to Northampton. We had a microwave meal and I said to them if we play like a Sunday League team, then we might as well be treated like one with our pre-match meals.

But coming back, the mood on the bus was superb. They knew they had played well and that there was not that much wrong. Hopefully we had sorted it out and given ourselves a platform to get back on the promotion trail before the end of the season. We couldn't afford to lose on Saturday against Chester. We needed to get the bandwagon going again.

Turned the corner? Eyebrows, not to mention questions about the manager's sanity, were being raised. Warnock was either going to look extremely stupid or extremely astute. Chester City, who still occupied one of the three automatic promotion slots, would provide the sternest test of his brave assertion at Home Park on February 3.

Actually, it turned out to be no test at all. Argyle returned from their mid-season break with a 4-2 home victory that fully justified their eve-of-season billing as promotion favourites. It was just a shame that none of their championship rivals also took January off.

The Pilgrims dismantled Chester with such chilling efficiency and single-minded purpose, it was impossible to believe their opponents were from the same division, let alone one place better off than Argyle in the promotion battle.

Four brilliantly created and classically executed goals ended their run of six winless matches and the overall performance proved Warnock to be astute, rather than stupid. The only whinge came from the notoriously hard-to-please Griping Greenies, who complained that Argyle, 3-0 up at the interval, actually conceded the second half to their visitors.

They discovered Warnock in complete agreement. "The goals we gave away were sloppy," he conceded. "I am disappointed we didn't keep a clean-sheet. I would have been happy with 1-0."

Had the manager's wish been granted, he surely would have found it impossible which of the four Green's goals to select as the match-winner: Martin Barlow's deadly drive in the 12th minute; Ronnie Maugé's emphatic finish to some sweeping wing play 80 seconds later; Scott Partridge's cool solo run on goal 13 minutes before half-time; or a length-of-the-field move started and finished by Paul Williams midway through the second half.

It was going to be Argyle's afternoon from the off. The midfield – Gary Clayton sitting in front of the defence; Maugé and Ian Baird in the centre; Barlow and Partridge out wide – snapped in the tackles, crackled with menace and popped around telling passes at will.

Scott Partridge celebrates his goal against Chester

Barlow, Warnock's fiddler's elbow of a selection, was the orchestrator of much that was good about Argyle, and Warnock, who had earlier pushed the midfielder so far out in the cold that his next stop was Siberia, paid generous tribute to his skills. "When he's bright, there's no-one better," he said.

Warnock also attributed Argyle's upswing in form to the absence of Littlejohn. The striker's unavailability had forced him to adopt new tactics, with Michael Evans now playing as the only out-and-out striker, and Scott Partridge and Martin Barlow occupying wide attacking roles.

Warnock explained. "Because Adie has done so well for us, I think a lot of players thought we should get the ball to him as quickly as possible. With him being out, it has made us realise we can play a lot more. We *want* to play more. I've stressed how important it is for us to pass the ball around. I think some of the lads were believing the myth that I'm a long-ball manager."

It was a credit to the persistence of Barlow, and of Warnock, that everyone at Home Park had been able to enjoy the former's vision and controlled passing. At the beginning of the season, the pair had fallen out so badly that Barlow nearly left the club.

"You can't hold grudges in football," said Warnock. "Martin took his bat and ball home but I told him the only way to get in the team was to show me that he wanted to be in the team.

"He did well against Wigan, where he scored and I dropped him the week afterwards for tactical reasons, but he stuck at it. He's been a breath of fresh air in training and he picked himself." The ball, if not the bat, remained in Barlow's court.

NW: *On the Thursday we were going to do some training and finishing, but heavy frost put paid to all our plans. Whenever you have any plans, the weather always puts paid to it. We ended up using the main pitch down the middle, where it was rock hard, just to see if we could do something.*

We just managed to train on the main pitch and we worked just on crossing balls and passing movement. I told them to believe in themselves and try to turn it on at home. I knew when I said that we had turned the corner after losing 1-0, people thought I was going around the twist but I just had to hope that the lads could continue with it.

Mark Saunders failed a fitness test at 1.00 p.m. so I brought Ronnie Maugé back in, which I wasn't too disappointed with because the way we were playing, Ronnie could make his runs into the box.

You could see the lads were all geared up for it. Bairdy had been captain for the previous game, but with Ronnie Maugé coming back in, I had a chat with him and just said I thought he ought to concentrate just on his game. Then I thought "To hell with it. There is only one real captain at the club and that is Micky Heathcote." I didn't go with him because we lost the first six games, but I said to Mick "You put the arm band on and let's go from now until the end of the season."

We got three goals before half time and I think Micky Heathcote would honestly say that he missed probably the easiest of chances in his career, from a yard out. We played some good stuff. Martin Barlow continued where he left off at Northampton and Scott Partridge scored his first home goal at Home Park, although we conceded two goals in the second half.

I thought for both goals Andy Petterson just tried to do what he didn't have to do, and came for a couple of balls and made a mess of them. It was really why we conceded two goals. So I wasn't too disappointed with the back four at home.

It was a great team performance and now although we had two hard games coming up, as I said to the lads at half-time, I wish we could have been on the bus to Scunthorpe for the following week.

It just seemed that we had wasted a month and I couldn't see any reason why we can't continue playing like that.

Martin Barlow, born in Barnstaple during his father's posting with the RAF but raised in Plymouth, was not the only local boy who had made good during the season. Striker Michael Evans had also not figured in Warnock's early-season plans, but, like Barlow, had become a valuable member of the team.

His improved form was rewarded with an improved $2^1/_2$-year contract, which he signed on the eve of the Pilgrims' visit to Scunthorpe on February 10 – 18 days after the two teams had met at Home Park and Warnock had subsequently issued his "shape up or ship out" message.

For Evans, the 90 minutes at Glandford Park proved to be a topsy-turvy affair. One minute – the 23rd to be precise – he was celebrating the award of his extended contract with his ninth goal of the season; the next – or, rather, the 90th – he found himself victim of one of the harshest sendings-off of the Endsleigh League season.

Martin Barlow

The high spot of Evans' afternoon came after Mick Heathcote had challenged goalkeeper Lee Butler – on loan from Barnsley – for Paul Williams' 23rd-minute free-kick. Butler served the ball up to Evans, who composed himself before shooting through a crowd of players and the ball deflected off Michael Walsh into the net.

Eyebrows were raised in the 64th minute, when the mild-mannered Evans was booked for an innocuous-looking challenge while helping out his defence. The greater significance of this moment was realised as the hard-fought tussle entered its final minute. Scunthorpe defender Paul Wilson appeared to bottle out of an aerial challenge with Evans deep inside his own half, and fell to the ground in truly theatrical fashion.

Rookie referee David Laws, officiating in only his sixth league match, bought the act and decided Evans, one of the least malicious players he is likely to encounter if he officiates until the age of 100, had to go.

Still, Evans' goal ensured a hard-earned point for the Pilgrims from a 1-1 draw after they had fallen behind to a fourth-minute Scunthorpe goal which was a carbon-copy of one of the three they had conceded at Home Park less than three weeks previously. Walsh, whose throw-ins looked questionably one-handed, catapulted the ball into the Argyle box and Richard Logan's attempted clearance fell at the feet of the number nine Iron Andy McFarlane, who drilled the ball past Andy Petterson.

The Pilgrims had chances to go on and win the game. Scott Partridge had an effort hooked off the line by David D'Auria and free-kick specialist Ian Baird thundered a dead-ball set-piece against the opposition crossbar.

Afterwards, Warnock approached referee Laws and asked him to review his application of the law against Evans after considering the match-video. Laws, to his credit, agreed.

"Evans was sent off for a second bookable offence – the referee said that he played the man," said Warnock, "but Martin Barlow then heard the referee ask the player [Wilson] 'Did he catch you?'

"If he said that, he could not have been 100 per cent sure. I think Wilson did not want to be brave, so he conned his way out of the challenge and got a man sent off." Action replays suggested Warnock's appraisal of the situation was spot on, and that Evans did not deserve to be pulled up for a foul, let alone cautioned for a fatal second time.

The loss of another two points had Warnock conceding what Pilgrims fans had known in their hearts for some time – that Argyle were unlikely to win the Third Division title. However, he remained convinced he would be in charge of a Second Division side the following season.

"We can go up," he said, as he prepared the Pilgrims for a second successive away game, at Doncaster. "We don't want to panic even though teams have got games in hand on us and we're not moving into second or third place. The games we are playing at the moment are difficult and our rivals are going to have to face difficult games of their own.

"If we can tick over and still be in the hunt at the end of March, I'll be very happy, knowing what's coming. I've said to the players, 'You've just got to believe me. I've done it before – not many of you have – and I'm telling you, we can go up.' "

If anything was going to cost the Pilgrims a place in the top three at the end of the season, it looked like being their away form. A 0-0 draw at Belle Vue against a Doncaster side with similar promotion aspirations became their 10th successive winless game on the road.

Excellent defence, in which Mick Heathcote and Richard Logan were proverbial pillars of strength – especially against a strong first-half wind – was not matched by the forward play. Ronnie Maugé did find the net, seizing on a loose ball after Doncaster goalkeeper Perry Suckling had parried a shot from Michael Evans, but he was ruled offside.

"A draw was probably a fair result," conceded Warnock afterwards. "Whilst we may not be winning on our travels, we have at least drawn our last two away games. We are not getting beaten."

NW: We decided to leave it alone against Scunthorpe because the players had done so well in the previous two games. We knew it would be hard, having got beaten easily down at Home Park by them, but we thought "Well, let's be positive and try and go for a win."

We got kicked in the teeth again. Four minutes to go and we lost a goal which they got with a long-throw again. We battled back and Micky Evans, who I had just given a new two and a half year contract to scored his first goal since November. You could see he was pleased.

Then in injury-time, he got sent off for a second bookable offence which, to be fair, Scunthorpe conned the referee. There is no way that Micky Evans deliberately tried to do the lad. We sent him a video of the incident in the hope that he would change his mind.

I got a telephone call on the Monday from Norman Medhurst – Adrian Littlejohn had got a broken toe. Apparently a horse trod on it 10 days previously but it only affected him after he started running.

The Youth Team did great, although they lost in injury-time to Crystal Palace. I had a chat with Steve Coppell during the second half, and he said they were keeping every player apart from the goalkeeper as a professional after all being second-years, and there was us with school kids in and first-year professionals. It was a really tremendous effort, I was ever so pleased.

Once again at Doncaster we had our chances to win. I knew they would be physical and they tried to around us but we played some decent football and had some great chances again. But it was not to be. We were really up against it – four points behind Chester again, but had Bury and Barnet the following week at home. Bury got seven the previous Saturday at Lincoln, and Barnet got five, so they were two in-form teams.

"A HORRIBLE GAME, BUT WE KNEW IT WOULD BE"

THE Pilgrims were back at Home Park three days later to face Bury, the side against which their season had really started and one of the 11 teams still in with a realistic chance of promotion.

The match marked the return to the West Country of a former Argyle player of the year, goalkeeper Steve Cherry, whom Warnock had borrowed from Watford after letting Andy Petterson return to Charlton.

Petterson had excelled himself as a penalty-saver – as well as stopping one on his debut against Colchester, he had kept out Nick Richardson's last-minute effort in the 4-2 win over Chester (having also conceded both spot-kicks) – but done little else to persuade Warnock to put him on the pay-roll.

Warnock knew all about Cherry, who had been his number one at Notts County during the Magpies' flight from the old Third Division to the First under Warnock's management at Meadow Lane. Since leaving Nottingham, Cherry, now 35, had been understudy to Watford's Cornish-born former Exeter City 'keeper Kevin Miller at Vicarage Road.

"I had him for three years at Notts County," confirmed Warnock. "He's overweight – always has been – but he's got a presence about him which we are going to need with the games we've got coming up."

Also back in the Argyle fold was leading scorer Adrian Littlejohn, happily recovered from his hernia operation and a subsequent bizarre injury sustained while recovering from it. Littlejohn had been out walking near his Cornish home when a horse had stepped on his foot, breaking his little toe. After showing up Third Division donkeys all season, the equine fraternity had exacted some sort of revenge.

Littlejohn began the match against Bury on the substitutes' bench but played a crucial part in a 1-0 home victory which maintained Argyle's hot favouritism for a play-off place on a freezing cold night.

A goal 11 minutes from time was enough to warm the hearts of Home Park's lowest – and coldest – crowd of the season. Chester's 1-0 defeat at Hereford, which progressed the Pilgrims to within one point of the automatic promotion places, was the icy icing on the cake.

Bury had scored seven goals the previous Saturday, but showed themselves equally adept at the defensive side of the game and supporters disgruntled with the Pilgrims' single-goal return will have done well to remind themselves that this was the Lancashire side's first away defeat since September – and that was at runaway leaders Gillingham.

Argyle's territorial supremacy was such that the biggest problem posed to Cherry on his return to Home Park after seven years, was from the icicles forming on the end of his nose. Opposition goalkeeper Gary Kelly was, on the other hand, kept warm by a succession of Pilgrims' attacks.

As the match went on, Argyle's threat cooled so manager Warnock attempted to stoke up their efforts by sending on Adrian Littlejohn and Chris Billy for Michael Evans and Scott Partridge in the 75th minute. Warnock could, therefore, take some credit for Argyle's winner four minutes later. Littlejohn forced a corner which Martin Barlow swung into the six-yard box and Kelly, the first-half thorn in Argyle's side, rose to punch, plucked fresh air, and left Heathcote to hoist the ball over his own shoulder into the net.

"One goal was always going to be enough, with Bury putting so many people behind the ball," said Warnock afterwards. "We just had to remain patient. It was an important win for us and has put us back in the promotion frame again."

Gillingham still led the table, with 60 points, ahead of Preston (54), Chester (47), Darlington (47), Argyle (46), Doncaster (46), Wigan (44), Bury (43), Colchester (42), Northampton (42) and Barnet (40).

NW: *I decided to let Andy Petterson go back to Charlton. Last week they wanted him back for the cup game just in case they got an injury and I thought if they were going to call him back at a second's notice, I needed to get somebody I knew who knew what was what for the month. I signed Steve Cherry for a month even though I had one or two letters from people saying they thought Cherry let them down when he left Plymouth to go to Notts County, where I signed him.*

I also knew the story from Cherry's point of view – there were one or two in the dressing-room that didn't get on so well and it wasn't all Cherry's fault that he wanted to leave.

Adrian Littlejohn joined in training on the Monday before the Bury game for the first time, and he was shattered but he didn't do badly. Keith Hill looked sharp. He was playing in midfield then and I wanted to include him as well.

Littlejohn said his broken toe was the worst thing but I said if that was the only thing, he would have to have an injection and I would put him on the bench. He was quite happy about it.

It was a freezing night and I went against all my superstitions. I had a big overcoat, gloves and nearly a hat on as well. Bitterly cold, 4,500 crowd, what a fabulous crowd, a bigger crowd than had been at Blackpool, who were going for promotion the next division up.

We played superbly in the conditions and their goalie made four or five great saves. I said to them at half-time, "Just be patient, carry on playing and your chances will come." Lo and behold Micky Heathcote came up with with an overhead kick and we went 1-0 up.

That morning we had been in the gymnasium because it was too hard to train and Micky Heathcote was like a man possessed. He scored from every angle, tap-ins, 20-yarders, he was scoring for fun. We had never seen him like it before – we thought he was on drugs – and he ended up scoring the winner that night.

So when we got back into the dressing room I sat him down and said: "Well Mick, there is one thing for sure, you'd never have scored when you were facing the goal. I have seen that many you've missed." Everyone had a laugh.

We just said we had got to get on to bigger things. We needed to concentrate on Barnet being the next obstacle. I knew we had played extra games but we couldn't worry about that. We just had to get on with ourselves and not to worry about others.

After we scored with six or seven minutes to go, the crowd behind the Devonport End goal just kept chanting my name. I gave them a wave and then they went quiet and I got them going and I said "Come on," waving my hands, "Get shouting again." They all got together again and started shouting "Argyle, Argyle", which I thought was tremendous. It's a two-way thing.

Steve Cherry made his debut and hardly had anything to do. Near the end there were a couple of dangerous long-throws and I could hear him screaming at his defenders where to go and what to do – we managed to clear them – which I think is the difficult part for goalies when they haven't got a lot to do.

It was nice to have him on board because I knew him inside out. Even though I knew there were some people who say that we shouldn't have taken him back because of how he left in a cloud. I know the run of circumstances that didn't make him very happy in Plymouth at that particular time with other individuals at the club.

He didn't want to go public about that, so it had never come out and I think it was a bit unfair, but I didn't think I should say anything publicly about it. I had one or two letters saying I shouldn't have taken him back, but as a manager you get the best players who you think can fill that position and at that moment I thought it was Steve Cherry.

Two pieces of news which suggested Argyle were becoming an increasingly forward-looking club emerged on the day of their next match, at home to promotion outsiders Barnet, the following Saturday.

Firstly, the *Western Morning News* revealed exclusively that the club was at the forefront of discussions with Plymouth City Council over the development of a new super stadium, at the heart of which would be the city's professional football club.

Warnock was at the forefront of the discussions, which had also involved talks with Plymouth Albion Rugby Club about a possible ground-share, and his involvement was significant. While manager of Huddersfield, the club moved from Leeds Road to the award-winning Sir Alfred McAlpine Stadium.

The "Alf" as it is known in the local community, boasted facilities for a wide range of sports, as well as business conference facilities for up to 450 people, and was due to host open-air rock concerts. If the enthusiastic Warnock was to use his well-known powers of persuasion to convince the local authority that the West Country was crying out for a similar scheme, it could well be seen as an achievement every bit as great as winning promotion for Argyle.

On the same day as the news of the super stadium broke, Martin Barlow put pen to paper on a new $2^1/_2$-year contract, his previous difference with Warnock now consigned to the past. "I have been delighted with Martin's response and attitude since I issued him with the challenge to get back in the side after he could not agree terms with Cardiff," said Warnock. "Throughout the last two months, he has been a credit."

"I did not want to leave," said Barlow. "With the new manager coming in, it was a case of having to prove myself to the boss all over again."

Barlow continued in his rich vein of form against Barnet but even his midfield promptings were not enough

Martin Barlow signs his new contract

for the Pilgrims to gain more than a point. The game finished 1-1 but the reactions of the two managers afterwards told you all you needed to know about the game's balance of power.

"I think a draw was a fair result," opined Barnet's Ray Clemence which, as we all know, is managerspeak for "We copped a right hiding but somehow managed to get away with it."

"We're going to hammer somebody soon, there's nowt as sure as that," was the expurgated version of the view of Warnock, who chose to employ the football shorthand for "we were over them like a rash but could not score for love nor money."

The high expletive-count in Warnock's post-match Press briefing was indicative of his unhappiness, not only at his own side's inability to take advantage of some scintillating approach-play, but also at referee Mick Fletcher.

Fletcher made an extraordinary decision early in the second half which was compounded by an equally amazing apparent admission to Warnock after the game.

With Argyle leading through Scott Partridge's seventh-minute goal and Barnet hanging on for grim death, Pilgrims' striker Adrian Littlejohn was hauled back by his marker Alan Pardew as he broke for goal. Fletcher played a questionable advantage to Argyle, which did not accrue, and, when play broke down a minute later, went back to caution Pardew.

"He [Fletcher] said if he'd stopped the game instead of playing advantage, he would have sent him [Pardew] off," seethed Warnock. "What's the difference? The lad is through on goal, and he's pulled him back. Give us a break." Clemence claimed he did not see the incident, which made him probably unique among those at Home Park. Clearly his eyesight has deteriorated rapidly since he dominated the England and Liverpool penalty areas, gimlet-eyed and aware of all around him.

It was the pivotal moment of the game. Had Pardew not fouled Littlejohn, Argyle's leading scorer would surely have increased his tally; had Pardew been dismissed, Barnet's suffocating defensive blanket would have been torn apart and the Pilgrims would almost certainly have been able to make the breakthrough their promptings threatened.

However, if Argyle were not helped, they did not help themselves, conceding a soft equaliser in the 72nd minute when Shaun Gale lofted Steve Cherry's weak punch back over the Argyle goalkeeper's head from 25 yards.

Barlow dictated play so much that his marker, Alex Dyer by name and dire by nature, stopped him only once – with a bodycheck – and when Barnet were late coming out for the second half it can only have been because his team-mates were having trouble persuading him the second 45 minutes could not possibly be as painful as the first.

NW: *In training for the Barnet game, I put Chris Billy into the side because I felt Scott Partridge was just a little bit below par but then we found out the referee wouldn't change his mind about Micky Evans' sending-off and he definitely missed the Barnet game. I decided to go for Adrian Littlejohn up front. Mick and I thought that one change was enough, so we persevered with Scott Partridge and put Chris on the bench.*

Obviously he was disappointed when I told him, but then Scott scored after about 10 minutes, so it was not a bad decision. We had a couple of offside decisions against us which were very, very close, to say the least, going against us.

Then we had two awful decisions. In the second half, Adrian Littlejohn was pulled back and the lad should have been sent off. I just couldn't understand it. The referee tried to play an advantage of some sort which was never an advantage in a million years and then just ended up booking the player.

Then Cherry was impeded for the equaliser, but the ref said to me after the game that he didn't even see the challenge, so I have had to send him the video. It was disappointing. We had so much of the game so many chances. I don't think they had more than one chance.

Partridge's goal proved to be his last meaningful contribution to Argyle's 1995/96 cause. With Adrian Littlejohn back to speed and Michael Evans having served his penance for his outrageous dismissal at Scunthorpe, Warnock returned Partridge to Ashton Gate with much thanks to Bristol City manager Joe Jordan.

Evans and Littlejohn were thus reunited for the first time in seven matches when Argyle travelled to Brisbane Road to play Leyton Orient the following Tuesday, and, clearly, the

Pilgrims were in need of the partnership to start providing a cutting-edge to their promotion bid. They had scored just three goals in their previous four matches, which had been enough to garner six points out of 12, and had found the target only once in their last three away matches, in which they had dropped seven points out of a possible nine.

Despite Warnock's assertion that Argyle were due to hammer someone soon, he had revised his opinion on the day of the game at Brisbane Road. "I'd settle for getting one more than them," he said.

His wish was fulfilled by defender Richard Logan, who headed the only goal of the game in the 63rd minute to boost Argyle above the rapidly fading Chester into fourth place in the Third Division table. Logan's run was perfect as he met Mark Patterson's excellent right-wing cross to power a pin-point header past the helpless Orient goalkeeper Ron Fearon.

"It was a cracking win," enthused Warnock afterwards. "There won't be too many sides who come to Leyton Orient and take three points."

However, Warnock was not too happy with his team's showing in the first-half, their performance earning a 15-minute ear-bashing during the interval.

"The lads responded well," said Warnock, "but they should not have needed the kick up the backside. I was disappointed with our first-half display – only three or four of the team played – but luckily the centre-halves kept us together."

Victory was no more than the Pilgrims deserved as, eager as footballers ever are for the quiet life, they stepped up a gear after the tongue-lashing and gave Warnock little to find fault with in the second half.

NW: *Before we went to Orient I had made up my mind to bring Micky Evans straight back in and put him up front.*

We trained the Monday and went through set-pieces for Tuesday. I decided not to train on Tuesday morning as we normally do, because we trained before we went to Northampton and and we lost that one. I am superstitious. So I thought we could do a little bit more of a warm-up when we got there instead.

In the first half at Orient, Mick and I felt there were only three or four players that were anywhere near playing. We had talked a good game before we went out but we weren't hungry enough, we didn't want to know enough.

There were over 600 supporters there for a midweek game, which I thought was fantastic, so we had to kick some butts at half-time. I was disappointed with all the forwards, but in particular Micky Evans and Adrian Littlejohn. I thought the full-backs – Mark Patterson and Paul Williams – could have put more balls in the box rather than being too pretty. We were being over pretty.

So second half we did that and, to be fair, we started dominating. We had some great chances again, and missed out and it looked like once again one mistake would cost us dearly. But, a corner went back out to Patterson, he played a great ball in and Richard Logan scored a good goal and celebrated with all the fans at the back of the goal.

I knew with 20-odd minutes to go that if we could hold out and get the three points, it would be a major result for the remainder of the season.

We had one or two nervous experiences near the end – a couple of penalty appeals which weren't penalties but could have gone against us with inexperienced referees but fortunately the referee didn't give a penalty this time. It was the same referee that gave a penalty with 10 minutes to go at Gillingham. So, I suppose you win some, you lose some. I knew it when the final whistle went that it was a vital three points.

All right, all the other results didn't go for us. But we felt that it was nothing to do with other results – it was up to us.

We didn't get back from Orient until 3.30 a.m. We ended up going through the middle of London, around Tower Bridge and Westminster, on a nice guided tour because where Gary Clayton comes from, he'd never seen anything like that, so we asked the driver to give us a guided tour of the town.

The spirit from the lads on the bus was very, very good and Mick and I were at the front and were reminiscing on how we had turned things around at Huddersfield and what the bus was like on the trips. Really, when you come on long distances, it is important that the spirit is right. When we got together, it was cracking that night. You could feel the hum and everybody was excited, knowing that the three points were vital to us.

Depending on your yardstick, Gillingham, the team which represented the best or the worst of the Endsleigh Third Division, were the next visitors to Home Park as the promotion-race entered March.

A glance at Gillingham's goals-against column was enough to tell you why Kent's only professional football team arrived in the West Country leading the Third Division, six months after facing bankruptcy.

"To have conceded only 13 goals going into March is incredible," admitted an admiring Warnock. "I suppose we should feel we've done well if we manage to score against them, never mind win the game."

Yet, it was an unseen statistic which, when allied to the Gills' defensive suffocation, helped you understand their success: a clutch of red cards, more than 70 yellow, and upwards of 300 penalty points represented the worst disciplinary record in the country and pointed to an aggressive, hungry side.

To appreciate that hunger, you needed to know that Gillingham was a club in chaos when manager Tony Pulis took over at the start of the 1995/96 season, training without proper kit on public parks, where stray dogs chased stray passes.

Pulis, a combative midfielder in his playing days, had instilled in his team the simple philosophy that drove him on at Newport, Bristol Rovers, Bournemouth and Gillingham – "commitment, passion and pride in the shirt: I don't think it's a lot to ask" – and worked a minor miracle at Priestfield.

"We know they are uncompromising and will take no prisoners," said Warnock. "We haven't to get involved, just get on with our game. We know what to expect – there were one or two unnecessary incidents when we played them at their place – but we will just try to impose our own game on them."

One of the "unnecessary incidents" was the alleged racial abuse delivered to Pilgrims' midfielder Ronnie Maugé by one of the Gills' players, although Warnock's threat to report him to the Professional Footballers' Association was subsequently dropped.

Given the tension generated by the top-of-the-table clash, it came as no shock that Home Park stewards had to eject three people for unruly behaviour. The surprise was that none of them were employed by Gillingham Football Club.

The men from the Hop County stamped their offensive brand of ale-house football on the game and so thoroughly cheesed off a crowd entitled to expect more from the divisional leaders that it was an absolute pleasure to see their borderline thuggery rammed down their throats by Martin Barlow's third goal of the season.

If Gillingham did go on to win promotion they would do it without winning any friends in the West Country. They played throughout on the outer fringes of legality – leading with forearms; following through with legs; chipping away at the officials; winding up opponents; delaying dead-ball situations – and demonstrated precisely why they were uncomfortably the country's worst disciplined players.

Opposition manager Quentin Tarantino ... sorry, Tony Pulis, said afterwards he thought his side's performance was the best for some time, in which case Home Park punters should have offered profound thanks they did not produce their worst. It is a sad day indeed when a manager sincerely takes pride in which the aimless lump forward vies with your centre-forward's elbow as your most potent attacking weapon.

Pilgrims' manager Warnock would sooner walk naked down Royal Parade in 20 degrees of frost than be termed a football purist, but Argyle looked like a combination of the best parts of Ajax and AC Milan compared to Gillingham. The Gills could not play and had obviously decided to kick their way out of the Third Division. The pity was, they looked like succeeding.

Warnock took special pleasure that his players faced up to the abject nastiness of their opponents and declined to find fault with referee Gurnam Singh, who somehow managed to keep a lid on the bubbling physical encounter. Singh booked one player – Leo Fortune-West, marking his return from a three-match suspension by elbowing Mick Heathcote – but could have added many more.

Neil Smith escaped detection for similarly knocking Mark Patterson senseless in a first half in which the most memorable highlights were those in Argyle goalkeeper Steve Cherry's newly-dyed hair. Tony Butler hit Argyle's crossbar following a flicked-on long throw, but thereafter the Pilgrims coped admirably with the stream of set-pieces that represented Gillingham's only chance of scoring. They were incapable of creating anything in open play.

Even Pilgrim Pete, Argyle's oversized cartoon-come-to-life mascot, got a piece of the aggravation when he was clobbered in the back by a ball being knocked around by Gillingham's substitutes during the half-time interval, and the relentless aggression continued into the second period.

The game's only goal came in the 70th minute, when Adrian Littlejohn collected a pass from Ronnie Maugé on the left, cut inside Richard Green and crossed for Barlow, who steadied himself before ramming the ball into the centre of the goal. Sweet.

Gillingham were in far too negative a frame of mind to respond to the blow and Argyle controlled the remainder of the game with some ease. Barlow – man of the match for the third game in succession – ran the ball into the corners, keeping possession without trouble as Gillingham, all brawn and no brain, proved themselves witless to the end.

"It was a fantastic performance and a fantastic result," said Warnock afterwards. "I dare anybody to play well against Gillingham. You've got to stand up to them and play when you are allowed to. You have to smile at them with no retaliation and then come out with the points."

NW: *We knew that Gillingham was going to be a massive test and I warned the players that it would not be pretty. But the way we were, it didn't really bother me who we were playing and it couldn't really have come at a better time.*

At 10.30 a.m. on Saturday, I got a telephone call from Mark Patterson. He had been up all night with sickness and diarrhoea. I asked the doctor to go round. He spoke to me about noon and said he had given Patto something and he thought he would be okay. I told Mark that I would rather he start off and I had Chris Billy on the bench just in case. This he did and, to be fair, he got through the game.

It was a great result from a tremendous performance. It was a horrible game, but we knew it would be and we tried to play as much as we could, even though we knew they would try and stop us from trying to do everything.

We managed to get the goal – Martin Barlow scored a cracker – and I thought we fully deserved it. Very professional at the end, the best we had ever been in the last five minutes of a game.

We had still got to play those extra couple of games and it was in the hands of everyone at the club. I knew that Darlington were still a point above us and they had got games at Fulham and Torquay on Saturday, so we had just got to cross our fingers and hope that we didn't get left too far behind.

I got a lad down from Eastwood, Neil Illman, who I was looking to sign. I'd just got a thing about him. He was a striker who I thought would score goals and was a right little hard nut.

In the build-up to the following Saturday's visit to Cambridge, Warnock allowed centre-back Andy Comyn to leave Home Park on a free transfer. Comyn, who cost Argyle £165,000 when he was signed by Peter Shilton from Derby County in August 1993, had been on a weekly contract while recovering from a back injury. Having recovered, Comyn was offered a two-year deal which was not to his liking and so was allowed to leave to try his luck elsewhere.

Argyle extended their unbeaten run to eight matches at the Abbey with a battling 3-2 victory that at last lifted them into an automatic promotion spot. Third place represented their highest league position of the season and it had taken them 35 matches to get there – after giving the rest of the division a 12-point start.

The match was a pulsating one, as Warnock admitted afterwards. "When the doctor came into the changing-room at the end of the game to put some stitches in Mick Heathcote's cut eye, I almost asked him if he had his blood-pressure gauge with him," he joked. "If he had taken a test then, I'm sure I would have been at double the normal rate. It was an incredible second half."

Argyle got off to a flyer when Chris Billy fired them in front after eight minutes with a 20-yard shot, and Billy followed up his early strike with a shot on the half-hour which Jody Craddock cleared off the line. Had that effort gone in, second-from-bottom Cambridge might have folded. As it was, they equalised early in the second period through Micah Hyde and continued to put pressure on Argyle's defence, in which former Cambridge captain Heathcote, with blood streaming from his facial injury, was inspirational.

Gary Clayton, another former Cambridge player, helped the Pilgrims regain the lead against the run of play in the 69th minute when his mishit shot was deflected past goalkeeper Martin Davis by Richard Logan, but still the home side was not finished.

They equalised from the penalty spot five minutes after Logan's lucky strike, when Martin Barlow brought down winger Tony Richards. Canadian international Carlo Corazzin converted the chance – and he would later prove his expertise from 12 yards in front of Pilgrims supporters again.

Argyle took the lead for the third, and decisive, time nine minutes from the end of the game when Ian Baird hit a wayward shot from the left flank which fortuitously bounced off the back of a Cambridge defender and nestled in the net.

"There was a suggestion of fortune about two of the goals, but you make your own luck in this game," Warnock said. "Cambridge were fortunate to still be in the match when we scored."

Warnock remained faithful to the same 11 players who had retained the winning habit at the Abbey for the visit of Northampton to Home Park the following week. Since losing at Sixfields on January 30, Argyle had been unbeaten in six weeks and were confident they could maintain their third place in the Third Division. "The lads are full of themselves," confirmed Warnock.

For the second successive home game, the Pilgrims were confronted by a side whose idea of daring was to switch briefly from a nine-man defence to an eight-man one, for whom 0-0 away from home is bliss and 0-1 heaven itself. Gillingham without the testosterone.

They frustrated the living daylights out of Warnock, his players and the crowd but patience has its own rewards and Michael Evans' complete mishit from three yards eight minutes from time was a somehow apt way to settle a wholly unmemorable encounter 1-0.

At the end of the match, Warnock made a point of directing his players to applaud the Home Park fans. It was his way of saying: "Thanks for putting up with that load of Cobblers."

Warnock's comments on the Cobblers' demise were laced with irony and delivered with tongue firmly in cheek. "I thought the goal was an absolute classic," he dead-panned. "I'm glad it wasn't a 25-yard shot into the top corner. I thought the goal was absolutely what the game deserved."

Northampton obviously thought they deserved better. Stuck on the away dressing-room wall as a pre-match motivational aid was a Desktop Published mock newspaper headline: "Northampton 2 Plymouth Argyle 1 – Cobblers storm towards play-offs."

"They must be joking," sneered Warnock. "How were they going to score two goals from one attack? Mind you, I'm glad their one chance didn't go in, otherwise they'd have had all 11 behind the ball."

The Pilgrims' players' frustrations at being unable to break down their stubborn opponents were unleashed in the 82nd minute. Martin Barlow, retrieving the ball following the breakdown of one of Argyle's many corners, cut back on David Norton and floated over a precise far-post cross which Mick Heathcote had claimed for his forehead from the moment it left Barlow's right boot.

The ball hit Heathcote's marker's back and rolled down the Argyle captain's arm before plopping almost ashamedly in the middle of the six-yard box; Evans cocked the trigger, took aim, and completely misfired, swinging far too early.

Had he connected, the ball could probably have broken a window in Milehouse Road. As it was, it caught his hip following through and span into the net between defender and post. He will score better goals, but none sweeter. The Cobblers had come unstuck at last.

NW: *I gave the players Monday off and on Tuesday I found out that Ronnie Maugé and Gary Clayton had both gone down with 'flu symptoms; Micky Heathcote had got stitches in his foot from the Orient game and couldn't train; and Ian Baird was having an injection, so we were a bit depleted.*

I had a laugh on the Tuesday morning when Sharon found a pigeon damaged near our house. It was a homing pigeon because it had a number on its foot. So we chased it up over the weekend and found out it belonged to somebody in Bournemouth. I spoke to them and said "Leave it to me, I have got a lad who can return it." I had to smile.

I asked Ian Baird to take it back over to Bournemouth. I telephoned him urgently and said to him that I needed him to drop somebody off in Bournemouth, but I didn't tell him it was a pigeon. He said that was all right with him.

When he got to the ground, he said: "Are you joking gaffer or what?" Anyhow he took the pigeon over and it got home safe and sound.

I also went to the Plymouth Supporters Association Fans' Forum at the ground. It was an interesting night. I think they learnt a bit about me and I answered a lot of questions. I don't think it does you any harm to go and see the public.

The week was absolutely chaotic. Ray Card, one of our sponsors died. He was only in his 40s and the funeral was on the Friday at noon. We were leaving at 10.00 a.m. to go up to Cambridge and Mark Patterson and Keith Hill both wanted to go to the funeral, which you would have expected. So I let them go. Micky Heathcote went up on Thursday to see the guy who did his back; Steve Cherry travelled down from Nottingham; and then we had a load of lads who had not trained all week, for one reason or another.

We had another meeting on the Thursday with the lottery people, along with the Plymouth Sports Council. It was a very, very interesting meeting and you could see how well organised Dave Renwick of Plymouth Council was.

That lasted a couple of hours and I had to rush off back home because Radio Cornwall had asked if they could come and look in my cupboards and do an interview with me for a half-hour programme scheduled for the Friday morning. They came and asked me certain questions in each room of my house.

I was also trying to pay Micky Ross up. I agreed something with him and I was trying to organise how we could get it done on the Friday as we were leaving to go to Cambridge. I agreed a settlement with Mick whereby we would cancel his contract.

I also decided that I was going to put Chris Leadbitter on the bench. I knew he was a local, with him coming from Cambridge, but he looked sharp in training even though he has only had one game and I feel that if Ronnie Maugé was going to be out, we might just have needed 20 minutes from him.

We left at 9.30 a.m. from Plymouth and got onto the A38 and had to divert off to Totnes – because of snow – to within a mile of Torquay beach, then we got back onto the A38 further up North. We had asked for two drivers and had to go into Bristol town centre to pick another driver up. We had been travelling for three hours and we still hadn't cleared Bristol. Can you believe that?

Mark Patterson and Keith Hill arrived at 8.15 p.m. after they went to Ray Card's funeral, because of the traffic hold-up. When we went to bed there was a lovely disco banging downstairs until 1.00 a.m., but sometimes these things help to get your mind off the game.

It was raining on the day of the match the following morning and the lads had a warm-up themselves which was voluntary. It turned out to be a great result and yet it's a wonder it didn't give me a heart attack, the way we almost threw it away.

We were winning 1-0 and could have been three or four up and cruising, and at half-time I got that feeling in the dressing-room that no matter what I said, the players were thinking it was going to be easy. Within 10 minutes of the second half, Cambridge were level and we are up against it.

We came through it in the end with a 3-2 victory and I went bananas at the end. We had a corner kick in extra-time and we crossed the ball into the hands of the goalkeeper, who knocked the ball downfield to give Cambridge the chance of an equaliser when we had just had it in the corner.

It was so unprofessional. So myself and Chris Leadbitter had a few words and one or two others joined in. It was all forgotten within half an hour but, oh my goodness, who would want to be a manager?

I let Ronnie Maugé have the week off because he couldn't do anything at all on his stress fracture. I was glad that we hadn't got too many games in March until the disciplinary-points cut-off time, and at least we had a chance to get at least one of the lads back within the next two weeks, hopefully Ronnie. Mark Saunders was struggling.

Two important dates now loomed for Argyle: their St James' Park Derby date with Exeter City on Saturday, March 23 and the season's deadline day for transfers the following Thursday, March 28.

Warnock thought he had successfully jumped the gun on the latter by beating off competition from a number of clubs to sign 20-year-old striker Neil Illman from Nottinghamshire non-leaguers Eastwood Town. Two days before the all-Devon encounter, he announced he had signed Illman for £5,000 and intended to give the former Middlesbrough apprentice his debut at St James' Park.

"He's a cracking finisher – he doesn't miss the target often – and he's quick, strong and nasty," said Warnock. "Mick Jones calls him an angel with a mucky face."

However, the bedevilled deal was put on ice the following day, with Pilgrims' chairman Dan McCauley claiming the deal had not gone through because of a "financial misunderstanding" between himself and his manager.

"I was presented with details [of the transfer] which were considerably different to the ones I had been told on the 'phone the previous night," explained McCauley. "I was expecting something which was within a certain financial framework, but this was different."

McCauley brushed off suggestions that the apparent breakdown in communications was similar to those which often blighted his relationship with Peter Shilton. "I would say that it is only a hitch, as far as I am concerned," said McCauley, who had recently been presented with a new reason to exercise caution with the club's finances – a £150,000 Inland Revenue bill for unpaid back-taxes over the previous six years, many of which he said had been built up during the Shilton era.

Instead of Argyle, it was Exeter who paraded a surprise new signing – Adrian Foster, the former Torquay United forward who had been borrowed on the quiet from Gillingham the previous day.

Foster proved a damp squib, but Exeter manager Peter Fox was a content manager after the 48th meeting between Devon's oldest rivals ended in an honours-even 1-1 draw. Exeter were outclassed, outgunned, outfought and outplayed by Argyle from start to finish but were never outfoxed, thanks to the home side's goalkeeping gaffer and his central defenders Mark Came and Noel Blake, and ultimately not out-pointed. They did not so much achieve a draw as survive one.

If Exeter felt like celebrating, and smuggling a couple of points away from their bitter, swankier, promotion-chasing rivals was surely worth a lager or two, it was sincerely hoped that Fox, Came and Blake did not have to dip into their own pockets.

Pilgrims midfielder Gary Clayton opened the scoring in the ninth minute with a swerving airborne drive that curled between the attempted blocks of Danny Bailey and Mark Cooper and flew past Fox. The strike, created by Chris Billy's thrust and Ian Baird's pluperfect lay-off, was all the more satisfying for dour Yorkshireman Clayton, given that six seasons earlier he had been told his career was over after damaging ankle ligaments at St James' Park.

Ten minutes later, Exeter equalised from one of their rare attacks. Mark Gavin swung a cross to the far post, where Cooper was lurking beyond Mark Patterson's nearly-clearance to control the ball and drive it into the net. Richard Logan, under no pressure, instinctively stuck out a leg and the ball lolloped over goalkeeper Steve Cherry and into the corner of the net.

The previous week, Logan had scored a crucial goal at the other end in a similar manner. Proponents of the luck-evens-itself-out-over-the-course-of-a-season theory were delighted to see evidence of their claims.

The match facts bore ample testimony to Argyle's dominance – and City's resolve. Argyle had 21 shots on goal, Exeter just four, but the two sides finished level in the only statistic that really counted.

Warnock was pleased with the whistle-to-whistle effort of his players, which maintained their third place in the division. He said: "A supporter said to me that, in these matches, Plymouth's attitude has not been as good as Exeter's.

"But I said to my lads that the game is important to supporters and that teams might beat us with ability and quickness of thought, but no team should beat us through effort and commitment. Unfortunately, we couldn't get the three points but I'm extremely delighted with the performance. We were disciplined and we dominated."

NW: *On Friday morning before Northampton, Micky Evans pulled up with a groin strain. We were hoping that he could get through Saturday because we hadn't really got anybody else to put in that position, with both Saunders and Maugé out.*

He played and we got the win. It was an absolute scramble but we knew they would be defensive and they were diabolical regarding attacking. I said to the lads at half-time, as they did their Wimbledon Apache dance: "Listen to this lot next door. Let's go out and beat them and then let's sort them out in the tunnel coming off, make sure we are loud and give them our song." That's what we did.

A late goal, a scrambled goal as we knew it would be, and then we didn't half let rip in the tunnel. In fact, their manager and players came out and scowled at us. What a horrible way to play, dear me. My most enjoyable Press conference and if ever football was just, it was that day.

Evans played with this groin strain and scored the winner, when he shouldn't really have played. Even though he has got his critics, I am a big believer in him and I thought he did ever so well. I changed Chris Billy before half-time from the left wing to midfield and I let Adrian Littlejohn go out there with Micky Evans up front, and I thought it worked a treat.

I knew Ronnie Maugé wouldn't be fit for Exeter, because he was still very sore, and Mark Saunders had got to rest. It looked bleak and I needed to try and get somebody in even though there was no money. The board had had this £150,000 tax-bill, which was a major blow because we were not flush with money. I would have liked to sign a couple of players, but I quite appreciated how the chairman felt regarding the tax-bill because it started from before his time at Plymouth.

I pulled Leadbitter out of the reserve game at Newport on the Wednesday because I daren't let him get booked – he was one booking short of a suspension. The lad Neil Illman who I wanted to sign from Eastwood, scored two cracking goals and both Mick and I thought he had got a right good chance. So I would have to try and level with the chairman again and see if I could have a dabble.

The chairman told me I could sign him so I got the lad down and agreed everything with Eastwood. Then on the Friday I was told that I couldn't sign him because the wages were too high and the chairman thought the agreement with Eastwood had changed.

We played ever so well at Exeter and drew 1-1. It was one of the best away performances I had seen regarding control but a deflected goal by Richard Logan gave them a share of the points.

It was an important game to the supporters and I made sure that the players knew that. It was ever so quiet in the dressing-room before the game. Peter Fox had done all the spouting off up there, about how they were going to be the hunters and not the hunted and I think we were all thinking about the game and how we wanted to approach it, especially for the fans.

We had loads of letters about how important it was to the fans and we went out there and dominated it from start to finish and yet we just couldn't get that winning goal, but I was ever so pleased.

Transfer negotiations dominated most of the following week as Argyle pursued strikers on two fronts. Warnock and chairman Dan McCauley came together to attempt to thrash out their financial differences over the Neil Illman deal and, at the same time, opened talks with Cambridge United for the services of 25-year-old Canadian international Carlo Corazzin.

Persistence paid on transfer deadline-day when, after what turned out to be years of trying, Warnock finally landed Corazzin for £150,000 and at last clinched the transfer of Illman, for an initial £5,000, after a week of negotiations.

Although Warnock and McCauley resolved their discrepancy over the difference on the Illman deal, Illman's crazy introduction to the world of professional football continued when he was immediately loaned out to Cambridge for the remainder of the season.

Warnock was delighted with his capture of Corazzin. "I have made at least four enquiries for him at three different clubs," he said. "I offered £250,000 for him at Huddersfield last season and the same amount for him *and* Mick Heathcote at the start of this season. I've always admired him because I think he's a lad who's very difficult to mark. He's always on the go, always threatening, and you can't take your eye off him. He's not a big lad but he's very good in the air. Centre-halves always think they are going to beat him in the air and when he beats them, it rubs them up the wrong way. He's got a bit of pace and he's a fresh-looking lad. He gives us something different in the squad, with his Canadian accent and everything. I think he'll give us a lift to everyone."

Illman would make his Third Division debut the following Saturday, though for Cambridge, instead of Argyle. Immediately after putting pen to paper on a two-year contract, he was on a train to East Anglia.

"He's looking forward to it," said Warnock. "It will give him the chance to settle into league football before coming back to us in the summer. I hope he'll also be able to score a lot of goals when Cambridge are playing our rivals for promotion. He can do us a lot of favours that way."

NW: *On Monday before transfer deadline-day, I was still trying to negotiate a deal that would get Neil Illman to Plymouth. I would have liked him on the bench against Exeter on the on Saturday because, the way he is, he could just turn a game.*

The chairman was also going to speak to Cambridge. They telephoned him about Carlo Corazzin and it was in the papers in Plymouth about how we had made an offer. We hadn't made an offer as such but the chairman was going to speak to them, just see where the land lay and how much they wanted for him.

I got a lad, Alan Errington from Vancouver, to come over and watch our reserves, and he agreed to sign Micky Ross and Ian Payne. They were both going to go to Vancouver so we agreed to cancel their contracts.

Steve McCall only managed the first half against Swansea. His calf just felt a bit sore. It would have been nice to have considered him because Gary Clayton was going to miss the Darlington game a fortnight later but if he was struggling with his calf, it was pointless starting with him.

Illman stayed down with us and played in the reserves, but Nottingham Forest wanted him to play for their reserves, so I had to make a decision. I had renegotiated a better deal, so hopefully the chairman would let us go ahead with it.

Micky Evans was struggling again. I had only got Danny O'Hagan as a forward to put on at Exeter, and didn't think he would be able to hold it enough against their experienced centre-halves.

Other results went quite well for us again in the midweek – Bury drew at Preston and Chester drew at home to Cambridge – so we were still there, even though there were only five teams within three points. It was very tight but we were hanging on, with some tough away games to come.

Transfer deadline-day was hectic. Carlo Corazzin came down and we did the quickest deal I have ever done financially. I told the player that I had just been to the chairman and what we could offer him, and he just accepted it. He wanted to play for us and we just had a bit of squabbling to do with Cambridge over the exact amount of the fee. We ended up paying what we thought he was worth – £100,000 plus £50,000 over 12 months – and he looked really bright. I thought he would do the squad the world of good.

Poor old Neil Illman – he had a right week. We ended up signing him but I agreed to loan him to Cambridge for the rest of the season. They said they were going to play him. I thought it would give him a good inkling into what the Football League was all about and we would be able to find out about him. It was a good idea for both parties. Cambridge were desperate, with Carlo going.

Neil Illman was not the only one letting the train take the strain that weekend. The Argyle squad, management, directors and 400 foot soldiers from the West Country regiments of the Green Army travelled to Fulham by rail. The Penzance-to-Paddington Express – specially chartered from Great Western – might have had the appearance of an early end-of-season jolly about it, but it was an experiment with a purpose.

"Coach journeys are getting longer for us, with the new laws governing coaches' speed and banning them from using the middle lane," said Warnock, manager of England's most southerly football club. "Travelling more often by train would suit us."

To where Argyle's tickets would be punched the following season rested at least partly on the match at Craven Cottage. The previous week's draw at Exeter had not cost them third place – nor, more surprisingly, had their midweek inactivity when promotion rivals were in action – but they could not afford too much more profligacy in front of goal if Peterborough and Wycombe were going to replace Leyton and Rochdale as destinations on the following season's timetable.

"Somebody will get hit with goals, the way we are playing," said Warnock, warming to a familiar theme. "Goals are important. If we've got more goals than our rivals, it's worth another point, really."

As cases of foot-in-mouth went, it was pretty serious. The way Argyle played at Craven Cottage did, indeed, ensure someone was hit with goals – themselves. The Green Army, having swelled Fulham's normal crowd to their largest attendance of the season, watched red-faced as the Pilgrims crashed to their heaviest defeat of the campaign – 4-0. The craven performance was described by Warnock as "a total disgrace" and "an utter shambles."

"I went into the dressing-room afterwards and said 'Well done'," said a sarcastic Warnock. "How they kept it down to four, playing like that… I thought they were magnificent."

The morning journey by train, as opposed to the overnight coach trip and hotel stay, had obviously affected the Pilgrims' preparations, although Warnock was too savvy to say so publicly. Any criticism of the Pilgrim Express could seriously affect the club's future commercial aspirations. Apart from the result, the train journey had been a great success.

Warnock suggested that his players pay penance for their on-field sins by being made to board the Pilgrim Express at the rear for the return journey to Plymouth and walking past all their supporters to take their seats at the front.

Actually, it was the manager who used the opportunity to talk to fans. Whether he was aware of the fact or not, his gesture replicated almost exactly that of former Argyle manager Dave Smith, who had boarded supporters' coaches after his promotion-chasing Pilgrims of 10 years previously had crashed 3-0 at Wigan at a similar stage of the season. Smith's side had gone on to go up.

NW: *We went up to Fulham on the Saturday morning by train. It was a well thought-out exercise by Steve Birley, the commercial manager – I think that 16 tickets out of 450 weren't sold – but it did mean an early start.*

My alarm clock went off at seven o'clock that morning. I like my lie-in on a Saturday morning in preparing for a game but I thought we would give it a try on the train. I thought the lads would walk about a lot more on the train and stretch their legs and it would be better for them.

In fact, it worked the opposite way. It was that tight with seats that everybody stuck to their own seats, and then there was breakfast coming past them and supporters coming for autographs. I had a sneaky feeling that it wasn't really the right preparation.

We got off the train at Paddington and they did tell us at first that we would be on a 25-seater coach so we planned who to take with us. When we got there, we were told that they had managed to get West Ham's team coach and we travelled on that.

We had been travelling for about five minutes when the driver started giving us a guided tour around London. We asked him to make sure he didn't rush because we didn't want to get to the ground before 1.30 p.m., so he started driving around London and telling everyone where this was and that was and there was Nelson's Column, Hyde Park Corner, etc. I just had a feeling that the preparation was all wrong because you just couldn't get your mind on the game. At a time when I wanted them to have their minds on the game, they were looking around at London.

I wanted us to have a walk because we were there early. We had been on the train all morning and I wanted them to get some fresh air. But Mick Heathcote wanted to get straight to the ground. So I thought "Okay, we will go straight to the ground for Mick, but then I will make sure that we have 10 or 15 minutes out on the pitch and have a walk."

Well, we got to the ground and by the time I had put my boots on they had not only been out, they had come back in again! So I made them go out again, but they were out for only two or three minutes, lounging around.

When we did our warm-up, you could tell that Fulham meant business. They were concentrating.

Our lot had such good support. We had over 2,000 people there as we were doing our warm-up, all chanting and clapping. It was difficult to put your finger on it, but I just had this fear that their attitude was wrong, their minds were just not on the game.

We were unlucky with the corner-kick for the first goal. It was certainly a goal-kick and the referee gave a corner. He was the only one that saw it as such and they scored from the corner. He must have made nine or 10 decisions in the first half which were wrong, and all went against us.

It was an absolute nightmare. We conceded a goal and I thought we could have sorted it out at half-time, but Ian Baird had come off injured after a quarter of an hour when he was doing ever so well. Carlo Corazzin came on but we were all at sixes and sevens and I was glad to get to half-time at 1-0 down. I thought we had sorted it out when the second half came, but, to be fair, apart from Micky Heathcote and Chris Billy, there was nobody that I thought did anything. It was too coincidental for nine or 10 players to be off. I had got to look deeper.

I know players and managers look for excuses but really our preparation for the previous few months had been spot on. So I had to look at the train and I think probably, because on the bus the players know that it is only themselves and they can relax a bit more and not worry about other people, the train journey probably took a little bit out of themselves. I wouldn't give them that excuse, but that is what I thought.

Argyle had an early opportunity to recover from the post-train crash in London the following Tuesday, April 2 – the last full month of the season, at home to Mansfield. Warnock made one change from the previous weekend's starting line-up, recalling fit-again Ronnie Maugé in place of Ian Baird, who had torn his groin at Fulham.

However, his two most interesting selections were on the substitutes' bench, where record-signing Carlo Corazzin rubbed shoulders with Warnock's immediate predecessor as Argyle manager, Steve McCall, who had been unavailable to his successor all season due to a succession of injuries.

Just as Dave Smith had urged his 1986 Pilgrims to forget the 3-0 humiliation at Wigan "as quickly as possible and concentrate hard on our next important home game", so Warnock had urged his players to "forget about [Fulham] and get on with the next games as if it had never happened."

History records that Smith's men returned to Home Park and trounced Bolton Wanderers 4-1 and while history did not exactly repeat itself, Argyle duly reaped their reward for perseverance. They won 1-0 in the most dramatic of circumstances after a superb display by Mansfield goalkeeper Ian Bowling had threatened to keep the scoreline blank. While Bowling did not stop a cricket score, he made enough splendid saves – including two breath-taking stops either side of half-time – to frustrate the Pilgrims almost beyond measure and all-but stump their promotion bid.

Warnock introduced McCall, to loud applause, in the 66th minute and within 66 seconds his first touch led to a chance for Adrian Littlejohn, which flashed over the crossbar. However, it was Warnock's second substitution which truly turned the game.

Corazzin entered the fray in the 87th minute and immediately found Bowling as impenetrable as his team-mates had, seeing the Stags' goalkeeper Bowling smother his header on the goal-line. Then, with the game entering time added on by the referee, Simon Wood brought down Corazzin for a penalty.

Michael Evans, Argyle's regular penalty-taker, had missed his previous spot-prize and did not look that keen on taking the pressure kick, so defender Mark Patterson took the ball from him and shaped to place it on the quicklime circle for the last-gasp vital opportunity. Warnock, though, had other ideas and frantically sent hurried instructions from the dug-out that Corazzin, whose last successful penalty had been *against* the Pilgrims for Cambridge, was to take responsibility.

It was not the best penalty ever taken but it was good enough to beat the otherwise impassable Bowling and new £150,000 signing Corazzin earned himself instant

Carlo Corazzin scored a dramatic winner against Mansfield

Home Park hero status by securing a vital 1-0 victory with only his third touch of the night.

Corazzin said: "I could not have written the script any better. When I got the penalty I thought I'd better stand back because every club has their regular penalty-taker and I am just the new boy. I didn't want to upset anyone, but when I turned round, I saw the gaffer saying 'Take it' – so I did."

Warnock said: "Carlo was not going to take it, so I stood up and told him to take it off Mark Patterson. You have got to give Patterson credit – he wanted to take it and I did not see many players running towards the ball – but I wanted Corazzin to take it. He took one against us when we played at Cambridge.

"Patterson was annoyed. He was still muttering afterwards, even though we won the game, which is good. He wanted to take the kick. He is a winner."

NW: *I asked Micky Evans, Gary Clayton and Ian Baird to come in on the Sunday after Fulham to have a look at their injuries. We thought Micky would play and I was going to try to play Carlo and Micky in the next match against Mansfield. I didn't think it was a time for change. I just thought we had got to say that Fulham was a one-off and try and do our best.*

On Tuesday morning, I announced the side and Carlo was in the team. I told Ronnie Maugé he was going to be on the bench with Steve McCall. I think you need somebody on the bench with who you can just change matches. I said to Steve that even if he only gave us half an hour, he might just be able to give us that influence that we needed to break down defences. He wanted to do it, so fair enough.

We had a practice match that morning and I tried to work with Carlo, just to let him know what we needed, but the lads were trying to knock long balls because of Carlo and there were four or five lads that had changed the way I wanted them to play.

That afternoon, even though I had announced the side, I spent two or three hours considering it and I decided that I was going to change my mind again and put Carlo on the bench and bring Ronnie Maugé in.

I just felt that with Gary Clayton, Chris Billy and Micky Evans in his deeper role, we hadn't got enough strength in midfield. So I explained that to Carlo. I knew he would be disappointed after telling him he was playing but I just thought that we ought to go with what had been good for 10 games before Fulham and shouldn't really go into changing things for the sake of things. He accepted it. He said that he thought that everybody was trying to look for him, and he had got to get used to us.

Their goalkeeper pulled off four or five cracking saves and we couldn't break it down so I put Steve McCall on with 25 minutes to go. I pulled Chris Billy off. I was ever so disappointed with the crowd. It was the first time that I had ever been disappointed with them. They not only got on Chris's back, but got on a few of the other players' backs, frustrated because we weren't scoring. But we couldn't help the goalkeeper pulling off breathtaking saves, and I thought it was unjust.

If they were going to be like that, I didn't think we would go up – whether by automatic promotion or the play-offs – because I thought they would put that much pressure on the players. If they put that kind of pressure on the players, then I didn't think we would get the right results and I had got to try to make sure the fans were aware of how important they were.

Anyhow, I put Carlo on with what must have been only five minutes to go. For about 15 minutes I had been trying to decide who to pull off. It could have been anybody really because they were all doing well and in the end I pulled Adrian Littlejohn off and shoved Carlo on because Micky Evans was winning everything in the air. From his first touch after a cross by Steve McCall, he pulled out a good save off from the goalkeeper. And then into injury-time, he got the ball onto his feet in the box, somebody fouled him, and we were awarded a penalty.

Mark Patterson was going to take it and I shouted on to Carlo: "You take it, I want you to take it." And he ran across to Mark Patterson and told him that I wanted him to take it and got hold of the ball and put it away. Instant hero. I don't think we could have written a better script really.

I just thought it was the right thing to do. Even if we had drawn 0-0, I would have still thought that it was the right thing to do because I think if I had played Carlo and things had gone totally wrong, the crowd would have got on his back.

McCall and Corazzin both impressed Warnock enough to earn places in the starting line-up for the Easter Saturday Home Park date against Darlington, as Warnock selected a squad of 16 players for the holiday double-header against the North Easterners and local rivals Torquay United. He then admitted that none of the 16 was as vital to the Pilgrims' promotion drive as more than 6,000 names not on the team-sheet.

"Our supporters can win us promotion," said Warnock, who had been criticised for having a go at fans whose frustrations had been given a vociferous airing against Mansfield. "All I was saying was 'Please be patient – supporters, management and players are all as one'."

The fans' evident displeasure at the Pilgrims' inability to break down the Stags until Carlo Corazzin's late, late strike, was directed largely at midfielder Chris Billy, not least of all because he was keeping favourite Steve McCall on the substitutes' bench.

"He had a bit of a 'mare," admitted Warnock, "but nobody has a 'mare intentionally. If the crowd is going to pick on individuals, I don't think we are going to go up. They will build up so much pressure on the players that they will not be able to play their normal game. All I am asking them for is some patience because, believe me, the players are so honest – they are trying so hard for the club."

It became evident that they would have to try even harder after the 1-0 home defeat by Darlington, who thus completed an impressive league double against the Pilgrims (no goals conceded), left them on the edge of the play-off zone in seventh place behind Chester, Darlington, Wigan, Bury, Gillingham and Preston. Snapping at their heels were Colchester, Barnet and Hereford.

Warnock accused his players of not gambling enough and then raised the stakes for the Easter Monday morning visit to Torquay. "If we don't win at Plainmoor, automatic promotion is out of the window," said Warnock. "It's as simple as that."

A goal of dubious legality proved the difference between Argyle and Darlington, and although the Pilgrims threw the kitchen sink at their opponents after Robbie Painter's 22nd-minute strike, their failure to convert a plethora of scoring opportunities looked likely to cost them the short route to promotion.

"The chances are there," said Warnock, "but we're not being ruthless enough. We're not gambling in the box. The forwards have got to take the blame. They've got to become winners, and to become winners, they've got to become more ruthless."

Painter and his forward colleague Robert Blake were obviously offside when they combined for the former to shoot past goalkeeper Steve Cherry from the edge of the box. The defenders had stopped, naïvely waiting for a flag or a whistle which never came, and Cherry made a half-hearted attempt to stop Painter's scuffed drive which beat him rather too easily. Clearly, none of them expected the strike to stand but, to stunned silence and general disbelief, referee Steve Baines allowed the goal.

Warnock has been a long-time advocate of professional referees. Whether he had changed his mind after a thoroughly inept performance from Baines, a long-time defender in the lower divisions, remained to be seen, but he was totally confused by the officials' post-match explanation of the goal.

"I haven't got a clue what's going on," he said. "At half-time, the linesman said he wasn't offside. At the end of the game, he said there was a guy offside [Blake] but he didn't think he was interfering. But Painter pushed him out of the way to shoot."

Warnock had no complaints about the result, having tried just about everything, including dropping Adrian Littlejohn in favour of Carlo Corazzin and starting with Steve McCall in place of Chris Billy.

McCall looked most likely to unlock Darlington's safe-box of a defence, with some delightful dinks, chips and reverse passes but Corazzin looked way off the pace in the danger area and Evans and Littlejohn – when he came on – were scarcely more effective.

"We have got six games left and we cannot afford not to win any of them," said Warnock, knowing that even that might not be enough to avoid the lottery of the post-season play-offs.

NW: *I had three or four letters from supporters. I had made headlines in the* Evening Herald *after the Mansfield game – "Warnock slams the fans" but what I was saying was if they were going to have a go at players I'd rather they did not come to the games. They had taken offence. They felt it was only a small minority who barracked and were appalled at my comments.*

I telephoned a couple of them up and just explained that I wasn't having a go at the majority, it's just that when they had a go at Chris Billy, in particular, against Mansfield, it was no wonder that there were one or two lads who were a bit apprehensive, with the stick they were getting. Everyone was frustrated. I was frustrated when we missed goals but the goalkeeper pulled off three or four world-class saves, so you had to put things into perspective and I thought that if we had got any chance of going up, the supporters had got to be really behind us or they would put us under pressure.

Against Darlington, we decided to go with Carlo Corazzin and Michael Evans and leave Adrian Littlejohn on the bench with Chris Billy and I was going to try and get as much as I could out of Steve McCall. I had been told he hadn't had a full game now for two years, so maybe it was asking a lot to see if he could get through one.

Ronnie Maugé hadn't trained again on Friday but he was going to try and give it a go to see if we could get him through, knowing that Gary Clayton could come back for the Monday game against Torquay, even though he had got an Achilles tendon problem for which he was having treatment.

After Darlington was the worst I have ever felt after a game of football. I knew we should have won. We had so much of the play again and failed to score and the result didn't give us any chance of slipping up now. We had to go to Torquay on Monday and win.

I was so disappointed with the goal. All right, we lost 1-0, but the goal was nothing to do with us. The work that we put in all week just went out of the window. The goal was so offside it was untrue. They crossed the ball and there were two guys offside – all right, one of them may not have been offside, I will give the linesman the benefit of the doubt. The other one, he said, was not interfering with play. He was stood still, two yards inside the box when the ball broke to this lad's foot at the edge of the box, the lad who was offside walked back towards him as if he was not active and then, when he got into a mix-up, the lad who was offside actually turned, shot and scored.

This linesman told me that he was never interfering with play. At half-time I went in and asked him and he said there was nobody offside. Then at the end of the game, he said that there was somebody offside, but he was not interfering with play. Then he said the player who was offside was at least three yards away from the ball. So am I to believe that a linesman who is 40 yards away from an incident – and an amateur – can apparently decide if a player is interfering or not? I can't believe the legislation of the Football League. If we have got amateurs like this expected to make decisions like that, he should flag and it should be left up to the referee, who was 10 yards away from the incident, and not left up to him.

The state of them as well. The condition of some is poor. Some are at least a stone overweight. We are asked to be professionals! Surely they can be professional enough to look after their own bodies and what can we do? Send a video off and they write back saying "Yes, you were right."

What good is it if you have lost the point? I am fed up with sending videos off, it is just a waste of time. We were getting the short end of the stick; we were getting first-year referees making mistakes, week in week out, and everybody said they needed experience and they had got to learn.

I know they have got to learn, but it is the same people suffering every week and there is no punishment. The linesman in this particular case cost us one goal, maybe three goals, because that goal gave Darlington a massive lift. What recourse have we got? He goes home, talks to his wife and goes to work the next day, it doesn't bother him. And he could have affected the lives of thousands of people, just because he decides they are not interfering with play!

We still could not score enough goals, not with the chances we were creating. Steve McCall got through the game, but it absolutely shattered him and I didn't want to bring him off because he was playing well.

"I JUST HOPE WE PLAY BADLY IN THE NEXT FIVE GAMES AND WIN THEM ALL"

THE Plainmoor Derby was a tighter affair than the previous all-Devon Endsleigh League Third Division clash against Exeter, as Torquay belied their lowly status to give the Pilgrims a run for their money. So bad was the Gulls' plight that many of their supporters had decided against attending the match in favour of travelling to see the GM Vauxhall Conference top-of-the-table clash between Stevenage and Woking. Torquay seemed certain to finish the season at the bottom of the Third Division but would escape relegation if Stevenage, whose Broadhall Way ground had failed to meet League criteria, won the Conference. The Hertfordshire side could not be promoted.

Ronnie Maugé heads the first goal against Torquay

The match was a typical Derby: a lot of huff and puff and not much quality. Torquay, whose players looked as though they had only just got out of bed for the 11.00 a.m. kick-off, went behind in the fifth minute when Ronnie Maugé headed home Martin Barlow's perfect left-wing cross.

For the next quarter of an hour it was all Torquay could do to get the ball out of their own half and Richard Logan spurned two opportunities to kill off the game before the mid-point of the first half. However, the Gulls gradually woke up and then controlled the game for the remainder of the match. The difference between the two sides ultimately proved to be the fact that Torquay wasted their scoring chances, while Argyle took their only other opportunity when Adrian Littlejohn out-paced the opposition defence to latch on to Steve Cherry's pumped clearance and seal the three points in the 76th minute.

"We knew it wasn't going to be pretty," said Warnock afterwards. "There are no easy games any more, but we couldn't afford to do anything but win. Our season could depend on this result. Now, we must beat Scarborough next Saturday."

NW: *I thought about starting with Carlo Corazzin behind the front three at Torquay. It had reached the point of do or die, so I was going to try and play Carlo behind Michael Evans, Adrian Littlejohn and Martin Barlow, just to see if we could get some bodies in and some goals.*

It was an 11.00 a.m. kick-off and I wanted to stop overnight if I could, just to get the players' minds right, but hotels and bed and breakfasts are too expensive, really, and the chairman and directors didn't want the expense of an overnight stop for such a short journey, so we travelled at 8.45 that morning.

I thought the pitch was good when we arrived. The crowd was already coming round and I had a good chat with about 20 of our supporters outside. As I was talking to these 20 lads, in the space of five minutes three different police officers came and asked every one of them to show them the colour of their tickets. And they explained they were only talking to the manager.

I couldn't understand the police. I said to the third officer: "With all due respect, this is the third time within the space of five minutes while I have stood talking to them. Can't you see that they are behaving themselves and that they are just having a chat with me? Don't you think that you are provoking them by asking them to show their tickets three or four times?"

I just said to the supporters to try and behave themselves and not to let the police have any excuse for anybody to be thrown out.

I thought they were very good that afternoon. The supporters were super. It was not a good performance football-wise, but we needed to have commitment to win games in which players were not playing well. I was delighted, even though certain people didn't think we were playing very well. We had just got to keep our nerve.

**With guest speaker Paul Fletcher at a sportsman's dinner
after the announcement of the launch of the new stadium**

If Warnock had one eye on the immediate future, his other was firmly on the Pilgrims' long-term progress. On Thursday, April 11, Plymouth City Council officially revealed their plans for a £25m, super stadium, offering state-of-the-art sport, leisure and business facilities and providing Argyle with a new ground to take the Pilgrims into the 21st century.

Along with a 23,000-seater stadium, the complex, which was due to open for business in the summer of 1999, would boast a banqueting hall for 500 people, hospitality suites, a golf driving-range, a cross-country course, a huge sports hall and an adventure play-area. With room for some 37,000 standing, it could also attract some of the world's biggest rock bands.

Funding for the project would come from a variety of sources, including the Football Grounds Improvement Trust, the Sports Council and the National Lottery – but not the tax-payer.

The ambitious plans, which would also create thousands of jobs across the West Country, had been modelled on the plans of Dutch side Ajax, who rose to become the best club side in the world on the back of a project designed to get people of all ages involved in sport and leisure at one venue, with football as the centre-piece. Their aim had been simple: to have the stadium used by as many people as possible for as much of the time as possible.

"Ajax are making their stadium a focus for the whole community and that is what we want for Plymouth," said Plymouth City Council director of programmes David Renwick. "Our aim is to get local people using the stadium seven days a week. If we don't do that, we've failed."

Warnock, whose enthusiasm had helped move the council towards their positive action, welcomed the project and did not mind that it had been based on the Ajax paradigm. "There is absolutely no reason whey we should not be playing Premiership football, or even getting into Europe," he said, "but if we are going to do that, we need a ground of Premier League standard – this is it."

Argyle chairman Dan McCauley concurred. "This is a tremendous vision for the future, not only for Plymouth Argyle Football Club, but for the whole of the South West of England," he said.

"Perhaps we'll be promoted to the Premier League at the same time the new stadium is opened," said the former Labour Party leader Michael Foot, Argyle's most famous, and arguably best-loved, supporter.

The widespread welcome that the announcement of the project received had been expected. What had not was the number of dyed-in-the-wool Greenies who objected to it superseding Home Park as Argyle's home, and the name given to it. "Tradium" – supposed to reflect the three-fold range of sporting, business and commercial opportunities – looked like a spelling mistake and sounded like the latest controversial tranquilliser from the USA.

With the end of the season fast approaching, Warnock knew he had to trade talk of the Tradium and its three-tiered approach for three points from the visit of Scarborough to Home Park. Three points which could prove vital building blocks for the immediate future.

Even Dan McCauley had been openly critical of the Argyle team's performance at Torquay, but Warnock, often a recipient of bouquets, was prepared to take the brickbats. "I thought the result was far more important than how we played," he said. "That applies to all our remaining games – how you play goes right out of the window. You're talking about scrapping for points and I couldn't have asked the players to scrap more than they did at Torquay. I was delighted.

"In an ideal world, it would be nice to play lovely football and win easily but we're not in an ideal world. I just hope we play badly in the next five games and win them all."

Argyle actually played well in their penultimate home game against Scarborough and won 5-1, although the victory was not as easy as the scoreline suggested: it was far, far easier.

Warnock's old club was on the shocking side of awful and although their former manager was charitable enough to suggest that Argyle made them look poor, Scarborough were shocking enough not to need any help. An injury-hit Marazion Under-12 side reduced to nine men would arguably have given the Pilgrims more of a contest.

The visitors only avoided being beaten by a cricket score on the opening day of the new first-class season because of some fine saves by goalkeeper Ian Ironside; the woodwork, which denied the Pilgrims twice; and referee Graham Barber's reluctance to punish Scarborough further after Mick Heathcote was clearly fouled in the penalty area.

As it was, five goals were enough for Argyle to overtake the goals-for tally of promotion rivals Bury and Wigan and give them a vital edge in the promotion stakes.

After the previous week's defeat by Darlington, Warnock had accused his players of not being prepared to gamble enough and the message appeared to have got through, even though it seemed to have become slightly misinterpreted.

Ronnie Maugé, nursing a broken bone in his foot, slammed home the 26th-minute opener after Michael Evans had hampered Scarborough's clearance of Richard Logan's free-kick, having placed a few quid on himself to open the scoring at 10-1. Chairman Dan McCauley also had a knack for predicting the right result, although he would ultimately have been out of pocket had Ironside not somehow got goalside to thwart Evans' header 10 minutes later.

Warnock missed Argyle's second, 23 seconds into the second period, as he was still making his way back to the dug-out after what must have been an inspiring team-talk. However, he later discovered that Evans was again involved, making a nuisance of himself after Jason Rockett's sky-high clearance of Chris Leadbitter's cross, and leaving Martin Barlow with the simple task of hooking the ball home.

Scarborough then shamefully raised the white flag. Evans, Mick Heathcote and Leadbitter went close before Evans wasted a glorious chance to register his name on the score-sheet. Adrian Littlejohn then showed his fellow striker how to finish when he capitalised on Steve Charles' missed headed clearance and finished with an insouciant flick past Ironside in the 71st minute.

Barlow extended the lead in the 77th minute with a left-foot shot from 25 yards which clattered in off the same post Maugé had headed against earlier, and Littlejohn completed the nap-hand in injury-time when he raced on to substitute Steve McCall's through-ball and put Ironside on his backside and the ball in the net.

The crowd bayed for a sixth goal and were surprised to see it come at the other end, when Andy Ritchie won a sympathy penalty against – ironically – Heathcote, and converted it himself.

"This was an important victory for us," said Warnock afterwards. "It was a game we had to win and win well. I'm pleased we achieved that."

The victory over Scarborough left Argyle, who had accumulated 69 points, in fifth place with four games to play – at Hereford, Cardiff and Rochdale, and at home to Hartlepool on the final day of the regular season. Ahead of them in the table were Wigan (70 points), Bury (72), Gillingham (77) and Preston (77); behind them were Darlington (68), Barnet (66), Colchester (64), Chester (63) and Hereford (62) – nine teams chasing three promotion places and the additional four play-off spots.

"It's very tight between four teams for the third automatic promotion place," summarised Warnock. "If we win our next game and Bury lose theirs, we'll go above them on goals scored. It's that close."

It was a lot less close by the following Wednesday morning. Reversing Warnock's hopes and intentions, Bury won their game on Tuesday, April 16 and Argyle spectacularly lost theirs 3-0 at Hereford.

The architect of their downfall was 37-year-old striker Steve White, who notched his second hat-trick of the season to leave Argyle six points away from third place with three matches to play.

White, who took his tally for the season to 29 when he rang in his treble against the Pilgrims, had nearly signed for Argyle two seasons previously and if he felt he had a point to make, he had certainly made it. He also scored the winner in Hereford's 1-0 victory at Home Park earlier in the season.

Warnock said: "It's the worst I've seen our back-four play all season and if we play like that again, we won't even get into the play-offs. We played all the football but we must remember we are in the Third Division and Hereford showed how it should be done."

The White-out started in the 12th minute when the former Swindon striker played a one-two with Richard Wilkins before drilling a left-foot shot past goalkeeper Steve Cherry.

Cherry's counterpart Andy Debont then made saves from Steve McCall's free-kick, and shots from Michael Evans and Mark Patterson, as Argyle went at Hereford like a bull at a gate, but the defence was again caught out in the 39th minute when White headed home after Tony James had nodded on Jamie Pitman's cross.

The home side took only six minutes of the second period to finish off their demolition job when White scored from the penalty spot, after Ronnie Maugé had fouled John Brough in the area, to keep the Bulls' late charge for the play-offs on course.

"We've shot ourselves so many times in the foot this season," confessed Warnock, "and we've now got to work very hard to make sure we get enough points to get in the play-offs. I think we need five points, and maybe six, to make the play-offs."

NW: *The presentation of the new stadium at the Council Chambers was a very, very good presentation and it really was all systems go. The councillors were very, very positive. They wanted to improve leisure facilities around the Plymouth area. The chairman gave it his blessing and we were trying our hardest altogether to get it off the ground.*

I intended to leave the team alone for the Saturday match against Scarborough. Chris Leadbitter had been doing ever so well, so I decided to leave him in and go for a bit of solidness, knowing that I had got Steve McCall up my sleeve and Carlo Corazzin, who still hadn't got rid of a chest infection.

We beat Scarborough 5-1 – a disappointing conceded goal in the last second from a penalty, but it was nice to score some goals. We were winning 1-0 at half-time and I said to the lads I felt we had to get a few goals to help our cause and they didn't let me down at all. In fact, it could have been double-figures if their goalie hadn't played so well.

The lads had asked if we could go up to Hereford in the morning and have a sleep in the afternoon up there, which we did, so they could have no excuses. We lost 3-0.

They had their afternoon. I went up in the afternoon and arrived there at tea-time. We went to the game prepared and I thought we were good to start with, we started by playing football. We were warned about the dangers of Steve White and their long-throws and then we started committing suicide.

With 12 minutes gone, Hereford had nothing more than a long-throw. We let play back in and they crossed the ball and White just took his chance. Then we attacked non-stop again and five minutes before half-time, we gave a corner away because we were messing about on the halfway line.

Everybody wanted to pass the ball but the pitch was bobbly. We had got Steve McCall in the side for Gary Clayton and obviously he passes the ball all the time but then other people thought they could do it. Paul Williams passed to Micky Heathcote, he let it run and slipped and White took it off him and brought a great save from Steve Cherry. They scored from the corner.

I could see us getting into the habit of everybody wanting to pass the ball. I think they had all been reading the newspapers about what the fans wanted. We were in Division Three and I could not believe it. We were losing 2-0, when we should have been walking away with it.

At half-time we said "Let's try and get a goal back if we can and put them under pressure." What did we do? Ronnie Maugé gave a Sunday League penalty away five minutes into the second half and the game was finished.

It was just a matter of playing for our pride. I felt so embarrassed after that that I had to go across to the crowd myself. I didn't even talk to the players, I had to go across to the crowd and thank them for the night, because they were super. They didn't deserve that. The back four were a disgrace. We were playing all the football, but I think people forgot that we were in the Third Division. I had never been so frustrated in my life and the worst thing was there were

only two players in their side – White and James – who would have got in our side.
Bury won on the same night, so we now had no chance of automatic promotion.

Warnock added youngsters Paul Wotton and Danny O'Hagan, along with central defender Chris Curran, to his squad for the next away match, across the River Severn in Cardiff, with the threat to make changes.

"I was disappointed with one or two players at Hereford," he said, "and I've told them I'd rather put the kids in to get 100 per cent commitment if I have to. The pressures are getting to some of them and you can't take pressure away from certain players, no matter what you do. Some cope and some go under."

In the end, neither Wotton or O'Hagan played, although Curran did as Warnock dropped Ronnie Maugé, Steve McCall and Martin Barlow – winner of six of the previous seven Argyle man of the match awards – in favour of the former Torquay player Curran, Chris Billy and Gary Clayton.

In truth, probably any 11 players Argyle had fielded would have beaten an unbelievably poor Cardiff side, who had not won any of their previous 10 matches. Warnock had to be grateful to a brilliant Michael Evans' goal on the hour for their 1-0 win, but the boyo who did most to ensure a successful trip to the Principality was Curran.

Curran, playing a free-role around the back four, superbly man-marked dangerman Carl Dale out of the game as the Pilgrims triumphed far from the green, green grass of Home Park. It was a role which he had played under Warnock at Torquay and the manager's willingness to change tactics at a vital stage of the season was superbly vindicated as 29-goal Dale was limited to one strike on goal.

Curran could do little to prevent that as it came from the penalty spot after Mick Heathcote had been spotted by referee Ian Hemley giving Tony Philliskirk a less-than helping hand. Goalkeeper Steve Cherry, facing his third spot-kick in three successive matches, saved Dale's thumping effort when the ball hit his trailing leg and ballooned to safety.

Evans, who would be a pretty porky professional if he had had more hot dinners than the number of times he had hit the woodwork in previous weeks, secured all three points when he received Richard Logan's pass in acres of space and bore down unchallenged on the Cardiff goal before unleashing a shot which, naturally, cannoned in off the post.

The picture at the top of the Third Division table was becoming clearer. For a start, Argyle knew they could not justify the bookies' pre-season favouritism and win the title – Preston and Gillingham were too far ahead to be caught. Secondly, despite needing two points to make mathematically sure of a play-off spot, the win had all-but ended fears the Pilgrims would not have a second crack at winning promotion if they failed to finish in the top three.

NW: *I decided to bring Chris Curran back in at Cardiff. I was not happy with the way the backs had played in the previous few away games so I went back to five at the back with Curran marking Dale, because I thought that we were that cavalier, we were giving goals away and losing games.*

So, sod it, for the remaining games I was going to try to be tight to see if we could win games 1-0. So Chris Curran came back in. I also left Martin Barlow out, even though he was not doing badly. I just thought that if we were going to play like that, we had got to play with one breaking from midfield – like we used to do at Notts County – and I wanted Ronnie Maugé to do that job, with Chris Leadbitter and Gary Clayton. I persevered with Michael Evans up front, even though Carlo Corazzin had come in. I just felt that there was too short a time to let Carlo get used to us.

I decided that I wasn't going to tell them the team until Friday and on Thursday night I got a telephone call from Norman Medhurst saying that Ronnie Maugé had definitely got a fractured toe and could be struggling. I telephoned him and asked him about having a painkilling injection and he said he would give it a go. Anyhow, on Friday morning we had a training session, he had a painkilling injection at 9.30 a.m. and came in and played and got through it okay and I told him what the team was going to be.

After the training session he came and saw me and said that he was very sore. I told him to see how it was overnight but I told Chris Billy that he would definitely be playing and that I didn't think Ronnie Maugé would make it and that's what happened on Saturday morning.

Mick Jones telephoned Ronnie and he said he wasn't fit, so Chris came in and in a way it was better, because I wanted a wide player to be that third forward, rather than having Ronnie running from the middle.

We did quite well to start with, we had three or four great chances. The goalie pulled off a couple of good saves and we hit the post and then a few minutes before half-time Micky Heathcote needlessly pushed somebody in the back and a penalty was given.

I didn't even look. I looked at our fans and waited for Dale to put the ball in the net. I thought to myself at that moment in time, I must have run over a black cat. But Steve Cherry dived and left his legs there, and it hit him and we got away with it.

We had some more good chances in the second half, and we scored one from Micky Evans. It was a great goal as well. Cardiff thought it was offside but I was convinced when they played it, their lads moved out at the same time as Micky went forward and it was onside. The goal stood and we came away with a 1-0 victory even though it should have been more. I don't think Cardiff had more than two chances in the whole match.

People started saying that it was not great to watch, but I couldn't see any game being great to watch at that stage of the season. It was little consolation afterwards to find out that Bury had lost because I still thought that we couldn't catch them, but it did mean that we were almost certain of the play-offs.

After Argyle's visit to play Rochdale at Spotland the following week – and a big helping hand from bitter rivals Exeter City, who held the Pilgrims' fellow promotion hopefuls Bury to a draw at St James' Park – all the theory and speculation regarding promotion had been reduced to a simple equation.

A 1-0 victory, through another goal from Michael Evans, left Argyle needing to beat Hartlepool at home in their final match of the season *and* hope that Darlington and Bury each failed to win their remaining game if they were to claim the third promotion spot behind champions Preston and runners-up Gillingham. Any other combination of results would leave the Pilgrims entered in the lottery of the post-season play-offs.

While the performance at Spotland had not been pretty, it had been pretty effective, much in line with Warnock's pre-match plans. "We need to be tight and grind out results," he had said. "The important thing is to get out of the Third Division, that's all."

On an awful surface that bore more of a resemblance to Blackpool beach than a football pitch, aesthetic football was impossible. Hard graft was the order of the day on a pitch which showed all the problems of football ground-sharing with rugby league – very little grass, plenty of sand and a surface that broke up far too quickly.

Perhaps the saddest casualty of a pitch on which timing and ball-control were everything was midfielder Gary Clayton, who mistimed a challenge within minutes of the start and sustained a knee injury which would curtail his season. His misfortune would, however, have a significant effect on the fortunes of fellow midfielder Ronnie Maugé and, consequently, the Pilgrims' progress in the rest of their campaign.

Argyle pressurised Rochdale throughout but a combination of the woodwork and goal-keeper Lance Key's bravery threatened to send them back to the West Country with no reward for their efforts.

The game was won in the 70th minute, when Paul Williams released Adrian Littlejohn down the left-hand touchline and Argyle's leading scorer's cross was side-footed home by Evans, who had been the subject of home supporters' anger throughout the game after clattering Key in the first five minutes.

There then followed the almost unique experience of Argyle's travelling support singing the praises of Exeter City, as news filtered through of a Grecians' equaliser against Bury back home in Devon.

The Pilgrims' defence withstood one or two late flurries from the home side as, appropriately on Spotland's appalling surface, the sands of time ran out.

"If we had played like this all season, we wouldn't be messing around with the play-offs now," mused Warnock afterwards, echoing the thoughts of Pilgrims' supporters everywhere.

The Pilgrims entered their final match of the season with a new director on board – Andy Dooley, a devoted 39-year-old Greenie and General Manager of Research and Development at computer giants Hewlett Packard – and knowing that, whatever the result, they could not lose. If they won the game, and Bury, who entertained Cardiff, and Darlington, who travelled to Scunthorpe, both failed to achieve victories, they would clinch promotion after their first stay in the country's lowest professional league. Even if the dream treble failed to materialise, they were guaranteed of home advantage in the crucial second leg of the end-of-season play-offs.

"All we can do is our best," said Warnock. "There's no pressure on us – we're already in the play-offs – so I've told the players to enjoy themselves and get the three points. I can't see Cardiff getting owt at Bury, to be honest. I think Scunny have got a chance, but I think Bury are going to beat Cardiff – and if they draw, we'll probably shoot ourselves in the foot by drawing as well. At least we've got a chance, even if it is small."

Kidology or not, Warnock's laid-back approach had transferred itself to the players. Defender Mark Patterson, who missed out on promotion with Argyle two seasons before when the Pilgrims won 8-1 at – spookily – Hartlepool, only to be thwarted by Port Vale's win at Brighton, was confident.

"We're in the ideal position," he said. "We're definitely at home in the second leg of the play-offs – which is a big benefit – and if things go for us, we might just sneak in at the back door."

The Pilgrims resolved their portion of the three-part equation by summarily dismissing Hartlepool 3-0 but their easy final-day dissection of the North Easterners counted for nothing from about 4.10 p.m., when David Johnson scored Bury's second against Cardiff to ensure the Shakers would avoid the play-off shake-up. Not only did Argyle miss promotion – by one point – they were effectively denied it on the ground at which they had registered their best win of the season.

One point. One lousy, miserable, little point. For the want of a tap-in from two yards in one of the 12 matches which the Pilgrims drew during the season, or a wrong-footing ricochet in one of the six games they lost by a single goal, or a reversal of one of the many errors by officials, promotion was lost.

Warnock, who had spent a large part of the season castigating officials, was in a more reflective mood after acting as MC for a post-match player of the season awards ceremony, conducted from the directors' box in front of hundreds of surprisingly cheerful supporters. "It's our own fault," he said. "I've no complaints. Over a season, I think you finish where you deserve to be."

He had a point. After an undistinguished start to the season, Argyle had been rock-solid bottom of the entire Endsleigh League (to appreciate how bad that was, ask yourself how good Torquay were during the season) and despite finishing with 11 wins and two draws from their final 16 matches, they were in the top three for only two weeks.

They eventually finished fourth, having accumulated 78 points from 46 matches, behind Bury (79 points), Gillingham (83) and Preston (86), winning 22 matches and drawing 12. They kept 18 clean-sheets, a figure bettered only by the top three, and scored 68 goals – the second best total in the division, behind Preston's 78 – and conceded 49, a total bettered by seven other clubs.

They had used 30 players during the league campaign with only one – Paul Williams – maintaining an ever-present record. Club captain Mick Heathcote missed two games through injury and Michael Evans was absent for a single game through suspension after his unlucky sending-off at Scunthorpe. Evans was on the substitutes' bench for the first four games of the season but came on each time.

Still, if you had to head for the play-offs, Warnock would be the man you would chose to take you there. Three times in the previous six seasons he had entered the post-season lottery; three times he had hit the jackpot.

"People think I do it on purpose," he said. "I can assure you I don't – it's not a piece of cake, sitting on the bench for 11 months – but I've never done anything easy. If you're going to go up, the best way is through the play-offs, but it's never easy. You have got to be mentally strong to survive."

And then some. Final day results meant that Argyle would now face Colchester over two legs. They were scheduled to visit England's oldest town – where, coincidentally, their 1995/96 campaign had begun – the following Sunday, with the second leg at Home Park four days later. If they were to prove successful, they would then face the winners of the other semi-final, between Hereford and Darlington, at Wembley. Their season's playing record against the other teams involved in the play-offs was: played six, won none, drawn one, lost five, goals for two, goals against ten.

Argyle owed Hartlepool one after squandering a two-goal lead at the Victoria Ground the previous November – at the time, Warnock turned to his assistant Mick Jones and prophesised correctly that the draw would ultimately prove costly – and they wasted little time in exacting revenge.

They could have opened the scoring within a minute when Richard Logan, the ex-brickie with a physique that suggested he had built himself, flung himself at Mark Patterson's expert cross to the far post. Logan, with remarkable juxtaposition, managed somehow to send the ball wide and end up in the back of the net himself.

With the very next attack, Martin Barlow – recalled to the side in place of the unfortunate Gary Clayton – fired in a pass which Michael Evans controlled on the full and played sweetly into the path of Chris Billy for the unmarked midfielder to register the day's fastest strike. "Argyle's opening goal, scored by Adrian Littlejohn," chirruped the public address announcer, with gay disregard for accuracy.

Two minutes later, Darlington went behind at Scunthorpe and, with Bury still being held by Cardiff, Argyle were momentarily in the all-important third position. "The Greens are going up," chorused supporters on all four sides of the ground, the Barn Park away terrace having been handed over to the home faithful.

Their passion cooled when David Pugh put Bury in the box-seat after 25 minutes but, with Darlington now two down and Argyle over Hartlepool like a rash, the afternoon remained pregnant with possibilities.

The Pilgrims began the second half with a determination that suggested Warnock had informed his players of the state of play at Gigg Lane and Glandford Park. Within four minutes, Mick Heathcote cemented his place in the affections of fans who had voted him their player of the season by heading in Barlow's corner, and Chris Leadbitter and Adrian Littlejohn then went close as Argyle showboated.

Suddenly, the Lyndhurst Side started cheering and dancing. There had been a goal at Bury. Cardiff had equalised. "The Greens are going up."

Blame the messenger. There had been a goal, but Bury had scored it. The game was up and Warnock knew it. With an eye to the immediate and long-term future, he dragged off Evans to give Carlo Corazzin a run-out, and Bury duly proved his instincts right by increasing their lead over Cardiff through Tony Rigby. Ronnie Maugé and Danny O'Hagan were similarly introduced from the bench either side of Argyle's third goal, a header by an altogether more coordinated Logan, direct from Leadbitter's corner.

A surreal atmosphere then descended on Home Park for the remainder of the match, after which Warnock affirmed. "I've got a good set of lads. They've all got their critics – except perhaps Martin Barlow – but they are as good as anybody in the division." The hope of the manager, and the supporters, was that they would be able to prove him right during the following three weeks.

Before the important post-season knock-out, there was time for some levity at Home Park, as Warnock's 1995/96 squad entertained Dave Smith's Third Division promotion side from 10 years previously in a charity kick-about to raise money for the Plymouth Argyle Supporters Youth Training and Development Trust, which had been established during the season.

A crowd of nearly 2,500 dipped into their pockets to help raise £10,000 for the Trust and witness Smith's men triumph 7-4. Each and every one of the Ciderman's old-stagers received acclaim as they were introduced by master of ceremonies Gordon Sparks, but the cheers turned to boos as the referee emerged from the tunnel.

Blowing the whistle on Ronnie Maugé in the PAYD charity match

Warnock, suitably attired in black, entered into the spirit of the afternoon and showed the crowd in the grandstand the red card, much to everybody's amusement. After a season in which officials had been the butt of much of his criticism, the Argyle manager was going to have his first experience of being the man in the middle.

His "inexperience" showed as he allowed the old 'uns to play the entire first half with 12 men, and they took advantage of the situation to race to a 4-1 half-time lead, with John Clayton, Tommy Tynan, Kevin Hodges and Gerry McElhinney scoring. Chris Leadbitter replied for the youngsters.

Leadbitter and Danny O'Hagan reduced the arrears in the second period before both sides started to make a plethora of substitutions. Warnock penalised Neil Illman for handball, allowing Tynan to score from the penalty spot; Martin Barlow scored at the other end; Tynan completed his hat-trick from close-range; and Adrian Burrows set the seal on the 85/86ers' win with their seventh goal.

However, the result was really irrelevant and the crowd rose to a man to applaud their old heroes on a lap of honour. The last man off the pitch? Well, of course, he was besieged by autograph hunters and admirers who really did not need reminding that "There's only one Tommy Tynan."

The fun of that Bank Holiday afternoon melted into the late Spring evening sunshine as Argyle supporters' minds turned their thoughts to the serious business of the play-offs. More than anything, they were hoping that Warnock's side could emulate the Smith team of 10 years previously that they had just witnessed, and win promotion.

NW: *A little bit of pressure was off us as we went to Rochdale on the Friday morning. Ronnie Maugé was still out with his little toe and Micky Heathcote had pulled up in training on Thursday and said that he had hurt his back. So I asked Keith Hill to come up with us and he could play the spare role if we needed him to. I decided to stick with the five at the back and to be solid, rather than just go all out and get caught.*

I thought we did ever so well. We gave them probably two chances in the game but once again missed four or five chances. We were more solid and Micky Evans scored the winning goal again, just when it seemed that we wouldn't get another chance.

I had just got Carlo Corazzin and young Danny O'Hagan warming up. They had just taken their tops off and I was going to put them both on up front, and Adie got around the back with Chris Billy playing him through and Evans scored. So instead of changing it again, we kept it the same and carried on. We should have put the result beyond doubt, but we didn't and then we had a couple of nerve-racking seconds in our own box.

The youngsters beat Exeter 2-1 in the League Cup final and I was ever so pleased for them because they had worked hard. Both Kevin Blackwell and Martin Hodge were proud of them because they wanted them to win something at the end of the season.

Gary Clayton got a nasty knock on his leg at Rochdale. It was a bit naughty really and in the first minute, as well. He played on until the second half but five minutes into the second half, he had no chance so he had to come off and Martin Barlow took his place. Gary was a real doubt now, not just for the following weekend against Hartlepool, but the rest of the season. Ronnie Maugé was going to give it a go in the reserves even though his toe was killing him and I wanted to play Martin Barlow in there as well, because I knew Gary Clayton would be missing.

Mick [Jones] was going to go up to watch Hereford. We telephoned for tickets and when we told them that it was the manager who wanted tickets, they refused. It was all-ticket at Hereford, so we would have to pay to go in. Mike Holladay made it clear that we were not happy about it and the next day they changed their minds and let us have tickets.

On Friday morning, once again, Micky Heathcote had an injury – his thigh this time – but not until after we had completed training. That was two weeks on a trot he had gone lame on a Friday.

I asked the chairman if we could have the player of the year awards after the game against Hartlepool, because I think it is great for the supporters to get on to the pitch and cheer the lads, and he agreed to it. Although I got criticism in the Sunday Independent *– Harley Lawer said that it was going away from tradition – I was sure they would enjoy it, because it was really for the genuine supporters.*

Every time you do something different, people have a go at you but sometimes it is for the best and Harley later admitted it had been a good move.

As we feared, Bury won 3-0. We were on the bench and we knew that Scunthorpe were winning 2-0 and Bury were 1-0 up, but then in the second half James Dungey came down on to the touchline and said that Cardiff had equalised. I couldn't believe it, but obviously I just hoped they had.

Within four minutes Kevin Blackwell came down and told me that they hadn't equalised, Bury had gone two-up, so that was it. I then threw on Carlo Corazzin straight away for Micky Evans, to let him have a game. I wasn't impressed with Micky Heathcote in that game if I am honest, so I thought that if he had got a thigh strain I would give the substitutes a game. So I put them all on in the end, Ronnie Maugé and Danny O'Hagan as well.

We ended up winning 3-0 against Hartlepool. They were decent goals but we should have won easily and it was a bit of an anti-climax.

We rushed off at the end and we got the lads out for the awards. It was quite funny when I said about us all getting criticised – apart from Martin Barlow. I think the crowd appreciated that and all had a laugh.

Then we had the game on Monday. I had a radio programme in the morning and got up at the crack of dawn. I got loads of telephone calls in the two hours and really enjoyed it. I spoke to Peter Fox from Exeter and Mike Bateson from Torquay and then we had the game in the afternoon against the old championship side of 1986, which I refereed. It was a cracking afternoon and everybody really enjoyed it.

I gave some silly decisions away, had a laugh with the crowd and then sent off Noddy, our supporter of the year. I showed him the red card, putting it up to his face when he shouted at me. Overall, it was a cracking day and we finished off the evening with a meal at the New Continental *for the lads, which was a super evening for them all. It was all in aid of the PAYD, so hopefully it would have given them a good start.*

"NOTHING CHANGES – WE DON'T MAKE ANYTHING EASY FOR OURSELVES"

IN the anxious build-up to the Pilgrims' visit to Layer Road on Sunday, May 12, Argyle supporters constantly reminded themselves that, when it came to the play-offs, there was no better manager plying his trade in the game than Neil Warnock.

Warnock, and his loyal assistant Mick Jones, had been involved in three successful play-off campaigns, twice in succession with Notts County and also with Huddersfield Town only the previous season. Moreover, Warnock and Jones had never lost a post-season game, having achieved five wins and four draws in the nine matches which County and Town played.

In 1990, they had taken Notts County from the old Third Division to the Second by beating Tranmere Rovers 2-0 in the final after knocking Bolton Wanderers out of the semi-final – drawing 1-1 at Burnden Park and winning the second leg 2-0 at Meadow Lane.

The following year County were promoted to what is now the FA Premiership after a 3-1 victory over Brighton at Wembley, with Dave Regis, who later joined the Pilgrims, among the goals. Previously they had accounted for Middlesbrough, drawing 1-1 at Ayresome Park and edging the return in Nottingham 1-0.

Warnock and Jones completed the hat-trick in 1995, when Huddersfield beat Bristol Rovers 2-1 in the Second Division final, which they reached by pipping Brentford 4-3 in a penalty shoot-out after 1-1 draws in Yorkshire and London.

Given his success, you would be reasonably sure that Warnock enjoyed the adrenalin buzz provided by the gambler's last roll of the dice that the play-offs represent. You would, however, be wrong. "No, I don't like them," he confessed. "I suppose I should like them more than other managers because they are good to me, but they are hard games mentally."

He looked drawn in the week before Argyle's trip to Essex, and although he put his tiredness down to long hours tending his Cornish garden, there was just the hint that the long season he had spent turning Argyle from a team on the slide into one on the edge of promotion – not to mention badgering Plymouth City Council into investing in a multi-million-pound sports complex – was taking its toll.

"It's been a long season, changing everything," he admitted, "and if we could sneak up – and that's how I see it, sneaking up – we won't have as many problems next season because the hard work's done this year. If we don't go up, it means we've wasted a year."

Argyle went into the four-team mini-tournament – which is what the play-offs boil down to – on the back of a 19-match run in which they had lost only three times. Worryingly, two of those defeats had been against fellow play-off contenders Darlington and Hereford. More worryingly, Argyle had not beaten any of the other sides in the play-offs during the previous season.

"Play-offs are nothing to do with league form," Warnock asserted. "If anything, we will have learnt more about the opposition by losing, than they will have about us by winning."

Learning is the name of the game and Warnock was keen enough a play-off practitioner to know that the semi-final required a two-game strategy. "We have got make sure we do nothing silly in the first leg," he said. "If we do go a goal down, we have got to dig in because if we lose by two goals we've got no chance in the second leg."

He would not, however, be sending his side out to play for a draw. He did not believe his players were capable of carrying out such a high-risk plan. "We can't go out and play for a draw like the continentals because we're not good enough at this level," he said, "but overall we know it's a game of two halves and we've got as much chance of winning at Colchester as they have of winning at our place."

Warnock's counterpart Steve Wignall believed his side would repeat their opening-day defeat of Argyle because Warnock and Argyle were simply too big for their size 10 Reeboks.

Following one of the matches between the two sides earlier in the season, Warnock was reported as saying that "little teams such as Colchester do not belong on the same pitch as us" and, although Warnock did not remember making such a statement, Wignall played the Plucky Paupers United *v* Arrogant Princes Wanderers angle for all it was worth.

He compared Warnock's spend of £1m on players with his own lone £2,000 purchase of Diss Town midfielder Paul Gibbs, and contrasted Argyle's plans for their £25m stadium with his club's mounting debt, which was accumulating at a rate of £5,000 a week.

"I would love to be able to have had the kind of money Neil Warnock has been able to spend," said Wignall, "but I look on the Colchester manager's job as a challenge and the fact that we're up there in the play-off hat with Plymouth at the end of my first season in charge is very rewarding. How many points did Plymouth take off us this season? And if having an endless pot of money means you are the best, somebody should ask Plymouth what they are doing in Division Three in the first place. I know which dressing-room I'd rather be in – and it's not the green and black one. The mere fact we are playing Plymouth is enough to get my players going."

Warnock declined to nibble at the bait set by Wignall. "All I am concerned about is getting my lads' minds right for the game," he said. "I'll let others do the talking. We're just focussing on the job in hand – a result that gives us a chance in the second leg."

To get his lads' minds right, Warnock knew he had to exorcise a memory which was ingrained deep in the psyche of the club's supporters – Burnley. Two years previously, Argyle had blown a golden chance of reaching the Second Division play-off final when, having drawn 0-0 at Burnley in the first leg of the semi-final and scoring first in the return at Home Park, they lost 3-1 in the second leg.

Of the Pilgrims' team that evening, only Mark Patterson, Keith Hill and Martin Barlow were in the squad for Layer Road but such was the impact of the unexpected reversal, it had permeated every pore of Home Park. Even Warnock felt compelled to mention it when he addressed supporters after the previous week's victory over Hartlepool – "Forget Burnley," he said.

If only Argyle supporters could. "For two years, people have continually talked about that game," said defender Patterson. "They said we should have got to Wembley and won promotion, and that we let ourselves down. I think they are right. We thought we'd done it all by not getting beaten away from home. There were 18,000 here. They did their part and we didn't do ours. The team is determined not to let the supporters down this time. Going to Wembley would mean so much to everyone."

Patterson also recognised a crucial difference between the Pilgrims' class of '96 and the factionalised dressing-room of Peter Shilton's play-off side of '94.

"The one thing we have got here is a very level-headed bunch of lads," he said. "You couldn't say that anyone thinks they are better than anyone else. If there's discontent among a team, it causes resentment, but there's nothing like that here. Everyone's together. Everyone's friends on and off the pitch. That can only stand us in good stead."

Warnock chose to take on Colchester with the same starting 11 that had ended the regular season with the sparkling victory over Hartlepool: Steve Cherry, his loan from Watford having been extended to cover the play-off semi-finals – but not the final, if the Pilgrims progressed that far – in goal; Mark Patterson at right-back and Paul Williams at left-back; captain Mick Heathcote and Richard Logan in the centre of the defence, with Chris Curran as sweeper; Chris Leadbitter in the centre of midfield, with Chris Billy and Martin Barlow outside him; and Adrian Littlejohn and Michael Evans up front. Keith Hill, Ronnie Maugé and Carlo Corazzin were substitutes.

Remarkably, the 11 had never played together as a unit before the Hartlepool match, with Curran having come late in the season to his roving defensive role and Barlow having regained his place in the starting line-up only because of the injury sustained by Gary Clayton at Rochdale in the Pilgrims' penultimate game.

Ten of the squad had previous experience of the play-offs, with four of them ending as Wembley winners. Billy had scored Huddersfield's winner against Bristol Rovers the previous season; Cherry was Notts County's goalkeeper on each of the Magpies' successful visits to Wembley; Curran was a member of the 1991 Torquay United side which won promotion to the old Third Division after a penalty shoot-out against Blackpool; and Leadbitter was part of the Cambridge United side which won promotion from the old Fourth Division by beating Chesterfield in 1990.

The quartet of unsuccessful Pilgrims' play-off participants included Maugé, who represented Fulham at the end of the 1988/89 campaign; and Patterson, Hill and Barlow, who were in the Argyle side browned off by Burnley in 1994. In addition, Paul Williams had been involved in play-offs with Stockport in 1992 and '93 and Mick Heathcote with Sunderland in 1990, though had not actually made it to the field of play.

Colchester's tiny Layer Road meant that only 1,200 tickets for the match were made available to Argyle's travelling Green Army, although hundreds more would be able to watch the drama unfold live on a giant television screen at Home Park. "The demand for tickets was 5:1 on what we received," explained commercial manager Steve Birley, "so we've put this on at Home Park to get as many Argyle supporters as possible to see the game live."

It would be uncharitable in the extreme to say Birley should not have bothered, but the pictures beamed across the country from Essex cannot have made pleasant viewing as, for more than an hour, the Pilgrims were overrun by the home side. Too many players who took Argyle to the brink of promotion in the regular season had a play-off off-day and Colchester were arguably unlucky not win by more than the 1-0 margin that separated the two teams.

However, Argyle hung grimly on to their Wembley dreams and would have taken heart from a strong finish and gained some satisfaction from knowing they had to claw back only a one-goal deficit the following Wednesday. For a while after Mark Kinsella's strike at the end of the first half, they wobbled badly.

Warnock said: "I felt in the two minutes after they scored, we could have lost the tie altogether. I'm glad the referee blew for half-time. I said to the lads at the interval they could go one of two ways: they could go under or they could come out and show why they're a good side. I thought we showed a lot of steel and character in the second half."

If Argyle needed any further incentive to escape from the Third Division, they had only to look around them at the tawdry surroundings as they stepped out at Layer Road, and under their feet, at the rutted playing surface. The parts of the ground that were not being pulled down or put up (it was difficult to tell which was which) were just this side of derelict and the pitch looked for all the world as if Colchester's famous garrison residents had been using it for manoeuvres since Christmas.

However, the home side played with a passion and commitment that belied their humble surroundings and the Pilgrims had to work extremely hard to make good their manager's promise that sides of his may be out-played or out-thought but are never out-fought. They were out-played and out-thought, too.

Perhaps they were surprised by a Colchester formation which was more attacking than they had expected, but they sat too deep in the first period and surrendered the midfield to the home side's quartet, which included Tony Dennis, who had a brief spell at Plymouth earlier in his career. The upshot was that there was too much pressure on a defence in which Heathcote was far from the composed figure that won him the supporters' player of the year award and a place in the Professional Footballers' Association Third Division Team of the Year. Curran, though, assumed the extra responsibility handed him by the skipper's abdication and played for two men.

The first signs of creaking among the rear guard exhibited themselves when Heathcote and Leadbitter were involved in a bout of push and shove which resembled nothing more than Bill and Ben having a squabble over the affections of Little Weed. The two former Cambridge United team-mates, apparently the best of friends, had to be separated by team-mates and referee Micky Pierce as they heatedly discussed the merits of clearing their lines.

They ended up grinning, rather than arguing, but it was a dubious psychological message to send to the home side, who immediately tightened the screw of the rack upon which they were torturing Argyle. Curran twice mopped up what Ron Atkinson would call "dangerous situations" as the last man; Williams bravely headed away Paul Gibbs' teasing cross; and goalkeeper Cherry picked off a teasing cross by Kinsella.

Cherry had no answer to a shot from Dennis which narrowly missed the target as Colchester continued to crank up the tempo. Argyle with their now apparently lightweight midfield chasing shadows, looked as though they would weather the storm into which they had been facing with gritted teeth and reach the sanctuary of the half-time dressing-room on level terms.

They were within moments of doing so when Billy was caught in possession – illegally, he seemed to claim – and Kinsella seized on the unexpected gift to rifle a 30-yard shot past a startled Cherry, who was unable to do anything except watch the bolt from the blue and white thunder past him.

Colchester gained even more strength from the goal and put the Pilgrims under great pressure for the remaining minutes of the first half and the opening quarter of an hour of the second period. Just after the hour, Barlow lost possession just outside his own penalty area and opposition striker Robbie Reinelt was on the ball in a flash to lash a shot which beat Cherry but thudded back into play from the post. It was the moment the two-legged tie turned.

Had Reinelt's excellent snapshot followed a path a mere two inches inside its eventual line of flight, the Pilgrims would have been 2-0 behind with half an hour still to play on their opponents' home patch, and facing football's equivalent of conquering Everest.

Warnock read the runes and decided to act. Off came Barlow, whose ball skills had never been a major factor on a surface and against fired-up opponents that put the highest premium on time and space, and in his stead arrived Ronnie Maugé. Maugé, despite being a virtual ever-present during the regular season – when injury allowed – and captain for much of it, would not even have been on the substitutes' bench had it not have been for Gary Clayton's unfortunate injury but, having been introduced late to the play-off action, he made an immediate impact.

His first significant act was to flatten – legally – Dennis. It was the first time all afternoon that the Colchester midfield had not had things entirely their own way and the shift in the balance of power had a galvanising effect on the previously beleaguered Pilgrims, who then spurned two glorious chances to equalise.

After prompting from Billy, Patterson won a free-kick on the right-hand side which Leadbitter swung deep into the opposition penalty area. Heathcote arrived on cue, his head zeroing in on the delivery, ready to bury his differences with Leadbitter and the ball in the back of the net in one movement. Unbelievably, from inches out, he missed making contact with the ball by inches. Worse for Argyle, Evans lumbered in too late at the far post and, obviously taken aback by Heathcote's profligacy, was also unable to apply the significant touch.

Evans soon recovered his composure and immediately flicked the ball into the path of Billy, whose perceptiveness had enabled him to read the pass well enough to gain space behind the last line of Colchester's rapidly wearying defence. The man who scored Huddersfield's winner at Wembley little more than 12 months before now had a gilt-edged opportunity to atone for his earlier error.

As the Green Army massed behind the goal on which he bore down held their breath and hundreds more back at Home Park rose from their seats in mounting anticipation, Billy controlled the ball well on the uneven surface, and, with defenders bearing down on his heels and goalkeeper Carl Emberson rushing towards him, looked up and took aim. He cut his shot across Emberson from right to left but the ball was never wholly on target and, to groans from Essex to Devon, it wobbled wide of the far post, with no amount of urging from supporters behind the goal able to persuade it to change direction.

At last Argyle began to play, sensing that Colchester's earlier all-out effort had drained the home side's legs of energy. Maugé drilled the ball wide and set up some scrambles in the opposition penalty area which the home side were grateful to clear as the Pilgrims continued to plug away against a visibly wilting defence.

Colchester, though, wanted another goal as insurance against an improved Argyle performance in the second leg at Home Park and the Pilgrims had to be alert to soak up late breakaways by substitute Adam Locke – which Williams snuffed out – and Tony McCarthy, whose shot Cherry did well to beat out.

The 1-0 defeat and poor performance meant Argyle would need a much better attitude back at Home Park the following Wednesday night. "Nothing changes this season," said Warnock. "We don't make anything easy for ourselves but it's still in the melting pot and at least we are still in the tie. It's only half-time. Time will tell."

Warnock also revealed that his players had been subjected to additional pressure by the partisan home supporters. "They were a hostile crowd," said Warnock. "One of the lads got hit by an apple before the game, and coins were thrown and everything." His claims were backed up by referee Micky Pierce, who had briefly halted play during the first half of the game to ask Colchester officials to broadcast a public address appeal urging supporters not to throw missiles.

Chris Billy agonises over his miss at Layer Road

"The crowd is so close to the pitch and can be very influential with the officials. I would like to think our Home Park crowd on Wednesday could be just as influential," said Warnock, seeking to maximise home advantage for the second leg. "Let our supporters be just as hostile. No missiles, though – I would like our fans to show their hostility with their voices."

On the subject of hostilities, Warnock said he would be taking no action against Heathcote or Leadbitter for their on-field argument which led to a lecture from referee Pierce. "I was pleased, if I'm honest," he said. "It was the first time Heathcote had been angry all afternoon. I thanked Leadbitter at half-time for getting him going."

Heathcote, too, was dismissive of the clash. "It was just heat-of-the-moment stuff," he said. "It was forgotten as soon as we walked away, and a couple of minutes later we had a good laugh about it. It happens in games which build up tension."

NW: *We found out that Colchester would not be issuing any complimentary tickets for the players. Then I saw a report from a Colchester paper talking about money-bags Plymouth and how it was a Paupers against Princes play-off semi-final. I also got a video of their coach having a go at us, saying how they beat us earlier and drew at our place and missed a penalty, and they thought they would go through. We just kept quiet.*

The preparation was good. I decided to go with Martin Barlow in midfield even though I knew we wouldn't be really strong in the physical department with Chris Billy, him and Chris Leadbitter, but his attitude had been good, so I just went with it.

I was disappointed in the first half. We nearly held out until half-time and then Chris Billy gave the ball away needlessly and Martin Barlow dived in. The guy shot from 30 yards and the ball rocketed into the net.

I was disappointed with four or five players. I thought we were a little bit overawed. The crowd was a bit hostile and as we came out for the second half, I said to Mick Jones, "There will be a lot of questions answered now because we can either go under two or three-nil or we can fight back and show them what we are made of."

I am pleased to say that we did fight back. We hung in there and we created two great chances in the last 20 minutes, although we missed them both – probably the two easiest chances we have had all season.

"I MUST ADMIT, I SHED A TEAR OR TWO"

THE second leg of the Endsleigh Third Division play-off semi-final on Wednesday, May 15 was Argyle's 55th match of their season. It was also their most important game since Neil Warnock's arrival. Defeat by Colchester, and the Pilgrims could pack up for the summer one match from Wembley and two from possible promotion for which they were favourites when the 1995/96 campaign began.

A draw would also see the Essex men progress at the Pilgrims' expense and even a one-goal home victory would not be enough to maintain their interest in the season if Colchester scored again. The visitors would take the tie on the away-goals rule if the aggregate scores were level after extra-time – unless the sides were locked at 1-1, in which case the whole shooting match would go to a penalty shoot-out.

Small wonder Warnock was calling for heroics from his players before the match. "I want them all to be men," he said. "I want them all to stand up and be counted."

Since Argyle wore their Sunday worst at Layer Road, Warnock had scoured the cloud of defeat for a silver lining and come up with a couple of plusses from what was a pretty negative performance. "I think we played with only six players, and to lose only 1-0 and miss the best two chances of the whole match speaks volumes for the other lads," he said. "Now, if we get those other five lads playing with the rest of us, I think we've got a chance. And if we had drawn on Sunday, I think we might have gone into the second leg a bit overconfident, whereas now we know we've got to win. Nothing else is acceptable."

However, he was ready – willing, even, in the kidology battle surrounding the all-or-nothing game – to bestow favouritism on the visitors. "If I was a betting man, I'd say the tie was 70:30 in their favour," he said. "They've got nobody to please; they've got the goal and know if they score an away goal, we've got to get three; and we haven't beaten them all season. I think they've got a lot going for them, but we've got to make sure we're ready for them. As we found on Sunday, they were very physical early on and I think the physical content to their game was slightly over the top. All right, they got away with it. I thought the referee was a bit lenient but they were at home and that's how things are. We've got to make sure we don't get into retaliation but we've got to be ready for the stick they are going to give us and not let ourselves down on that aspect."

Mark Kinsella's 45th-minute strike at Layer Road meant Argyle had to score one goal to get back on level terms, and former Notts County manager Warnock borrowed a memorable quote from his one-time counterpart on the other side of the River Trent to signal a cautious approach. "It only takes a second to score a goal and we have got to be patient," he said. "If we concede an early goal, we will have played right into their hands and I think that would be very amateurish."

Warnock's opposite number Steve Wignall was not of the belief that Argyle would sit back for too long. "Plymouth have got to come out and score, which will be the better for us," he said, "and the longer we go without conceding a goal, the more the pressure will mount on the Plymouth boys. Whatever system he decides on, Warnock has got to push men forward in search of goals, but we will be ready for anything he wants to throw at us."

If things were not going to plan, Warnock had already made up his mind to throw a whole lot at Colchester. "If we're on level terms or a goal down, to hell with it, we might as well lose by having a go," he said, "but I don't want us to go out and concede goals early on because we've got a mountain to climb then."

Wignall was also aware that an early goal from his side would put added pressure on the home side. "If we can nick one, they would have to score two, or possibly three if it goes to extra-time," he said.

Nevertheless, he pledged to go into the game with an open mind and an open plan. "We've never gone and defended in any game this season," he said. "We'll be looking to get a goal."

Despite Wignall's assertion that his side was not good enough to defend a one-goal lead, statistics showed that there were few teams in the Third Division better equipped to grind out the result they needed. Colchester were among the entire Football League's away draw specialists, along with Gillingham – already promoted to the Second Division – and Darlington, another of the sides involved in the Third Division play-offs. Colchester and Gillingham each drew 11 of their 23 away league games during the regular season, with only Darlington (12) achieving a higher figure from among the 72 league clubs.

Pilgrims' captain Mick Heathcote was aware of his manager's call for the players to stand up and be counted, and he saw no reason to doubt that he and his team-mates would respond positively. "The outcome of this game is so vitally important I don't think any player needs any motivation," he said. "We all know the job that has to be done.

"It's a massive game. When you think that we've had all those matches and it's been whittled down to this one game with everything depending on it… We came together at the beginning of the season as a new group of lads, and it's been a long, hard season. It would be heartbreaking to not have anything to show for it."

Heartbreaking, not just for the players, but also the supporters, especially those who could still not quite shake off the memories of Burnley's visit two years previously – despite the fact that the staff and most of the players had been at other clubs on that fateful night.

Warnock was only too aware of the part the crowd could play. "I'm hoping they will be another player and we can play with 12 men," he said. "I think the players found it difficult at Colchester, not having the crowd with them, but they've got no excuse at home because everyone's rooting for them. I hope we make it as hostile for them as it was for us up there, only three times louder.

"I hope the Lyndhurst Side get as bad as they did against Gillingham; I hope the Devonport End take the roof off; and I hope the conservatives in the stand clap loudly." What was about to unfold in front of their almost unbelieving eyes certainly gave them no excuse not to.

Before he sent his players out for their date with destiny, Warnock had to make an important decision about the composition of his midfield. The trio of Chris Leadbitter, Martin Barlow and Chris Billy had scarcely been effective at Layer Road, and the balance had certainly improved when Ronnie Maugé replaced Barlow just after the hour.

However, Barlow undoubtedly possessed the skills to unlock a stubborn defence and the feeling must have nagged away at the manager that, if things were going against his side, a frustrated crowd might just turn on Billy, as they had done for most of the season.

He decided to persist with Barlow and against selecting Billy – despite play-off goals in both the previous year's Second Division semi-final and final. Thus, Maugé for Billy was the only change to the Pilgrims' starting line-up from the previous match at Layer Road. Billy took Maugé's seat on the substitutes' bench, alongside Ian Baird, who had returned quicker than expected from a groin injury to displace Keith Hill in the squad.

Warnock's thinking was that if the vital goals were not forthcoming, he could change his forward line wholesale, bringing on Baird and Carlo Corazzin.

Colchester manager Wignall stayed faithful to the 11 that had won the first leg but he, too, made a significant change on the bench, bringing in leading scorer Tony Adcock, who had been suspended for the clash at Layer Road. The scene was set and a crowd of more than 14,500 waited expectantly.

They did not have long to wait – 159 seconds, to be precise. Argyle, showing a positive attitude which contrasted sharply with their sluggishness at Layer Road, went for the jugular and drew blood.

Their perfect start was initiated by a less-than-perfect kick-out by goalkeeper Steve Cherry who, gripped by nerves generated by the occasion, horribly hooked his kick towards the Devonport Road end. Instead of arching gracefully upwards and dropping inside the opposition half, the ball skewed off to the left on a low trajectory.

However, Chris Leadbitter was alive to the situation and, back to goal, he stooped into the flight of the ball. His head connected perfectly and lifted the ball back over his head, and over the heads of most of the Colchester cover, into the path of Michael Evans.

With the tall, gangly, shaven-headed Peter Cawley chasing him, Evans looked for all the world like the pursued innocent in *The Hills Have Eyes*, but he outpaced the cover, waited for Leadbitter's assist to bounce, and larruped a left-foot shot past Carl Emberson. Argyle were straight back in the tie and the only true Plymothian on the pitch had put them there – with a "despised" route-one, long-ball goal, too.

The goal, and the crescendo of noise which greeted it by rattling window panes in Stoke Village half a mile away, clearly rocked Colchester and twice in the next five minutes Argyle came within inches of stretching their lead: United defender Gus Caesar headed Chris Curran's free-kick just wide of his own goal-post, and Martin Barlow's resultant corner was nodded a similar distance past the opposite upright by Ronnie Maugé.

The Pilgrims' early strike opened up the game. Colchester knew from as early as the third minute they would now have to score a goal to win the game – or run the risk of a penalty shoot-out – whereas before the kick-off, it would have been possible to reach Wembley merely by keeping a clean-sheet. Unlikely, but possible.

However, the more Colchester edged forward, the more Argyle took advantage of Home Park's green acre to counter. Desperate defending denied Adrian Littlejohn the chance to finish off a cross by Barlow, who then ended a sparkling run down the right with a drive that flashed wide of Emberson's near post.

The Pilgrims' preeminence was due in no small part to Warnock getting his selection spot-on. Their near total control of the second leg was down to their midfield dominance – a stark contrast to the anonymity of four days previously. Maugé and Leadbitter terrorised the centre of the park and Barlow was a constant thorn in Colchester's right side.

Leadbitter, the brave provider of Argyle's first goal, doubled the Pilgrims' lead on the night and put his side 2-1 in front on aggregate in the 41st minute with a goal that was as rehearsed as the opener had been improvised.

Mark Patterson challenged for the ball with Paul Gibbs on the right-hand edge of the penalty area which Colchester were bravely defending and won a fortuitous free-kick. Fortuitous because, as Patterson explained afterwards, he felt Gibbs' challenge was legal. Certainly, the Colchester man felt aggrieved and was subsequently booked by referee John Kirkby for voicing his displeasure at the perceived injustice.

If Gibbs was simmering with discontent then, he would have been boiling seconds later as Argyle dipped into their training-ground repertoire and fished out a set-play which gave them the overall lead in the two-leg tie for the first time in more than two hours' play. Barlow shaped to take the kick but dummied over the ball and Leadbitter stepped up to curl the sweetest left-foot shot ever seen at Home Park past the wall and beyond the reach of a grovelling Emberson.

The timing of the two first-half goals could not have been better: Evans' early opener settled the nerves; Leadbitter's late set-piece after near-constant Pilgrims' pressure gave the visitors plenty to mull over during the half-time interval. Opposition manager Steve Wignall clearly saw the need to change things and when the two sides retook to the field to a standing ovation, he had made two switches – 17-goal leading scorer Adcock and Adam Locke replacing Robbie Reinelt and Caesar.

The double-change made little difference as Argyle took up where they left off, with Barlow jinking his way into the penalty area and firing a shot over. The splendid Barlow then won a free-kick in an identical position from where Leadbitter had earlier converted successfully, and the midfielder nearly repeated the dose. This time his attempt was more opportunistic than planned as he took advantage of Colchester's disorganisation to unleash a quick low scudder which ripped into the side-netting. Had the shot been on target, out-of-position goalkeeper Emberson would have been helpless to prevent a goal.

Leadbitter was again at the centre of affairs when the match exploded into controversy just before the hour. Littlejohn, having latched on to Leadbitter's pluperfect release from deep, was clear through on goal with Cawley and Tony McCarthy struggling to catch him. McCarthy attempted to tackle the disappearing Littlejohn from behind but succeeded only in clipping his heel. If ever there was a tackle which merited the red card, this was it. However, referee Kirkby wrongly deemed the offence only worthy of a caution and McCarthy escaped an early bath.

Adrian Littlejohn goes down after being foiled by Tony McCarthy

Kirkby's decision sent Warnock apoplectic with rage. The linesman patrolling the touchline on the dug-out side copped an earful of invective, as did Kirkby when he strolled across to find out what all the fuss was about. Kirkby decided it would be better for all concerned if the Argyle manager removed himself from the dug-out, but if he thought Warnock would meekly take his place in the stand, he had another thought coming.

Warnock spontaneously clambered over the perimeter fencing and leapt into the crowd on the Mayflower terracing, just to the right of the Colchester bench, from where, flanked by security personnel and with assistant Mick Jones and the trusty Kevin Blackwell for company, he directed operations for the remainder of the game.

His palpable sense of injustice was heightened almost immediately when Mark Kinsella capitalised on a rare Colchester excursion into the Argyle half of the field to score his second wonder-goal of the tie, a 25-yard strike from nowhere which zinged past Cherry. The manner of Colchester's celebrations suggested they were only too aware of the implications of Kinsella's 66th-minute goal. It meant the two-leg tie was now level at 2-2 (Argyle 2 Kinsella 2) on aggregate, and that the visitors had the considerable advantage of an away-goal which would take them to Wembley if no-one else scored.

Argyle responded positively to the shock and Chris Curran came within inches of an immediate riposte when he flung himself towards another Barlow free-kick for a header which beat Emberson but bobbled agonisingly wide of the far post. The Pilgrims were now attacking from every quarter. If it was not exactly Total Football, it was totally committed, as was demonstrated when defender Patterson finished off a goalmouth scramble with a toe-poke that lacked only the power to trouble Emberson.

With extra-time looming and Colchester visibly preparing themselves to defend for the additional 30 min-

Paul Williams begins the victory celebrations after his winning header against Colchester

utes, Barlow launched himself on another mazy right-wing dribble and crossed into the penalty area. Barlow's delivery across the face of the goal proved too elusive for Emberson and little Paul Williams, "Charlie" to his team-mates and 5ft 6in in his stockinged feet, proved the man for the big moment as he dived into the ball and sent it curling into the net from his head. Warnock bowed his head in silent thanks as Home Park erupted. 3-1 on the night, 3-2 on aggregate.

Colchester strode forward in numbers, as they had to, and forced two corners which Argyle's defence imperturbably batted away, before Littlejohn and Evans took advantage of the yawning gaps at the back and combined to force Emberson into a brave save. Then referee Kirkby blew his whistle for full-time and the field of play was transformed into a sea of green and white as Pilgrims' supporters swarmed on to the pitch to acclaim their heroes. "*Que sera sera*, whatever will be will be, we're going to Wembley, sing *sera sera*."

The dramatic victory and scenes of celebration that continued long after the final whistle brought Warnock to tears. "I've only cried three times in football and tonight was the third," he admitted. "It was very emotional."

Argyle would follow Huddersfield and Notts County (twice) as clubs Warnock had taken to play-off finals at Wembley, but he said: "The best thing is that it will be the biggest turn-out of any of my clubs at Wembley. I will be very, very surprised if we don't take 35,000 to 40,000 people. Everybody in the West Country will want to go.

"I was ever so proud of the supporters for the way they got behind the team, and I was ever so proud of the boys. Once again we shot ourselves in the foot – we gave Colchester a goal and they were in the driving seat again – but it was one of those nights in football when you realise why you are involved. You can't put into words your feelings. You are emotionally drained as a manager, but when you see supporters like that after the game, it makes it all very much worth while. We won the game by ability and tremendous support."

Warnock was unrepentant over his outburst at officials which temporarily boosted the Home Park crowd by one during the second half. Television replays suggested that the Argyle manager was justified in disputing the decision of referee Kirkby not to dismiss McCarthy, but Westcountry TV's pictures also gave supporters a rare glimpse of Warnock, agitated to the point of losing it altogether, in full, angry flow.

"If you haven't got passion, you haven't got hope," he said, without a trace of regret. "I've always been passionate. It frightens other people – they think I'm going to have a heart-attack. I probably will one day, but if I don't get like that, it wouldn't be me. If you haven't got passion and emotion, you shouldn't be in the game. If I ever lose that, that's the time to put me out to grass. It won't do supporters any harm to see how I am, and I expect officials to referee within the rules of the game. To them, it's just another decision and tomorrow's tomorrow and they go back to work. But to us, you're talking about 10 months, careers, livelihoods. All right, he gave what he thought was an honest decision but referees are right, even when they're wrong, aren't they? You work hard for 12 months and all you expect is that the rules that are laid down are applied. The ref said he thought I would be better off keeping away from the linesman and asked me to go away from the dug-out. I have known him for some time and he said he thought it was in my best interests, but deep down, Paul Williams got him out of a situation."

Warnock's reaction to Mark Kinsella's tie-leveller was similarly all-consuming. He said: "I thought everything was on top of me. I can't get on to the bench; I might not be able to get on the pitch to talk to players if it goes into extra-time; and there's a team that should be down to 10 men playing with 11 who've got the lift of an away goal. The one redeeming factor is that we've got a bit of spirit. We've always played with spunk and I think we've got stronger as the season's gone on. To see us come back like that… It was a cracking goal by Charlie. For a left-back to be there… he's been my man of the season – it couldn't happen to a nicer lad. Underrated – he could play a lot higher when he's got the confidence, and I think I've given him the confidence since I've had him.

"I just felt it was meant to be after everything else that had gone on out there."

The object of Warnock's praise was suitably modest about his winning strike. "I just knew we had to get bodies in the box," he said, of the moment he saw Martin Barlow launch his 85th-minute raid down the right. "I'm just glad it landed for me. The gaffer has always told me to get to the back post and gamble because you never know what's going to happen. That's what I did, and, to be honest, I should have scored a few more in the past couple of weeks – but it's nice to score at the right time.

"I couldn't have timed it any better and we're there. I knew deep down it wouldn't go to extra-time and it was really nice to get the winner. I hope all the fans will enjoy themselves at Wembley and we can get promotion to Division Two. They were magnificent, especially when we needed them most."

Local boy Michael Evans, who had given the Pilgrims such a wonderful start, was also pleased for the supporters. "I'm glad I scored and delighted we won because I know how much it means to Plymouth people," he said, before recalling his nerve-settling third-minute strike. "The ball came across to me and I didn't get a good first touch. I let the ball go under my feet then I just hit it with my left foot. Fortunately, it went in the top corner. To be the only local lad in the side on a night like tonight is brilliant. I can't wait for Wembley."

The Pilgrims' other goalscorer Chris Leadbitter put his Wednesday night special free-kick down to hard work on the training ground. "We practice those free-kicks in training every Thursday," he revealed. "Their wall seemed a bit smaller than normal – it appeared to have

Dressing-room celebrations after the play-off semi-final victory against Colchester

shrunk – so I thought I'd go for it. I tried to put a bit of pace and bend on the ball and as soon as it cleared the wall, I knew the 'keeper wouldn't get there.

"We were so much on top in the second half but then they scored which knocked us back and put a spring in their step, but we did well to get back into the game. It was a great cross by Martin Barlow and a superb finish by Paul Williams."

The modest streak which seemed to run through Warnock's players extended to Barlow, whose wing play and delivery for Williams' header had been crucial. "I just had to get past the defender and get a cross in," he said. "I put it in a dangerous area and Charlie came from nowhere to get in a great header. In fact, all three of our goals were great. There was a possibility I might not have been playing. I was just happy to be out there. It is the best night I have ever had. I wanted to do it for the supporters because I knew how much it meant to them. They have got to be the best fans in the country and it is superb for everyone at the club."

Ronnie Maugé, who, with Leadbitter, won the battle in the centre of the park revealed that Williams had told him before the game, he would score. "He told me he was due a goal and thankfully he turned up trumps," said Maugé. "When Colchester got their strike, I thought it might be one of those days but, fair dues to the lads, we rolled up our sleeves and we went at them again. We did not want extra-time and thankfully Charlie turned up with the winner."

Chris Billy, the midfielder at whose expense Maugé won his recall to the side, was grateful to his team-mates for helping him to forget his miss at Layer Road four days previously. "They've got me out of a hole," he said. "It wasn't a bad miss and I don't want to think about it too much because it doesn't matter now, but if I could do it again I'd definitely hit the back of the net.

"I can't believe I missed it, but it's history now and we've won, so I'm very happy."

His happiness was mirrored in faces throughout the city and all across the green-and-black areas of the West Country. Chairman Dan McCauley, who had watched the game sporting a giant Pilgrims' stove-pipe hat, said: "I was crying, to be honest. I tried hard to hold back the tears but in the end I couldn't. The excitement was too much.

"Steve Birley [Argyle's commercial manager] assures me it's good for us financially to get to Wembley but that is of secondary importance. The most important thing is for us to get back where we belong." McCauley was tasting his first success since taking over as Argyle chairman nearly five years previously. Two relegations and a play-off semi-final defeat were all he had had to show for his vast investment in the club.

"When I appointed Neil last year, he assured me he would get us promotion," he said. "I didn't think he would do it this year, to be honest, but he has got us this far and let's hope we can do it."

Veteran politician Michael Foot, too, had known the bad times at Home Park but he was also riding the crest of the enthusiasm that had begun rolling through the city which he represented in Parliament for many years.

"Argyle would have beaten Manchester United or Liverpool on that form," said the former Labour Party leader. "They are right up to Premier League form. It was a wonderful day. They were three great goals and the team played magnificently. That was the best game of football I have seen for years. It was the best for about 10 seasons."

The famous victory also gave impetus to the multi-million-pound plans to build a new stadium for the club and city. By accident or design, council officials were due to meet with the Argyle board and manager Warnock the day after the victory over Colchester to discuss the latest developments of the plan. With the jubilant scenes of the previous night still fresh in the minds, it would have been a brave person who would have poured cold water on the scheme.

Certainly David Renwick, the council's director of programmes, was in no mood to do anything but press ahead with the utmost urgency. Renwick, whose five-year-old son Paul had led the Pilgrims on to the field for their vital game as the Argyle mascot, said after the game: "Tonight showed what the fans of Plymouth Argyle want and what they deserve. There was an electric atmosphere and we want to build on that. The Tradium will happen."

Chris Mavin, chair of the council's leisure services committee, echoed Renwick's views as he revelled in Argyle's triumph, joining in the post-match celebrations in the Green Room. "The fans proved tonight that Plymouth deserves this stadium," he enthused. "I'm absolutely overjoyed with the result. I'm a born and bred Plymothian and I know the fans need this new stadium. They deserve the best."

The city council immediately promised a civic reception for Argyle if they won their play-off final, although the invitation was later extended to them whatever the result of their final match of the season.

Incoming Lord Mayor Sylvia Bellamy, who was actually to receive her chain of office two days after Argyle's triumph, said: "If they win, I will definitely hold a civic reception for them. It's a great excuse for popping the champagne corks. I think it is wonderful they have got this far and wish them every success at Wembley.

"You have to support the home team and I want to say to Argyle: 'Keep the flag flying – we're right behind you'."

Council leader John Ingham backed Councillor Bellamy's proposals, saying: "It's good for the city. Clearly we want to see a successful football team by the time we build the new stadium and we are well on the way to that now."

NW: *The first-leg defeat threw all the onus on us again. The massive lift for me was that Ian Baird was fit again. I didn't tell anybody that he was available and I was going to put him on the bench for the second leg. We had a practice match and he and Carlo Corazzin looked very good together. If I thought Bairdy could have got through 90 minutes, I might have even started with him in the second leg because I was so disappointed with Micky Evans and Adrian Littlejohn at Colchester.*

But I had a chat with them both and told them that they had got to play as if the first 45 minutes were the last and we had got to see if we could get that goal back. I said to the lads I knew Colchester had got a great record away from home, but we were playing well and even if they got a goal, it was not beyond us to get three. We had got everything to play for and it's not as if we had got a choice.

I was hoping the crowd could be hostile. I had tried to pump them up a bit as well, because I thought they were very important to us.

I slept quite well and woke up at 6.30 a.m. with a splitting headache, tension at the back of my neck. What can you do about that? It is what you get paid for.

I told the players the team on the Tuesday, and the team was I was going to play had three up front – Adrian Littlejohn, Michael Evans and Chris Billy – but as I got home on the Tuesday night, I thought we would be better off starting with Martin Barlow and keeping their left-back occupied, because he was such a busy player.

We could have a go in the first half with what we had got, knowing that we had got Carlo Corazzin and Ian Baird up our sleeves and we could take an extra defender off, if need be. So I had Martin Barlow over to my house on the Tuesday night to tell him, and I had to tell Chris Billy on the morning of the match that I'd changed my mind. It was not one of the most difficult tasks, but it came close and had to be done.

I told Chris Billy. Obviously having told him the previous day that he was playing, he was devastated, but as I said to him, it was important that he kept his chin up and didn't let the lads see he was disappointed. He did. He was brilliant, and went training with a great attitude.

In fact, he really got carried away on the bench as well, with Carlo Corazzin and Ian Baird. They were all really pushing us on and after the game I remember Chris saying thank goodness they had got him out of the cart when he missed his sitter at Colchester.

Obviously Martin Barlow was chuffed to death with me telling him that he was playing and it was appropriate that he then proceeded to create the winning goal.

He was back to how he was when he first came in the team. I am not saying he had gone off, but he was actually electric and I think with him thinking he was out of the side, it actually gave him that little bit more to show what he could do. He had a great game, as did every player. I couldn't fault any of them.

It was a great performance to win with so much happening on the night. It was unbelievable. We had already talked and planned that if it was 0-0 at half-time, which meant we were still losing 1-0, I was going to bring Ian Baird and Carlo Corazzin on together.

I had kept it from the newspapers that Ian Baird was fit and he looked ever so well. I decided that I was going to put Adrian or Evans wide on one side, play 4-2-4 and have a go at them because obviously we needed to score goals.

That's why I gambled with three forwards on the bench. I thought we had nothing to lose. But we scored within the first three minutes with a Micky Evans goal. I gave Micky Evans and Adrian Littlejohn a swig of whisky before the game. I pulled them both to one side before the game, and said "I want you both to take a swig of whisky and breathe on the defenders you are playing against, so they think you're pissed!"

Obviously scoring in the first three minutes must have done some good. Just before half-time we scored a great goal from a free-kick which is what we had worked on. It gave me a lot of satisfaction and it was great to see it work, to go two-up.

I knew that one goal would pull us back and I reiterated at half-time how much concentration we had to have but I wasn't aware of what was going to happen.

Adrian Littlejohn went through clearly and was tripped – a deliberate professional foul when there was no chance of anybody catching him. I just turned to Kevin Blackwell and said "The referee can't do anything but send him off. He can't just book him." To everyone's amazement, the referee just booked him.

To me, their right-hand side had just started causing us trouble and I thought that if he was sent off that would be it, that would be the end of the game as they would have had to drop the other right-hand player back.

I just couldn't believe it. I just thought everything was going against us, what with the offside goal against Darlington when we played them at home, and then a decision like the one against McCarthy. I stood up and confronted the linesman and asked him how anybody could not get sent off for the foul. The reserve official came out and asked me to sit down and the linesman asked me to be quiet and I just said, "It's all right being quiet, it's our livelihoods at stake. You can go to work tomorrow."

Anyhow, he flagged and the referee came over, and said to me "I think you ought to go off the bench." So I did, it was no good staying. I said "I can't believe how you can't send him off" and he said he thought there was a player who could have got back – he saw him out of the corner of his eye – and I said I just couldn't believe it.

I jumped over the back of the dug-out and stood in with the crowd and watched the rest of the game. I feared the worst and within six minutes they went and scored a great goal. So now we had got to score again to win the tie and I was thinking, "I can't believe it. After all we've been through, a decision like that has cost us the game."

But then the lads showed even more resolve and they kept pounding away. We missed another good chance with a Chris Curran diving header from a free-kick but then Martin Barlow came up with another bit of magic, another great early ball in, and who was there but Paul Williams?

Leaving the crowd after the play-off semi-final second leg

What a brilliant goal from a header at the far post. I didn't even see any celebrations, I just put my head down to the ground. I was so chuffed for the lads, I knew what it meant to them. I then said a couple of prayers, if I am honest, and wanted the whistle to go.

It didn't seem long coming and I just cleared off into the dressing-room early. I felt ever so emotional and when the lads came in we had a great celebration. Then they told me the fans were still outside on the pitch so I made the lads that had got their shirts left go out and we went on the balcony and took a couple bottles of champagne and wet them through.

It was brilliant with the fans. They were absolutely out of this world and I must admit I shed a tear or two. The atmosphere was something else. I didn't have a drink afterwards, I didn't want to forget the moment and I was tired and drained but I also knew that I would soon have to get my head right and we had to get our minds on the play-offs.

However, when we got home we did open a bottle of champagne between ourselves, Sharon and I, and we did enjoy a victory toast. I think she, more than anyone, understood that day how much it meant to me and the relief, but I realise it must be difficult living with a football manager at times.

I went to the Lord Mayor's ball on the Friday night after the game against Colchester. We left at 12.15 a.m. and were driving around Toys R Us near the traffic lights, and there was a chap in the middle of the road. I said to Sharon "Watch out! There's a bloody idiot stood in the middle of the road," and as we pulled closer, Sharon said "Look! It's Chopsy [Martin Barlow]."

So I said "Stop the car. Quick!" and we got out to have a look. Hilly was there too, so I shouted "All right, Hilly?" When he looked he was obviously the worse for wear, but then Martin looked at me and I don't think he even recognised me. I found out later that he only heard my voice, he couldn't even see me!

So I thought that gave me a great excuse to give them a bit of hard work on Saturday morning before we went away. Of course, when I told all the lads the following morning, they all killed themselves laughing. Poor old chaps. I think it was funny because on the Sunday, I noticed that when the lads were having one or two drinks, Hilly and Barlow were on water. I had to smile.

"THEY CAN CLOSE DOWN THE SOUTH WEST ON MAY 25"

IN the wake of all the euphoric scenes at Home Park on Wednesday, May 15, Argyle supporters woke the next day reminding themselves that the club had not actually achieved anything. For everything that winning a place at Wembley for the first time in the club's history meant, the season would still be one huge anticlimax if the Pilgrims did not win promotion.

To do so they would need to beat Darlington in the Endsleigh League Third Division play-off finals on Saturday, May 25 and no Argyle follower needed telling they had lost both earlier games against the North Easterners in the regular league season. Worse, they had failed to breach the Quakers' defence in three hours of play.

Darlington had progressed to Wembley by beating another of Argyle's bogey sides, Hereford, 4-2 on aggregate, winning both legs of their semi-final 2-1. Like Argyle, they had never before played at Wembley.

Warnock began his preparations for the play-off final as the club's fans were still nursing hangovers from the previous night's celebrations of the semi-final victory over Colchester. He was up before 7.00 a.m., planning for the next 10 days and, while he urged supporters to enjoy their day out in London, he warned his players they could forget about doing likewise.

"Although the city will be thinking of a day out, we've got to try and do the next bit and beat Darlington," he said. "It's been a long slog and I don't want to waste 10 months by not coming out with anything. I know it's a great day out for supporters but it's not going to be a great day out for us. That's not how I look at it. It's not a place to lose, Wembley."

If that was a strange observation from a man whose play-off finals record was second to none of his peers – three appearances, three wins – he explained: "I haven't lost but I've seen it in other people's faces, walking away from their dreams, and I don't want to experience it. I want to manage this club at a higher level and, hopefully, my players want to play at a higher level. We're playing against the best away side in the league, who we haven't beaten this season, but it's a one-off job now."

Warnock's assistant Mick Jones, the quiet power behind the Pilgrims' promotion drive, a calming sounding-board for his more overtly passionate colleague in the office next door, had been at Warnock's side during play-off successes with Huddersfield and Notts County and he prophesied the Wembley appearance would be the making of the club.

"It's the first time this club has ever been to Wembley, just like when we were at Notts County," he said. "They were the oldest league club in the world and they'd never been to

Wembley. And it was amazing how one Wembley appearance changed the whole fortunes of the club. Their new stadium, getting to the Premiership, everything was on the back of that Wembley appearance.

"Huddersfield's success, the new stadium, was on the back of their first Wembley appearance in the Autoglass Trophy because the place just came alive. It just brought something out in the people of Huddersfield. The same thing will happen here, it's a certainty. They can close the South West down on May 25."

Jones also believed the experience he, Warnock and a surprising number of Argyle players shared of preparing for a visit to the self-styled Venue of Legends could only stand them in good stead. "You can't put a price on experience," he said. "The only difference in our preparations this year will be that we are travelling north, instead of south. Neil will have everything in place. Playing at Wembley is different in every way, shape and form. I know one thing, though – it's a piece of green grass with two white sticks at either end, some string at the back of them, and four flags in the corner. And that's where we do our job, week in, week out. I really think Wembley can be the platform for this club to go where everyone thinks it should be, but it's like everything – it's easier said than done."

As he spoke, the first symptoms of a previously unknown epidemic were being diagnosed in Plymouth. Few people were expected to avoid the effects of Wembley Fever, which, experts predicted, was threatening to sweep across the city and spread throughout the West Country.

The day after the victory over Colchester, the club had already chartered a train and booked 100 coaches to ferry the Green Armada up to London. Ticket-office staff prepared to deal with the first of more than 30,000 applications for tickets, and the club shop was clearing its shelves to create space for the arrival of already-ordered Wembley memorabilia – everything from green bubble wigs to smart polo shirts. Operation Wembley was in full swing.

Warnock, who had bemoaned his luck so often during the season, was now beginning to feel the green tide turn: he won the toss for choice of Wembley dressing-rooms and plumped for his "lucky" North dressing-room, from where he would lead his Pilgrims out straight into the massed ranks of Argyle supporters, who had been allocated the Tunnel End of the ground.

Wembley tickets, starting at a seat-only £14 and rising through a wide range of packages up to a £91 per head luxury package that included a four-course lunch at Wembley Conference Centre, went on sale at Home Park on Saturday, May 18. The box-office opened at 8.00 a.m. to a queue which stretched a quarter of a mile back into Central Park. It did not get any shorter for most of the day as a steady stream of fans from Penzance to Taunton converged on the ground clutching cash, cheque-books and credit cards.

The first of the 30,000+ queueing for tickets at Home Park

By the following evening, the club estimated that in the region of 20,000 tickets – about two-thirds of the club's allocation – had been snapped up. Another three private trains had been chartered by Argyle commercial manager Steve Birley, including one that would set out from Cornwall, and extra coaches had been laid on to cater for supporters living in North Devon, which would leave from Bideford.

Birley also said that the club had taken around £10,000 in the club shop as supporters clamoured for Wembley memorabilia. "The whole thing is unbelievable," said Birley. "The Football League has never heard of anything like it."

Birley estimated that the Pilgrims' first ever visit to the Twin Towers could net the club a cool £1m if Warnock could inspire his players to victory over Darlington. Even if the unthinkable happened and Argyle lost, he reckoned that merely reaching the play-offs had paid off to the tune of £$^{1}/_{2}$m.

"We're looking at getting something in the region of £250,000 from ticket-sales and I expect to make at least £150,000 from other enterprises. Every bum on a seat in a coach or on a train, every souvenir bought at the club shop, brings something into the club. What is important is that the profit-making goes on. If we win at Wembley, there's 'We won at Wembley' tee-shirts, the video of the day, improved season-ticket sales next season. That could well bring in excess of £$^{1}/_{2}$m. When do you stop measuring success? If we get the right result, we will still feel the benefit in a year's time. People will say 'That's when it started, the day we went to Wembley.' We all knew the club was big but we didn't realise how big it is and how big it can be."

Big enough for the club to demand more tickets from the Football League after the Argyle ticket-office sold out of seats in the mid-price range. Despite shifting more than 28,000 tickets in three days, Pilgrims' chairman Dan McCauley was convinced the club could have increased that massive sale if the League had given them more tickets in the £22 and £26 price-range. After pestering from the Pilgrims' chairman, the League relented and sent Argyle a further 2,000 tickets for the mid-price seats. "I really had to push them," said McCauley. "Our supporters were getting the cheaper tickets they would rather not have, while the League was sitting on tickets which they were planning to sell on the day.

"Up there at League headquarters in Lytham St Annes, among the golden beaches and the golf clubs, they are not living in the real world. They have no vision, and it is no wonder that football is in a mess when people like that are running the game. They are incompetent."

A spokesman for the League declined to be drawn on the competence or otherwise of his colleagues. "If Mr McCauley is unhappy with the allocation of tickets, he should take it up with us and it will go through the proper channels," he said. "Plymouth indicated to us they would be able to sell a large number of tickets, which they have done. It should be a marvellous occasion."

With Darlington confident of selling around 15,000 tickets to their supporters – more than seven times their average home attendance – it promised to be the best-attended Third Division final in the play-offs' brief history. It also meant that more people would watch Darlington v Plymouth Argyle than had attended the previous six England home matches.

The demand for tickets and mementos might have surprised everyone from Wembury to Wembley, but not Argyle manager Warnock. "Nothing that has happened has shocked me, really," he said. "I knew this could happen. That's one reason why I came to Plymouth."

Warnock had ensured that the tee-shirted, bewigged, hat-wearing supporters would not be the only well-dressed people at Wembley by doing a deal with *Louis Bernard's* – owned by Argyle vice-chairman Peter Bloom – to kit out his players with special blazers and ties for their visit to the Twin Towers.

On an altogether different sartorial note, Dan McCauley confirmed he would be wearing his lucky stove-pipe hat in the Royal Box throughout the play-off final. The Pilgrims' large as life chairman had donned the topping titfer on a whim, moments before the victorious play-off semi-final at Home Park, and had continued to wear it for much of the following week.

"I'm definitely wearing it at Wembley," he said. "I'm getting like Neil – more and more superstitious. You just get the feeling that wearing it in the semi-final might have added

At Wembley in new club blazer

something. You don't know, it might not have done, but it's not worth the risk. I've got to wear it now, whether I like it or not."

McCauley revealed that it was down to his wife, Ann, that he took his seat in the directors' box wearing the hat. "I was going to wear a green wig, to be honest," he said, "but my wife said 'Don't take it and don't wear it.' There was a hat down in the boardroom and she said 'Well, that looks better than the silly wig' so I thought I'd wear it, but I didn't realise it would be such a hit with supporters."

McCauley also revealed that his impish sense of humour would not stop at wearing the unorthodox headgear in the Royal Box. He planned to present other VIP guests with mementos of the Argyle mascot. "I've got some Pilgrim Pete teapots to give away to the chairman of Darlington and our mayor," he said. "Now the League has agreed to putting up a cup for the winners, they'll have a Pilgrim Pete teapot to fill it with if they want."

Warnock decided from past experience that his players would benefit from being removed from the fervent activity at Home Park in the early part of the week leading up to the play-off final, so he took them away for a few days' break at the *Belfry Golf and Leisure* complex, near Sutton Coldfield in Warwickshire.

"There's a long time between the semi-final and final, too much to just keep training," he explained. "So we trained to get rid of the semi-final celebration drinks, then we have been relaxing, playing a bit of golf, and socialising. There's no better place – away from Plymouth – to do it. The ticket-office wherever I've been before has been absolute bedlam and whenever players go in, they get pestered by every Tom, Dick and Harry to do things. All our ticket requirements have been sorted out, so all they've got to do now is go in, train, and go away again."

For players like Steve Cherry, Gary Clayton and Richard Logan, the home of the 1985, 1989 and 1993 Ryder Cups provided welcomingly familiar surroundings in which to unwind. "It's exactly the same preparation," said Cherry. "He [Warnock] hasn't changed anything. It's all going to plan."

Clayton added: "The lads are all relaxed. There aren't any cliques or little gangs. Everybody is together at this club. It's a credit to Neil."

While he was up at the *Belfry*, Warnock managed to deflect a potential blow to his play-off plans dealt him by a Football League ruling that Argyle would have to play at Wembley in their second-choice yellow shirts.

The League had decided that the white sleeves on the Pilgrims' shirts were identical to those on a new Darlington kit which the North Easterners had unveiled to cash in on their first Wembley appearance, and, fearing a rash of hand-balls in which the referee would be able only to see the players' arms, decided that Argyle must change their colours.

Warnock was aghast but acted swiftly to ensure the Pilgrims would be able to wear their traditional green on the big day. "We were desperate to wear green," he said. "Green is our colour and the fans expect us to wear it. Plus, I don't like wearing yellow. We've never done well in it. We sent Kevin Blackwell [Argyle's youth team coach] all the way to League headquarters in Lancashire with some alternative proposals, which basically means we will wear some green and black flashes on the sleeves. Luckily for us, the League agreed." Goodness knows what Dan McCauley would have said if the men among the golden beaches had not acquiesced.

Even more amazingly, Warnock had persuaded the company who made the Pilgrims strip to hurry through the changes, despite the club having already agreed to switch manufacturers for the following season. "They are confident they can get it out in time," said Warnock. "If not, we'll paint it ourselves. We're definitely wearing green."

Whatever, with a new kit due the following season, the Wembley kit would be a one-off. Worn once and then… well, the destination of the unique shirts would prove to be the topic of much debate long after the final whistle at Wembley.

Warnock and his players returned from the sunshine at the *Belfry* to a soggy Home Park for two days' training – basically working at set-pieces – prior to travelling up to London. Martin Barlow and Adrian Littlejohn both stayed behind after the work-outs at Harper's Park for attention from physiotherapist Norman Medhurst to tight hamstrings, but both were expected to be fit.

Whatever the result of the play-off final, Warnock knew that he would have to break up the side. Goalkeeper Steve Cherry would be leaving after the match, despite having joined the Pilgrims on a permanent transfer after his 18-match, three-month loan from Watford.

Since his loan period had expired, signing Cherry on a full-time contract was the only way Warnock could secure his services for the play-off final, but, because Cherry favoured a move back to his native Midlands, Warnock had agreed to give him a free transfer in the summer after he fulfilled the shortest of short-term contracts.

"In my contract at Watford, I had it written in that I was on a free and it's the same at Plymouth," explained Cherry. "I want to see what my options are in the summer. The only reason I've signed permanently is because I've had to do that to play in the one match. The problem is, I don't want to move house and it's very difficult training away and playing at Plymouth. I think you've got to be more settled to be able to keep playing as long as I want to. All I want to do is to go out on a high and hope someone is watching at Wembley. I'm sure people have picked up that I've spent three months on loan and that those three months have been successful."

NW: *I think I went to bed at around 1.30 a.m. after the play-off semi-final, reading the match programme, and I woke up at 6.15 a.m. I couldn't sleep anymore. I knew what we had to do. We had so much planning to do that day. I wanted the same preparations as we had at Huddersfield and Notts County, so I wanted us to go to the* Belfry *for a couple of days but I wanted to work hard first.*

I wanted to organise the hotel at Wembley to stay the night before and I wanted to get all the preparation for the wives and directors done. I knew how difficult it would be. I wanted to speak to the bus company about an executive bus for the wives and our own bus. Then we had a board meeting. I got in at 11.00 a.m. I had also hurt my back about six or seven days before so I had to see a chiropractor at 11.45 a.m.

We were told that we couldn't play in our green and white strip because Darlington were playing in their new shirts and the colours were too similar. So I telephoned the kit people to see if they could get a strip in all green. I was determined not to play in the yellow strip. I asked the kit people if they could do us a plain green one, just for Wembley, so the fans could see that we were playing in green. Because I thought there would be that many green and white scarves, we didn't want to be playing in any other colour, really.

Then the next day Sharon made a good point. She said: "I don't believe that you want to play in all green." I asked her why and she said " because, if you remember rightly when we were there last year when the sun was out at Wembley, you wouldn't have seen the players, just like the Manchester United grey kit." And I had to admit that she was right.

That is what a good woman is for. Anyhow, I didn't want to play in yellow so we got the video out. I was up two hours in the morning looking at the video of Darlington and their strip was almost all white.

I went in first thing and telephoned the Football League and asked if we could put some more green flashes on the white sleeves and a bit on the back just so that we could play in our normal strip.

We were that convinced that it needed a good representative to put our case. After speaking to the chap at the Football League – David Cookson at Lytham St Annes – we decided to send Kevin Blackwell up with the shirts, shorts and socks and Mick Jones drew a sketch of what the amended kit would look like, to try and put our case over to them.

We decided to try and get some screening done on the actual original shirts so we could play in those. Blackie set off at 10.30 a.m. to go to Lytham St Annes. I just felt that it was that important.

We had a meeting as we always do to try to get players to know about what tickets they wanted for wives, etc., because there is more hassle in these situations when you are not organised.

Fortunately we had been through it all before and I managed to get straight on the telephone the next morning to where I wanted the players to stay – the same place as I had stayed with the three previous successes – and then I rang the Belfry up, because I had stayed there three times – it has got a good leisure complex as well as the golf – and managed to get in there as well.

It was hectic trying to organise the tickets, because I knew I had to get all the heavy work out of the way. The people at the ground would wonder what had hit them, they would be so busy. That is why I wanted to get the players away – to sort out the tickets and try to concentrate on the arrangements, because there is more hassle if you upset people.

We got up to the Belfry and two people were not at the meeting. We all checked in apart from two players, and you could put your money on it being Adrian Littlejohn and Ronnie Maugé. I had a meeting with them all to tell them all about extras, because if anyone signed my name on my room for extras, they would all be paying for it.

So Gary Clayton says: "Gaffer can I ask you, what happens if you sign for it in somebody else's name?" Trust him to think of that.

Being interviewed by Hamish Marshall, of the BBC, at the Belfry

I arranged for all the Press, television cameras etc., to go up on Monday lunchtime when some of the lads were teeing off, to get all the interviews out of the way, and then it left us the rest of the week to concentrate on the task ahead.

We had all the players round our house on the Saturday night for a barbecue because I thought we had to get the wives together and talk about the arrangements for Wembley, and get the kids out. So we had the kids and all the wives around for a barbecue.

It was fine for most of the night, but it finished up chucking it down with rain for the last half an hour. We had Micky Heathcote's lad Liam holding an umbrella above Carlo Corazzin and myself while we were cooking.

It went ever so well and all the girls made a contribution and I actually arranged for all the tickets to be handed out that day. I did that in the afternoon so they could take their tickets home before they went away and then, like I said, we could get on with everything else.

It was nice to hear the wives planning to go out on their own together while the lads were away at the Belfry.

We travelled up on Sunday morning to the Belfry. I fixed up for some of the lads to play golf but my back was still killing me so I couldn't play. We arrived there and the Benson & Hedges golf tournament was on the television, beset by gale-force winds – it said that only 20 professional golfers broke 80 – and it was just as bad at the Belfry. It was absolutely blowing a gale, but 15 went out and played.

The hotel assistant manager said when I went in, it was good to see me back again and I said to him that it was my fourth time. I said that while we kept winning, I couldn't see why we would not keep coming back. And he said that it was funny, because every other football club that came to the Belfry always ended up losing.

That evening we had a meal but I kept out of the way and had my meal later on with Mick. I told the players at first that they weren't allowed to go out of the hotel and then Gary Clayton and Chris Billy reminded me that the previous year I let them go out as long as they were all back in at a certain time. Knowing how superstitious I am, they were smiling broadly because they knew I'd agree, and said "All right, but get back in for 11 o'clock," which they did. Then we had a drink around the bar and there were only a couple the worse for wear. There is no need to say who it was.

I do think the Belfry is an ideal place to stay. Obviously I like St Mellion and the other courses in the West Country, but I think you have got to get away completely from the area for two or three days, because with everything happening in Plymouth, you would have gone in there every day and there would have been some hassle.

I let them have a free night on the Monday. There was a nightclub in the complex and they could let off steam, but I said to them that it would be the last time and I didn't want anybody getting into trouble. I didn't like to let the Belfry down – I had been there four times and I asked them to respect that. I also had a chat with the hotel night-porters – any hassle and I wanted them to telephone me.

On Monday night we looked at the video of the highlights of the Colchester game. The lads were killing themselves laughing at Charlie's celebration run and also at my voice, which was near to breaking. They were killing themselves laughing.

A few of the Sky lads – Andy Gray and Richard Keys – were playing golf there, and George Graham and Frank McLintock and a few other celebrities were also there.

We travelled back down to Plymouth on Tuesday in readiness for the final assault on Wednesday, Thursday and Friday. There would be no Press whatsoever on Thursday and Friday, but I fixed up to leave at noon on Friday, so there would be a few fans who wanted to see us off. And I had already sorted out a civic reception on the Sunday at 12.30 p.m. – win or lose.

We saw the Notts County lads, who were also in the play-offs. They were also visiting the Belfry and on the Tuesday as we were leaving, they were just checking in. They said that they were struggling to sell 10,000 tickets and their chairman was quite amazed when I told him that we had already sold 25,000.

**Mark Patterson, Steve Cherry, Carlo Corazzin, Chris Curran and Richard Logan
ready to tee off at the Belfry**

Gary Clayton set off at 6.30 that morning to travel down to London with Norman to see a specialist in Harley Street. Then I had to clear the bill up and I was surprised to find that none of the lads had actually signed on my room for some of the drinks. All the extras had been paid and I was pleasantly surprised that they hadn't tried to stitch me up.

On the Tuesday we still needed a form signing by Watford regarding Steve Cherry's transfer, so Kevin Blackwell travelled to Watford and their secretary did everything for us and faxed it off. Then we found that we also needed another form signing by Steve, so we had to get that off as well.

Radio Five Live telephoned me. They wanted to interview us on Wednesday regarding the play-offs. They were doing a little programme on the Saturday.

Then we had to go for the blazer and slacks fitting at Peter Bloom's Louis Bernard's *on Wednesday lunchtime. We had got to try and get that out of the way so that there was no messing about at the weekend.*

Then I found out that Steve Cherry couldn't get down to the Wembley hotel until the Friday night, so there was no chance of training with him. He had a couple of offers with other clubs and wanted to talk to them. It was not the best preparation defensive-wise, but there was nothing we could do about that because my agreement was to suit him really.

As I thought, it had been chaos at the ground so I was glad we had been away with the lads. I know this was my fourth time, but I hadn't got a clue how people seemed so organised. I think I am so organised, but there is so much to do. All I wanted was for the players to go home and relax and get ready for the game.

I managed to keep it away from them, but everything at the ground just seemed to be piling up. Mick and I just seemed to be there non-stop, but we got on with the training all right. Everything was organised, everything was out of the way.

We had a great session, in fact we had to stop it after about half an hour. We played the reserves and the reserves were just so fired up that I was frightened of an injury. Everybody was so keen to get on with the play-off final, it just felt so good. The lads believed in themselves at last, and I think it couldn't come quick enough for most of them.

After their final day's training in the West Country, Warnock signalled an all-out assault on the Endsleigh League Second Division by naming five forwards in his 14-man squad for the play-off final. He selected the same starting line-up that won through to the promotion decider by beating Colchester in the previous week's dramatic play-off semi-final second leg, which meant that Michael Evans would partner leading scorer Adrian Littlejohn up front.

Warnock decided to throw caution to the wind by opting to have three more forwards on the substitutes' bench, meaning that the loss of any defenders or midfielders due to injury at Wembley would have to be covered by shuffling his starting deck.

Carlo Corazzin, who had only started one match since his £150,000 transfer from Cambridge on deadline-day; Ian Baird, who had trained in earnest for the first time in the week preceding the play-off final after missing the final weeks of the season with a torn adductor muscle in his groin; and Chris Billy, who scored a Wembley winner for Huddersfield in the previous season's Second Division play-off final, would comprise the Pilgrims' substitutes.

"Why should I want to change anything?" asked Warnock. "I haven't got any defensive cover, that's all. I'm probably being a bit brave, having three forwards on the bench, but that's how I feel. It's everything or bust now. I think everything that could have gone wrong for us this season has gone wrong. I feel we've just got to be strong now.

"As I've said to the players, all I can expect from them now is honesty and 100 per cent commitment. I've felt we've improved as the season's gone on. I think I'm learning about players all the time – some of them I've only had under my wings for a few weeks – but I feel we're getting stronger and we've got as good a chance as Darlington, even though we haven't beaten them and haven't even scored against them."

The encounter had been billed as something of a culture clash, with Darlington having acquired a reputation under manager Jim Platt as a passing side and Argyle still trying to shrug off the long-ball stigma that arrived with Warnock. Warnock rejected the notion. "They are a good passing side but I think you'll find we'll play as much as them. In the Colchester game, with all the pressure and tension, you can't say we didn't play football. It's all in the minds of people who want to invent things. I think we play as good football as any team in the division but I'll always get a certain label because of who I am."

"IT'LL BE A WASTED YEAR IF WE FAIL NOW"

THE eve of the play-offs dawned bright over the city of Plymouth and a healthy number of Pilgrims supporters unhealthily skipped lunch to give Warnock and his players a hearty early afternoon send-off from Home Park.

A little more than eight months previously, after Argyle had been beaten 2-1 at Colchester on the opening day of their 1995/96 campaign, Warnock had asked those supporters to suspend their assessment of his new-look side. "The time to judge us is at the end of the season," he said.

Fifty-five games later, the Green and White jury was poised to deliver its verdict on his hastily-assembled collection of lower division journeymen and wannabes. Ninety minutes at Wembley the following day would decide whether they were heroes or villains.

Even taking Argyle to Wembley for the first time in the club's, frankly, mundane history would not mitigate against failure to win promotion to the Second Division *via* the Endsleigh League play-off final – not in the supporters' eyes, or those of Warnock. "It'll be a wasted year if we fail now," he said, as Argyle journeyed to the *Wembley Hilton* hotel, which Warnock had used as a base from which to launch his previous play-off successes with Notts County and Huddersfield.

Warnock was making his fifth trip in six seasons to the home of football. As well as winning three times in the play-offs, he was beaten in an Autoglass Trophy final by Swansea. "I lost the only cup game that I played at Wembley and I didn't give a damn – we lost on penalties so I've never lost an actual game – but the play-offs were so important to me. The league is so important. The play-off final is all about 10 months of hard work in one afternoon, really."

Hard work, and then some. While, back in the previous Autumn, everyone was rating Argyle favourites to win the Third Division, Warnock had been contemplating what he had often referred to as "my most difficult job in football."

"To make us favourites when the lads that turned up for pre-season training would have finished in the bottom six is ludicrous," he said. "There was no heart; no passion for the club; they looked a mess; professionalism was zero. I know people will think I'm talking for the sake of talking but I feel it was a massive job. I don't think anybody – Glenn Hoddle, Kenny Dalglish, Graeme Souness – could have done more than what we've done here this year. I've had it thrown at me that I'm a lucky blighter but you don't get luck year in, year out. You don't survive on luck. I think we've given supporters their belief back. We've got criticism from certain quarters – and I'll bet the people that criticised me are going up to Wembley – but everywhere I've been I've had criticism."

Warnock loves Wembley. Having missed the opportunity of playing there by several bucketsful of ability, he now had a season-ticket for the manager's seat under the Royal Box and an annual reservation at the *Wembley Hilton*. "There's nowhere better to play," he enthused. "It's a tremendous achievement for a player. My ambition when I was a player was to play at Wembley; when I became a manager, my ambition was to manage at Wembley. The turf is like velvet, like no other turf in the whole world, and the stadium gives you a tremendous thrill. Going down the tunnel, even when it's empty, is exciting. To actually play on it is unbelievable."

Warnock's own knowledge of the Venue of Legends was repeated in no fewer than 10 of his 14-man squad for the play-off final. Goalkeeper Steve Cherry would be making his fifth Wembley appearance after two play-off finals (1990 and '91) and two Anglo Italian Cup finals (1994 and '95), all with Notts County, while full-backs Mark Patterson (Anglo Italian Cup with Derby in 1993) and Paul Williams (1992 Autoglass Trophy final with Stockport) had each played there once.

Central defenders Chris Curran and Richard Logan both scored on their Wembley debuts, Curran against his own Torquay side that played Blackpool in the 1991 play-offs, and Logan for Huddersfield in the 1994 Autoglass Trophy final.

Chris Leadbitter played for Chesterfield in the 1990 play-offs and his fellow midfielder Ronnie Maugé was substitute for Bury in the previous year's post-season knock-out.

Striker Adrian Littlejohn came on as substitute for Sheffield United in the 1993 FA Cup semi-final against Sheffield Wednesday, while substitute Chris Billy scored the winner for Huddersfield in the previous season's play-offs, and also played in the 1994 Autoglass Trophy final.

Ian Baird represented Leeds United in the Mercantile Credit Centenary Festival eight years previously, which left the third substitute Carlo Corazzin; local lads Martin Barlow and Michael Evans; and, surprisingly, captain Mick Heathcote as the four Pilgrims without Wembley experience.

Assistant manager Mick Jones had been to Wembley five times as Warnock's right-hand man and once in his own right as manager of Kettering Town, while physiotherapist Norman Medhurst had been acquainted with Wembley more times than all the other Pilgrims put together from his time as the England spongeman and curer of all ills.

All of them carried with them the similar hopes and dreams of hundreds of professionals from all over the world who had trodden the Wembley turf before them.

Cherry, the Wembley veteran who would be packing his bags and heading away from the West Country, whether he kept a clean-sheet against Darlington or did a Hammond and chucked a few in – "It's been quite strange. It's everyone's ambition to get there and, all of a sudden after years in the game I'm going there for the fifth time in six years. It has been good."

Patterson, out of touch and out of favour at the beginning of the season – "We didn't see eye-to-eye and it was my fault because what he [Warnock] was asking was alien to me. I was on my way to Blackpool for talks but I didn't fancy that because I felt it was a new era, that something different was about to happen."

Williams, "Charlie" to his team-mates and "Champagne Charlie" to West Country headline writers after his semi-final winner – "I know Plymouth people are going there for the day out and I hope they enjoy it, but at the end of the day we have got to get promoted. It will be devastating to lose."

Curran, teenage scorer of an own goal for Torquay in his previous Wembley final – "You look back and you think to yourself 'I'm really lucky, I've played at Wembley.' Some players never get to play there. It's fantastic."

Logan, the qualified bricklayer who had laid the foundations for a successful life inside and outside the game – "Scoring at Wembley is unbelievable. You can't put it into words – the nearest thing is probably sex. Every time someone mentions it, a big smile comes on your face. You've done it, and there's thousands who've played there and not done it."

Heathcote, the Wembley virgin with the captain's responsibility for being Warnock's representative on the pitch – "I think it's just a question of reminding the lads of their different responsibilities that the gaffer has given them, what his instructions are. Other than that, they won't need motivating."

Leadbitter, architect of Colchester's semi-final downfall – "It's winner takes all. It's been a long season and it's just another league game, except if you win, you're promoted and if you lose, you finish with nothing. It's a big game. We've just got to make sure we win, then we'll enjoy it afterwards."

Maugé, the midfield buzz-bomb with a golden-toothed smile and happy-go-lucky personality – "Everyone asks me whether I've made the wrong decision and tells me I should have stayed at Bury, but really and truly I don't think I have. I know what sort of potential Plymouth have, and I know there's better things to come when we go up."

Barlow, the Barum boy who had to find 45 tickets for family and friends and who had nearly moved to Cardiff earlier in the season – "I thought I'd try and prove myself to the boss. I'll be so proud. I never dreamt I'd be going to Wembley with all my family there."

Littlejohn, the saxophone-playing streak of lightning who loved nothing better than to put the wind up opposition defenders – "It would be fantastic to score – if I do, I expect I'll be ecstatic – but if no goals come and we get the victory which sends us up to the Second Division, I'll be just as happy."

Evans, the lone true Plymothian and, according to Warnock, a potential million-pound player – "My mates love it. Everyone's been trying to get hold of tickets to get to Wembley. There's been loads of hectic 'phone calls, and my mum and dad's 'phone's been ringing all the time from people asking how we were getting on."

Billy, the midfielder who, for reasons which mystified his manager and team-mates, had become the easy target for fans' abuse (a Billy scapegoat, if you like) – "If you get too nervous, you will try too hard and things won't happen for you, but we're all pros and know what it's all about."

Baird, the bargain-buy veteran striker with a career-long habit of scoring against Argyle in the past, back after injury – "I'm just happy to be in the squad, having been out for six weeks. As you get on in your career, I think you begin to appreciate it a bit more, so I'm just looking forward to it."

And Corazzin, the £150,000 deadline-day signing and Canadian international who had had to bide his time on the substitutes' bench since signing from Cambridge – "Hopefully, I'll get the chance to play for a couple of minutes to see what it is like. Everybody wants to score at Wembley and maybe I'll get the opportunity to put myself in that situation and make it count."

In the way of their hopes and aspirations stood the players of Darlington, a team which had twice beaten the Pilgrims in the previous nine months – 2-0 at Feethams on Saturday, October 28, when Wembley was the last thing on either side's mind; and 1-0 at Home Park on Saturday, April 6, when both still harboured hopes of automatic promotion and Robbie Painter's controversial goal proved the difference between the two teams.

They would step out on to Wembley's lush turf intent on extending one of the most remarkable sequences of the 1995/96 Football League season. In 23 league games away from their Feethams home, the Quakers had lost only once – 4-1 to Chester in November – which meant they were easily the best travellers in the English game. In qualifying for the Third Division play-off final, they had lost just once in their previous 22 matches.

Their manager Jim Platt, the former Northern Ireland international goalkeeper who understudied Pat Jennings for many years, was of the opinion that their current form and the fact that they had achieved the league double over Argyle, should have made them favourites to win the Wembley match. His feelings were at odds with the bookies, however. William Hill offered the Quakers' chances at even money, while Argyle were 8-11 favourites. Adrian Littlejohn was favourite to score the opening goal, at 9-2, with Evans 11-2, Baird and Corazzin 7-1 and Maugé 10-1.

"I can't understand it," said former Middlesbrough favourite Platt. "We have beaten Plymouth twice, and lost only once in the last 22 matches."

Warnock confessed himself an admirer, both of Platt and his charges. "Darlington have got a lot of good, young players. They'll enjoy it," he said. "And what have they got to lose? Who would have thought that Darlington would have been up there at the end of the season? I think Platty deserves the manager of the year award for what he's done. He's a smashing lad – it will make a change for me to walk out at Wembley with someone I genuinely like – and the club's a nice friendly club. They've got some good players: Mattie Appleby could play at a higher level; Gary Bannister's got a shrewd brain; Robbie Painter and Robert Blake are very live-wire up front; and they've got Steve Gaughan, who's very big and very strong."

Presumably, Warnock did not give the same glowing testimonies to his players in his Friday evening preparations for the big day, which consisted of a relaxing night at the *Wembley Hilton*, with a team meal together, followed by a video-viewing of past games and a review of the Argyle set-pieces that might be needed the following day.

A vital participant in the build-up to the final was Gary Clayton, who had journeyed to London in advance of the main Argyle party, not to recce the hotel, but to visit a Harley Street specialist for a consultation which would tell him whether or not his career was over. The knee injury which the 33-year-old midfielder had sustained at Rochdale in the Pilgrims' penulti- mate league fixture had proved a lot worse than at first feared.

However, the medical diagnosis relieved those anxieties and Clayton was told he would be able to resume playing after a month's complete rest. "It's great news," said Warnock. "We thought he had ruptured his posterior ligament but that is not the case."

The relief felt by Clayton will have offset his disappointment at missing out on a fourth Wembley appearance. Six years previously, he had been sidelined through injury when a Cambridge side that included Chris Leadbitter had beaten Chesterfield 1-0 in the Fourth Division play-off final; four years later, he was cup-tied when Huddersfield lost to Swansea on penalties in the Autoglass Trophy final, having played for Cambridge earlier in the competition; and a year previously, he had missed being part of Huddersfield's Second Division play-off success through another injury.

"I think I'm fated never to play at Wembley," he said, without a hint of obvious regret. "I'm getting used to it now. I'm gutted, but in a way I'd rather get injured second-to-last game of the season than second game. At least I've played in 40-odd games."

However, Warnock was insistent that Clayton would be part of Argyle's Wembley experience, with a brief to relax and entertain his nervous playing colleagues. It is a role which, like most of his life, he made light of.

"I'm just one of the lads," he said, modestly. "I like a laugh and a joke. When I'm playing, I'm more serious in the dressing-room, but when I'm not playing, I'll mess about."

Warnock said: "Clayts is the main man – he gets them going with his Northern sense of humour. Kevin Blackwell is another bubbly character, he has plenty to say – he's a Cockney – and Trigger (Michael Evans) gives us the flavour of the local accent. I'm not sure anybody understands what he says, actually."

Warnock was going to Wembley with the full backing of his chairman, who had been so desperate to secure his services 10 months previously. "There is no manager I would rather go to Wembley with," proclaimed Dan McCauley. "With a record like his at the Twin Towers – three wins in three play-off finals – you have got to be fairly confident of success."

The pair had been at Wembley together 12 months previously, Warnock guiding Huddersfield to victory in the Second Division play-off final; McCauley, less glamorously, to watch Argyle fans play in the Endsleigh League Supporters Challenge six-a-side competition, but both had plans for a future together.

McCauley said: "Neil said to me that day 'How would you like to savour some of this?' I told him 'I'd love to' but I did not think it would come so soon. He has done a great job. He virtually had to start from scratch, change the team and build a new spirit at the club, but maybe it was better that way. There was such a feud and split within the club at that time, he told me there was no way he could go ahead with that team, so it was possibly an advantage to start afresh. There were no players on long-term contracts, so he was able to move people out."

However, McCauley rejected the notion that Warnock's success had come from his reliance on McCauley's ever-open cheque-book. "Neil raised the money in the transfer-market," said the Pilgrims' chairman. "All the money was really spent in the Peter Shilton era, whereas Neil did bring in some transfer revenue to try and balance the books. Although that is not to say that the wage-bill is any less now."

Between them, the Argyle chairman, his chosen manager, and his manager's chosen players had succeeded in arresting an Argyle slide which, apart from one season of near-glory two years previously, had been more or less constant for five seasons. All they had to do now was contrive one more victory.

Warnock's preparations for the Endsleigh League Division Three play-off final against Darlington had been meticulous, as he had promised they would be. Everything was in place; the players knew what was expected of them; the supporters were planning to invade Wembley on a scale never before seen by fans of a Football League club. All that remained was to win a game of football.

NW: *I had diarrhoea for three days leading up to the play-off final and although I took tablets I just felt it must be stress underneath. I felt okay in myself, but stress must have been building up. I know you don't get nerves at certain times when you have done it all before, but I just seem to get worse as I get older.*

I touched the piece of grass I have had on my windscreen for a year now. My son picked it up at Wembley last year and he said to me: "Dad, keep that until next year when I'll get another piece." It was still there. It had dried up but I was hoping that it would last until the weekend. That is how superstitious I am.

Some lads want to switch off before a match, but when we had the pre-match meal I put Billy Connolly on. I did that the previous year, let them have a laugh rather than take it all seriously.

People said when I stopped at the Wembley Hilton *that it was too close to the ground, but I found in previous years that it was a different class. The head chef Narino is a big football fan and he had helped me out for years. I had never had one bit of problem there. Even though it is busy, the players have slept well.*

The traffic was bad on the motorway and it was only Friday. Apparently there had been a land-drain blocked on the M5 on both sides, but we by-passed it through Bristol and avoided most of it.

I didn't sense any nerves on the bus but as we got closer to London, I put Chubby Brown on just to break it up and then just before we got to Wembley I showed the players the highlights of Darlington versus *Hereford, where they were talking about beating us, etc. It finished just before we got to the hotel and then I showed them the Colchester game, because that was magnificent.*

Martin Barlow, Richard Logan, Carlo Corazzin and Chris Leadbitter kill time at the Wembley Hilton

I booked Sharon and the kids in to see Oliver. They went to a show the previous year while Mick and I went for a quiet meal and so we said "Let's do the same thing."

Sharon came back with the kids at about 11.15 p.m. and played the piano again, like we did the previous year. We all sat around the piano for the last half an hour, just relaxing, and then we shut up and went to bed.

It was quite difficult to sleep. It was probably the most nervous I had ever felt. I didn't know why my stomach was all to pot. I must have been getting old!"

"I'LL DO WHAT I ALWAYS DO – I'LL 'PHONE MY MUM FOR THE RESULT"

SATURDAY, May 25, 1996, 4.00 a.m. Long before the directors, management and players of Plymouth Argyle were roused by their morning alarm call at the *Wembley Hilton*, the club's supporters were awakening from their slumbers for the Pilgrimage to Wembley.

The sun had not yet risen on the day Argyle followers had waited all their football-supporting lives for as the first of hundreds of coaches, minibuses, vans and cars left Cornwall. In Plymouth itself, the Home Park car park was gearing up for the mass exodus from the city, rank upon rank of coaches waiting silently in the chill dawn to ferry the Green Armada to London.

At Penzance railway station, the first of the four specially chartered Pilgrim Express trains was gradually filling with passengers, eagerly, if somewhat sleepily, anticipating its 6.20 a.m. estimated time of departure.

Jason Martin, a 27-year-old from Camelford who had been crossing the Tamar for more than a decade to watch his beloved Pilgrims, epitomised the breadth of support for the Pilgrims in the Duchy. Argyle are, uniquely, the Football League team of a county which does not have a Football League team.

"It's the nearest league team to us," he said. "There's nothing in Cornwall and there are going to be a lot of upset people if they don't win. I have always said I would never go to Wembley unless Argyle are there."

Gradually, and with increasing regularity, the foot soldiers of Neil Warnock's Green Army began their march on England's capital city. Not since the days of Trelawny had London seen such a concerted mass determination to make a mark. "And shall we know the where and when, and shall the Pilgrims' dream die? Here's 30,000 West Country folk who will know the reason why."

Certainly, Argyle's first visit to the home of football had fired the imagination of West Country folk like never before. Only when followers of the Cornish rugby team had journeyed to Twickenham for the County Championship final had comparable numbers set out for a day in town with such a collective will to win. Then, as now, it was a case of: "Will the last one out of the South West, please turn off the lights?"

The A38, M5, M4 and M40 were awash with green and white, old bangers that had seen far better days plodding up the motorways alongside the luxury coaches, scarves and flags fluttering from open windows and tied to aerials, posters plastered to windows, united by the common desire of their occupants to see Argyle succeed on Wembley's field of dreams. Flippant, maybe, but the analogy with Dunkirk was unavoidable: a peaceful flotilla of ordinary men and women in all manner of transport doing their bit for Argyle's cause.

Not altogether everyone in the West Country was rooting for the Greens, however. "Good luck Darlo" read a banner draped across the footbridge near Exeter's Sandygate Service Station: "Love from City" continued the message at the next walkway.

Each and every service station between Land's End and Wembley was a seething, happy mass of Pilgrims who had stopped for mechanical and human refuelling and took the opportunity of the break to touch up their green and white face-paint in the lavatories.

A vast majority of the faithful Plymouth brethren journeyed to Wembley from Cornwall, Devon and Somerset, but such was the pride in Argyle's moment of history, those with green in their veins converged on Wembley from all parts of the country, all parts of the globe.

Fans like Dave Townsend, a member of the seven-strong Argyle New South Wales supporters club, who jetted in from Australia; like Andrew Williams, who cut short a back-packing holiday in South Vietnam, leaving his companion in the Far East; like Clive Foster, who emigrated to Canada 30 years previously and who was bringing his son Scott 3,500 miles across the Atlantic, hoping, no doubt, that his life-long enthusiasm for the Greens was passed on a generation; like Roy Barnes, who flew in from Turkey; like Alec Gribble, an attaché at the British Embassy in Kuwait. Plymouth Argyle might not be the biggest club in the world, but it surely boasts some of football's most loyal followers.

Those that could not be there sent their good wishes from all over the planet. Philip Marsh, founder of the New South Wales supporters branch, could not afford to join Dave Townsend and would be unable to tune into the BBC World Service because of the lousy reception 2,500 feet up Australia's Great Dividing Range mountains. "I'll do what I always do," he said. "I'll 'phone my mum for the result. That'll be about 1.40 a.m. our time."

From the Antipodes to the Caribbean, where HMS *Argyll*, the Devonport-based Type 23 frigate was on operations. "We will be listening closely for the result and hope all goes well," said *Argyll*'s Commander George Zambellas. "There will be a loud cheer from this part of the world if they win."

Everyone, even those on the periphery of the occasion, was caught up in the green dream. "I don't know anything about football," confessed John Dudley, of the Barbican's famous Cap'n Jaspers cafe, "but I think it's brilliant. I'll give half a yard of hot dog to each of the team if they win."

It was perhaps as well that Argyle's players did not fully appreciate the weight of expectancy that would be on their 14 pairs of shoulders as they walked out of the relative gloom and calm of the Wembley tunnel into the bright afternoon mayhem. Warnock had kept them as far away from the cauldron of hope as he could and he had yet another plan, honed from years of play-off experience, to further settle their nerves.

Teams playing at Wembley are not generally allowed access to the ground on the morning of a match but Warnock knew how to skip round the protective protocol. After a leisurely breakfast at the *Wembley Hilton*, he shepherded the players onto the coach and took them to the empty stadium. On the pretext of dropping off the kit, and with a nod and a wink to some by now familiar London faces, players and officials disembarked for a sneak preview of the stage on which would unfold the drama of a few hours later.

The players were back inside the sanctuary of their hotel as the first Argyle supporters parked up in the shadow of the famous Twin Towers. For many, the reaction of Cornish fan Andy Bond summed up the moment. "I've been waiting for this for 35 years," he said. "It's great – it's all I thought it would be." No matter that the national stadium is set among a sprawl of factories and warehouses, it still looked the most special football ground in the world.

Long before the Wembley gates opened, Argyle supporters had claimed the place for their

**Sneaking a look at Wembley
on the morning of the play-off final**

own. The outside perimeter of the stadium was a carnival of green and white which stretched out down Olympic Way as far as the eye could see, a raucous celebration of Westcountryness. Dads with lads, picnicking families, young girls with their fellows. Was anyone left back home in Plymouth? Darlington supporters were conspicuous only by their relative anonymity.

Among the 30,000 faces were some that were more immediately familiar than others. Michael Foot, the Rt Hon Pilgrim himself, who had followed Argyle through thick and (mainly, it has to be said) thin, but whose loyalty and devotion had remained undiminished; Kevin Hodges and Leigh Cooper, two of the club's most faithful servants, now just two more eager fans; Tommy Tynan, their former team-mate, a legend in his own six-yard box, who was doing the match summary for Westcountry TV; Andy Comyn, released by Warnock a few weeks previously, performing a similar duty for Plymouth Sound Radio; former Argyle manager David Kemp, assiduous as ever – "Wycombe'll be playing one of these teams next season, it will pay to take a look at them"; Frank Clark, Barry Fry, Steve Coppell, managers on the hunt for talent; and Marc Edworthy, the previous season's Argyle player of the year whose own Wembley experience with Crystal Palace two days later was to end in personal heartbreak.

A message over the public address system alerted supporters to the fact that the gates had been opened and the first of 30,000 eager Pilgrims made their way through the turnstiles. The sight that greeted them was heaven to the eye: the famous lush green turf glinting in the early summer sunshine, the Venue of Legends, the home of football – it belonged to them for the day. As hundreds streamed in, so hundreds more flooded up Olympic Way in full voice and fuller heart – "Green Army", "The Greens Are Going Up", "Drink Up Thee Cider". Football League officials proclaimed themselves aghast at the numbers, the enthusiasm, the sheer size of the Green Army.

Amongst all the good humour, there was one incident which cast a sombre shadow over the day. Kelvin Noon, a 24-year-old Argyle supporter from Salcombe, in Devon, was fatally injured in an incident right outside Wembley's main gates a few minutes before the match kicked off. Noon, a chef at Salcombe's Marine Hotel, died of a brain haemorrhage. Police later charged another Plymouth supporter with murder, which was later changed to manslaughter.

Most Argyle supporters inside the stadium were blissfully unaware of the tragedy outside as they tuned up their larynges and practised their banner-waving in support of the Plymouth Pilgrims Ladies team, who took on their Darlington counterparts in a six-a-side contest for the Endsleigh Insurance Wembley Women's Cup.

Never before in the post-war history of women's football in this country can a match involving the fairer sex have been so partisanly supported. Certainly, the Pilgrims Ladies, more used to playing in front of the proverbial two supporters and a dog, had never experienced such a reception. However, they duly kept their half of a pre-match bargain to make the day a double celebration for Plymouth by prevailing in a tightly-fought contest.

Despite twice going behind, they levelled on both occasions through Angie Pope and

Entrance of the gladiators

eventually lifted the Cup after a prolonged nervous penalty-shoot out which ended when goalkeeper Julie Brealy converted her spot-kick.

"The crowd were brilliant," said delighted Pilgrims' captain Mandy McCann. "We could hear them and it really lifted us." The crowd was, though, merely warming up.

The women's victory was watched by players from both sides. The Argyle contingent had arrived at Wembley for the second time that day in their *Louis Bernard* blazers and club ties, having been wished on their way by their families.

"We met up with the wives and girlfriends for about a quarter of an hour, so that they could have all their little kisses and cuddles and all that," said Warnock. "I have always thought it is good for players to meet up with their families just before a big game."

While the Pilgrims Ladies were enjoying their moment of glory, their male counterparts who would provide the main attraction an hour later had returned to the North dressing-room to get stripped for the warm-up. Their exits and entrances down the Wembley tunnel around which the West Country fans were congregated were greeted with full-throated cheers.

Those on the periphery of the action – Keith Hill, Paul Wotton, Neil Illman, Danny O'Hagan and the unfortunate Gary Clayton – stayed suited while their erstwhile colleagues got booted, drinking in the by now incredible atmosphere and no doubt thinking what might have been – and what might yet still be – for them. As their active team-mates left the pitch to pull on their new green and white shirts, a stray ball bobbled towards Clayton, who had been watching proceedings standing to the side of one of the goals. Clayton thumped the ball into the net, unleashing with one hefty swipe the hidden, but pent-up, frustration at once again missing out on a Wembley match.

As kick-off time approached, the traditional build-up to the start of a football match, known and loved by supporters the world over, swung into gear. The teams were announced to cheers from one end and jeers from the other. No last-minute surprises from either camp, no pronunciation cock-ups from the the Wembley announcer – "Number Four, Ronnie Mo-jay."

The dignitaries took their place in the Royal Box: Argyle chairman Dan McCauley, wearing, as promised, his oversized stove-pipe hat; his fellow directors, Peter Bloom, Graham Jasper and new-boy Andy Dooley, waving to friends in the stands; the Pilgrims' much-loved president Sam Rendell; and dear old Footy.

Then, the arrival of the gladiators. Argyle, led out by Warnock and his daughter Natalie, play-off mascot for the second year in succession, matching her brother James' earlier double with Notts County. The commander and his off-spring were followed by his

Leading out the troops with daughter Natalie

sergeant-major, Mick Heathcote, as the Pilgrims' ranks filed out for the pre-match preliminaries: Steve Cherry, Mark Patterson, Paul Williams, Chris Curran, Richard Logan, Ronnie Maugé, Chris Leadbitter, Martin Barlow, Michael Evans, Adrian Littlejohn, and substitutes Carlo Corazzin, Chris Billy and Ian Baird.

Darlington, led by Jim Platt, who despite three appearances at Wembley for Northern Ireland, admitted his knees would be trembling when he emerged from the tunnel. For the third time in nine months, Argyle supporters took stock of a team which had beaten them twice. "A lot of opposing managers have said we are the best footballing side in the division," Platt had said, "so it will take a very good team to beat us at Wembley."

Platt had just one change of personnel to the Quakers' team which had faced Hereford in the second leg of their play-off semi-final, bringing in Anthony Carss for Matt Carmichael. They lined up with Paul Newell in goal, defending a record of having appeared on a losing side only twice since being released by Barnet the previous January; a defence of wing-backs Phil Brumwell, once of Sunderland, and Mark Barnard; and centre-backs Andy Crosby, a failed Leeds United trainee, and Sean Gregan, at 22, the club's longest-serving player.

Mattie Appleby, Darlington's player of the year would patrol the area in front of the back-four and behind a midfield trio of Gary Bannister, the possessor of a shrewd brain after years at the top level with Coventry, Sheffield Wednesday and QPR; Steve Gaughan, who would have joined Carlisle on transfer deadline-day had the Cumbrians not pulled out of the deal; and Carss, who left Blackburn's reserves for Feethams the previous summer. Up front were 12-goal Robbie Blake and former Chester, Maidstone and Burnley striker Robbie Painter, who had scored six goals in Darlington's final 12 games of the season. Only Painter and former Newcastle player Appleby had cost Platt money.

On the substitutes' bench were Carmichael, the former Doncaster striker; Gary Twynham, a Manchester United youth-team player signed after serving a prison sentence for grievous bodily harm; and Paul Mattison, who had already been granted a free transfer by the club though, presumably, a hat-trick in his final match might be enough to earn him another contract.

"The players deserve the credit," said Platt, who took sole control of Darlington's future after Director of Coaching David Hodgson, the former Liverpool striker, resigned the previous December. "They have been fantastic all season. It's the players who win matches, not the manager. This season has surprised everyone at the club. I would have been happy with a mid-table position but we have exceeded everything that was expected of us."

Platt had nevertheless been obliged to work within tight financial restraints as he sought to bring success to Feethams. He had, for instance, been forced to sell midfielder Gary Himsworth to York City for £25,000 during the Quakers' promotion challenge and replace him with a player whose wage requirements were not quite so draining on resources.

Darlington's achievement was sportingly recognised by Argyle skipper Heathcote, a North Easterner whose family had travelled the same roads to Wembley as the Quakers' outnumbered support. "Our chairman has been tremendous, giving the gaffer money to get the kind of players that he wants," he said, "but clubs like Darlington struggle to survive and for them to get to Wembley is a credit to themselves."

Despite his meticulous attention to detail in the build-up to the play-off final, Warnock realised that, right at the very last minute, he had overlooked something important. A hurried word to Kevin Blackwell followed and the Pilgrims' youth-team coach scurried back to the dressing-room and emerged a few seconds later clutching the commemorative Pilgrims pennant which Heathcote was to present to his Darlington counterpart before the toss of coin to decide which team kicked off.

Before the kick-off, and after the national anthem – during which Argyle's players kept a chilling eye-contact with their opponents a few yards across from them – the two teams were presented to Football League president Gordon McKeag, League secretary David Dent, and Ian Passmore, sales director of Endsleigh Insurance.

Then Heathcote and Crosby stood toe to toe in a centre-circle across which had been laid a giant vinyl logo of the Endsleigh owl, separated by Scarborough referee Bill Burns and his linesmen. Photographs followed, then the toss – Argyle would attack their own supporters at the Tunnel End for the first 45 minutes – then a pause, then, as the officials made their final checks, an anticipatory growl, which built up to a roar as the second-hand on Burns' watch ticked round to 3.00 p.m.

Thirty-thousand voices, a chorus of hope amidst a sea of green and white, united with the single purpose of waking the West Country's sleeping giant. The disappointment that would be felt if the religious war between the Quakers and the Pilgrims that was about to ensue ended in defeat would be almost palpable.

If anyone owned shoulders broad enough to bear that weight of expectation, it was surely Warnock, three times previously a play-off champion. Been there, seen it, done it, wanted to do it again. The preparations had been spot-on; the players were up for it; the fans were ready to shout themselves to a standstill. It was time for all Plymouth brethren to have faith.

"BETTER THAN ALL THE REST"

THE 1995/96 Endsleigh Insurance League Third Division play-off final between Plymouth Argyle and Darlington was never likely to be a free-flowing epic peppered by a myriad of scoring opportunities resulting in a glut of goals. Since conceding three goals at Hereford seven matches from the end of the season, Argyle's defence, stiffened by the inclusion of Chris Curran as a man-marker, had conceded only two spectacular goals to Mark Kinsella: in seven matches that preceded Darlington's topsy-turvy 3-3 draw at Scunthorpe, the Quakers' defence had been breached just twice.

Warnock's Green Machine idled unimpressively for the first 20 minutes as Darlington's butterflied stomachs settled quicker. The veteran Gary Bannister, whose only other Wembley appearance had been as a virtual spectator when his QPR side were beaten 3-0 by Oxford in the 1986 Milk Cup final, produced the Quakers' first – and, as it turned out, only – goal-bound effort in the second minute. However, Steve Cherry, drawing on the experience of his four previous games at the national stadium, dived to easily thwart the attempt.

For Argyle, only Michael Evans hit the ground running and it was the young Plymothian who first had his West Country kinfolk and their affiliates off their bucket seats after 10 minutes, when he threaded a pass through to fellow striker Adrian Littlejohn. Darlington's defence was momentarily nowhere as Littlejohn burst through, unchallenged, on goal but the ball from Evans arrived on his forward colleague's right foot – i. e. his wrong one – and Littlejohn trapped the ball further than most players can pass it.

Darlington nipped as Argyle tucked in, with neither side able to make headway against resolute five-man defences until the 22nd minute, when Mattie Appleby decided on the direct approach. Shrugging off half-hearted tackles, Appleby strode out from defence into Argyle's half, his lank, long locks flapping around his face.

His thrust ended with Bannister receiving the ball on the left of Argyle's goal as Appleby continued his run into the six-yard box. Bannister crossed to Appleby's feet but the player who demonstrated a deft touch on almost every blade of Wembley's turf found his skills had gone awol when he needed them most. With Cherry bereft and the goal proverbially yawning, Appleby swept the chance wide.

The shock of being inches away from losing parity proved to be the jolt to the system Argyle's players needed. Roared on by an overwhelming majority of a 43,431 crowd – more than 2,000 greater than the previous Division Three play-off final best – they gradually gained a foothold on the game.

Michael Evans gets over a cross

Chris Leadbitter matched Appleby's surge with a forceful sprint into a shooting position and steered his shot wide of the target, but close enough to fool Argyle supporters on the blind side of the goal into believing he had broken the deadlock.

Martin Barlow, who had to deal with the problem of being double-teamed by Darlington's well-briefed defenders, for once escaped the unwelcome attentions of his two markers, and delivered a cross which found its way to Evans. Evans blasted the opportunity over, but his error was mitigated by referee Bill Burns awarding a free-kick for a foul on goalkeeper Paul Newell.

Then Littlejohn, with the ball now on his favoured left peg, cut in from the left and tried to bend the ball around Newell. The ambition was not matched by the result, however, and the ball continued in a straight line past the far post, steadfastly refusing to dip or curl.

The unwanted incursion of a streaker, not wearing colours but apparently a Darlington fan, distracted from the stalemate, and the first half ended with neither side having been able to claim actual or moral superiority. Both defences had been well and truly on

Martin Barlow and Mattie Appleby clash after Adrian Littlejohn is wrestled to the floor

top of matters, especially at set-pieces, a fact which led to Warnock sending out his players for the second period with special instructions to obey when they next won a corner on the right-hand side.

It was another 20 minutes before the opportunity arose to test the Argyle manager's theory. Barlow, so often shown up a blind alley by his two ever-present markers, for once saw daylight and his run into the corner forced Darlington to concede a corner at the expense of an immediate cross.

The Quakers retreated smugly into their penalty area, confident of dealing with another of Leadbitter's slinging left-footers. Near post or far post, they had been guzzling them up all afternoon like kids let loose in an ice-cream factory.

Such naïvety caused their downfall. Arch-tactician Warnock had not been on the bench soaking up the atmosphere and counting the crowd. He, like Baldrick, had a cunning plan. Unlike Baldrick, his cunning plan worked.

Leadbitter shaped for another long-shot and Mark Patterson, feigning indifference, turned his back on the apparent move and ambled back, uninterested, towards the halfway line. Suddenly, the trap was sprung. Leadbitter played the ball along the ground to no-one in particular and Patterson turned on his heels and sprinted forward to collect the angled pass.

Without a moment to compose himself, he whipped in a first-time right-wing cross as Darlington's mug defenders responded too late to prevent his delivery. Three of them, who had been patrolling the near-post area, ran towards him, creating space in the penalty area. At the same time, Barlow, who had been hovering provocatively on the edge of the area, withdrew, drawing another marker out of position.

Into this space drifted Ronald Carlton Maugé, the man who owed his place in the Pilgrims' Wembley starting line-up to Gary Clayton's misfortune. So unsure was Maugé of his role in the planned set-piece, he had checked with Patterson as they emerged from the dressing-room, post lemon-quarters, of his precise role in the plot hatched by Warnock.

Patterson had put him right and into the space vacated by Barlow and the wandering Darlington defenders, drifted Ronnie-come-lately. Too late, the Quakers' defence realised they had been duped. Patterson's cross winged its way towards Maugé's shaven head with the

Yeeeeeeesssss! Ronnie Maugé's play-off winner

accuracy of a Polaris, and a red number four flashed between the opposition's gangly defenders with a perfect leap.

Leather connected with cranium and the ball looped past Newell, who could not have been more flat-footed if someone had wandered onto the pitch and placed anvils on his Reeboks.

Cue mayhem. Leadbitter and Patterson embraced on the touchline like reunited family members on *Surprise Surprise*, at the same time making it-blooming-well-worked gestures towards a hugely satisfied Warnock. Maugé, who has lumps of gold where others have canines, joined them in their ecstasy, smile glinting in the sun. Littlejohn and Barlow soon joined the celebration party. Baird turned round to Warnock on the bench and said: "You're a genius, boss."

All this was enacted first in uncomprehending silence, then, as the truth dawned on 30,000 people that Argyle, their Argyle, had taken the lead, a huge cacophony. Thirty-thousand fans stood up as one and roared – a great, primeval roar from the pit of 30,000 stomachs. "Yeeeeeeesssss!"

The subsequent scenes and sounds of unbridled joy emanating from the Tunnel End were simply awesome. Thirty-thousand individuals became one giant voice, one huge united mass of bubbling passionate emotion.

The goal and the reaction which greeted it, unhinged Darlington and unlocked their tight formation. Argyle soared in confidence and only once in the subsequent nerve-frayed, nail-biting 25 minutes did they look in danger of relinquishing their hold on the game. That came when the flap-eared Steve Gaughan for once evaded the attentions of Curran to reach the left-hand bye-line. His cross evaded everyone in the Argyle penalty area, but was too heavy and too imprecise for Painter, lurking at the far post while the Tunnel End held its collective breath, to get his head on.

The furious response of Painter to Gaughan's gaffe was indication enough that Darlington were rattled and they further demonstrated their loss of cool with a series of uncompromising tackles to which Patterson and Leadbitter stood up unflinchingly. With the onus on the Quakers to score, Argyle were content to keep them at arms' length and not gamble on doubling their lead.

Cherry plucked off a threatening, hanging cross by Phil Brumwell and then watched as a shot three minutes from time by substitute Matt Carmichael soared over his crossbar, to the relieved mocking of the Argyle supporters behind the goal. By this time, the Pilgrims had inflicted the final ignominy on the rivals as the North Easterners aborted their much-vaunted passing game in favour of the hopeful hoof.

Those horrible long-ball merchants Argyle, meanwhile, passed the ball around to keep possession. 88 minutes. A life-time. 89 minutes. An eternity. 90. The final whistle. Bedlam. Tears. Most importantly, promotion. "The Greens Are Going Up." The single goal, scored by the player who had opened Argyle's account under Warnock back at Tiverton in July, was enough.

Bill Burns' last blast on his whistle did not so much signal the end of a football match, more the beginning of the biggest football party Wembley had ever seen. The eruption of sheer pleasure which greeted the end of the match cranked the decibel-level a notch higher and the full-throated singing brought a lump the size of the match-ball to throats.

Mick went up to lift the Endsleigh Cup, Maugé knocked the lid off it ("you can tell I'm not used to picking up trophies," he said) and then the real partying began. Warnock and his players paraded the play-off trophy in front of a sea of green and white. The Wembley public address system spurred on the supporters. *We Are The Champions, Simply The Best*, more incongruously, *Rockin' All Over The World*. Argyle were, of course, neither the champions nor the best but to 30,000 people, it certainly felt like they were and, anyway, no-one has written a song entitled *Simply The Fourth Best Team In The Third Division*.

Heathcote briefly left the celebrations to seek out his seven-year-old son Liam and, after an entirely forgivable breach of Wembley security, waded into the crowd to present his son with his first winners' medal. "I have won nowt in my football career but I always said that if Dad won a medal one day, I would put it around his neck," he revealed.

Warnock and his players took the trophy from one side of the ground to the other, savouring the moment, their every wave and triumphant gesture meeting with a similar response from the giant green and white karaoke machine. *Better Than All The Rest. Semper Fidelis* just would not have sounded right.

They were joined on the pitch by behatted chairman Dan McCauley, his fellow directors Peter Bloom, Graham Jasper and Andy Dooley, and club president Sam Rendell, who had lived and breathed Argyle for many of his 83 years. McCauley and Jasper danced like they had not done for 30 years, and, amid the mayhem, the proud look of contentment on Rendell's face etched itself into the memories of the day.

Having waited for 110 years to reach Wembley, Argyle's fans were not about to let the

"Is this what you want?" Mick Heathcote and play-off trophy

moment disappear. They simply would not go home. Even when, after the best part of half-an-hour, Warnock decided his players' stiffening muscles would benefit from a hot bath, many Pilgrims stood gazing at the empty pitch, savouring every last minute, trying to fix the memories.

Out in the car and coach parks, complete strangers hugged each other as they headed for home on the long, satisfying journey back to the West Country. "I've been watching Argyle for 40 years and I've been waiting for this," said Brian Quance, on the Cornish Supporters' coach. "It's been brilliant, absolutely fantastic."

Outside the Twin Towers Jon Copp declared "It makes me proud to be a Plymothian" and everywhere the lucky talisman Warnock was being hailed as the hero. "He's the greatest," declared John Jesson, of Launceston. "With his sort of record, who needs automatic promotion?"

Mark Davies put the thoughts of many into words. "One day, I will be able to tell my grandchildren all about this," he declared. "When they say 'Grandad, are you being serious? Did Argyle really play at Wembley?' I can say, 'They did, they won and I was there'."

As the fans were acclaiming Warnock and his players, so they were being acclaimed. "I've never seen anything like it and the officials said they'd never seen anything like it," said Warnock. "To be in unison like they were, with all the scarves and flags in the air, and everything, was inspiring. They were magnificent."

Warnock's Mick Jones, a veteran of five previous Wembley appearances, was flabbergasted by the size and passion of the support. "When we walked out, I thought 'Blooming Heck.' I never thought I would see anything that surpassed the following we had at Huddersfield, but that took my breath away. I'm known as a calm and collected bloke but I got a little bit carried away at the end because I wanted to enjoy it. I did not expect the reception we got when we arrived at Wembley, I did not expect the volume of support, and I certainly did not expect that response at the end. I felt that if the music had kept playing and we had stayed on the pitch, we could have been there until midnight. The support, for our division, was absolutely phenomenal."

"I hope now that Wembley is a platform for this club becoming the club that everyone talks about. People seem frightened of the word 'potential' down here but I love it. I think it is a waste of time if you talk about it but can't realise it. Let's not talk about it, let's go and do it. All this talk bores me to tears."

Argyle chairman Dan McCauley was similarly moved by the Green Army. "When I saw our supporters staying there at the end, it brought tears to my eyes because you could tell how badly they wanted us to win. No way did they want to leave the stadium before our players went off."

Mick Jones, Argyle's Assistant Manager

Striker Michael Evans, the only true Plymothian on the pitch, was another to pay generous tribute. "Brilliant, fantastic," he said. "They didn't stop singing all day. We've been relegated twice in three years so it was nice to give them something to sing about."

And Evans' fellow Devonian Martin Barlow agreed the experience had left the pair of them speechless. "Absolutely brilliant," he said. "Me and Micky couldn't speak after the game, it was just so much."

Defenders Mick Heathcote, Richard Logan and Chris Curran also marvelled at the encouragement of the Green Army. "The fans were fantastic – they deserve a Premier League club," said Logan. "When there's 30,000 people cheering you do do well, you can't beat that feeling."

Curran concurred. "The fans were superb from start to finish," he said. "They played their part to a tee." And skipper Heathcote added his own praise. "They have stuck with us through thick and thin and deserve something," he said. "The response from the whole area has been tremendous and I'm thankful that we came away with the right result for them."

As the supporters queued for the Wembley Park tube and began the slow crawl around the North Circular, at the same time buzzing and relieved, the ritual post-match dissection of the game was beginning. The Argyle camp was firmly of the opinion that the game was won and lost in the 22nd minute.

Rarely can the difference between success and failure have been as little as six inches, but that was the distance by which Mattie Appleby missed the open target of the Argyle goal when, with the game goalless, it appeared easier to score. "We were off the bench," said opposition manager Jim Platt. "We thought it was in."

"I felt we would have lost the game if they had scored that one chance," said Warnock, "because every time we've played them, they've had the lift of a goal and that would have given them a massive lift. After that miss, I thought we'd win the game. We started playing when they missed that chance. I thought we weren't in the game until that moment."

Mark Patterson, who set up Golden Boy Ronnie Maugé's Wembley winner, revealed that the scorer of Argyle's historic Wembley goal had originally been unsure of his role in the set-piece which killed off Darlington. Maugé had filled a different role in short-corner routines when Argyle had used the ploy during the regular season and needed to double-check the fine details of the move after Warnock had called the play during the half-time interval.

Patterson said: "It's a corner we work on in training but, strangely enough, Ronnie's never normally in that position because he's usually further in the box to start with. As we were coming on the pitch before the second half, he was actually asking where he went when we played the move."

Patterson played his own role in the move, a precision right-foot cross following Chris Leadbitter's short-range pass. "We've been trying it all season. It's about time I knocked in a good cross," he said.

"The manager said they were vulnerable to that corner, and he was right," said Maugé, who, despite the conviction of the Pilgrims' supporters who were sure the whole move took place in slow-motion, revealed that his promotion-winning moment went by in a blur. "Everything happened so fast," he said. "It's a set-piece we practice in training, week in, week out, and it paid off. Sometimes when we've been practising it in the rain and the cold, you think, 'Oh gosh, do we have to do this again?' But it was all worth it."

Warnock had decided to call the play after seeing a succession of dead-ball opportunities go to waste in the first 45 minutes. "I wanted to try it because I thought it needed a bit of quickness of thought," he revealed. "We've worked on those corners for ages but we never seem to put them into operation in matches. The players seem to have a block on them. I said to the players 'I want the next corner on the right-hand side to be the one we've planned.' We've tried it a lot of times but Patto's hit a bad cross or one of the defenders has won the ball, but it gives you so much satisfaction when it comes off."

The all-important strike was also appreciated by McCauley, who said: "It was a cracking goal, an engineered one, you could tell that. I thought once we were in front we would win because Neil would never let it slip."

And assistant manager Jones hailed the tactic as a master stroke. "You have got to give Neil all the credit going," he said. "We discussed it and said we wasted our corners and free-kicks and that we needed to try something different. Mark delivered a great ball and Ronnie's header, well ... what can you say?" You could try "Yeeeeeeessss!"

The goal was the culmination of a remarkable turn around in fortunes for Eastender Maugé, who had not figured in Warnock's play-off plans when the post-season knock-out competition had begun at Colchester 13 days previously and would not have been considered for a Wembley start had Gary Clayton not been injured.

"You need luck in football and Ronnie's had a bit of luck," confirmed Warnock. "He wouldn't have been on the pitch if Clayts hadn't been injured. He came on as substitute against Colchester, got back in the side, and he's ended up scoring the winner at Wembley. He'll never forget that moment for the rest of his career, and yet he might not have been in the side. That's football."

Maugé, one of Warnock's first purchases when he took over at Home Park, had been dropped for a six-game spell towards end of the season after previously scoring seven goals in 43 games. He jokingly put his axing down to McCauley. "We had a bet before the season that I would score 10 goals," he grinned. "When I started getting near the target, I reckon he had a word with the boss to drop me."

Play-off final winner, Ronnie Maugé

However, Maugé had also gambled at the beginning of the season, leaving Bury, who subsequently pipped the Pilgrims to promotion by one point. "I always knew leaving Bury, who were a good team, was a gamble but, with Neil Warnock and his record, I knew Plymouth were going to win things. We deserve to be in a higher division because of all the hard work and preparation that the gaffer's put in with Mick Jones. Neil Warnock took a bit of a gamble himself by coming to Plymouth and a lot of the players are glad to have repaid him and the fans. The way we played, we were the better team and we deserved to win."

Jones was also delighted for Warnock. "When everyone was celebrating the goal, my eyes were fixed on the manager because he deserves the credit," he said. "He dictated the corner and deserves all the accolades going. That was pure management. That is what management is all about."

Warnock's preparations for the play-off final were also recognised by Darlington manager Jim Platt. "We didn't play as well as we can," he said in his soft Irish brogue, "but you have got to give the opposition credit. We like to play with the ball down and get it on the deck, and they didn't let us. They got tight and prevented us from doing what we wanted to do. Simple as that.

"It was the first time they had scored past us as well. Aw, nobody likes to lose but somebody has to lose and today it was us." Each sentence was

Team work – the Manager and Assistant Manager

punctuated with a pause and in every interval were heard the sounds of departing Devonians intent on singing themselves all the way south.

Despite winning his bet with Maugé, chairman McCauley was counting the cost of winning promotion. "I bribed them to win," joked McCauley. "I told them before the Colchester game that there would be a pre-season trip to America as part of the build-up for next season if they won, and they did it. It will be worth every penny."

Although Argyle would share gate-receipts from the record 43,431 crowd, McCauley revealed that much of the money would be quickly swallowed up. "People will say we made a lot of money from the play-offs but, although commercially it will go on and on, I've been adding up the figures and there are a lot of knock-ons. We've got to pay extra money to Bury for Maugé, and to Cambridge for Heathcote because we won promotion and there were promotion-clauses written into their contracts. The manager and his assistant also get bonuses and good luck to them. They deserve it because they've done what they said they would do. That's all we wanted. What a day it was. You have got to give Neil credit. I think he's got us up a year ahead of schedule. It's hard to get a team to gel so quickly. I know he had freedom to get what he wanted but it's not always easy."

Testimony to that season-long graft could be gleaned by one look at Warnock, the colour drained from his pallid face and the hoarseness of relief cracking his voice. "Somebody said to me 'How do you do this? What's the formula?' and I said 'It's bloody hard work'," he croaked. "Ten-month seasons! There's no secret ingredient to success. You've just got to work hard and be better than the other side. In every play-off final I've been in, we've been the best side. The preparation was spot-on. I badly wanted to win because I did not want to have another 10-month slog in the Third Division next season. Mick Jones and I have turned things around at this club through sheer hard work. Only three players playing today were at the club when I joined it in the summer. I have rebuilt the side the way I wanted to and I have had the full support of my chairman all through the season. We have generated £1m in revenue, yet we have only spent £650,000 on players. Now that's what I call good business. I think the chairman is happy.

"I feel tired, I must admit. I'm looking forward to a long, long rest and plenty of fishing. In my contract it says I've got 42 days holiday and I think I'll have every one of them."

However, Warnock's busy day did not end with the reception for his conquering team in the Olympic Suite. He had to rush back to Plymouth later that night to be with his 10-year-old daughter Natalie, who had fallen ill. "It was tough for her, being our mascot," he said. "There has been a lot of pressure on everyone – players, management and supporters alike. I think it was just the emotion of the day."

As he arrived in the city at around midnight, the party which had begun a few hours earlier in London was still in full swing. Knots of Pilgrims' fans stood on street corners, waving flags, singing; cars were driven around to nowhere in particular, horns pumping, lights flashing. It was enough to wake a sleeping giant.

When she recovered, young Natalie would have a host of happy memories to look back on, as would 30,000 supporters and the players they had cheered to the echo for more than two hours.

Goalscorer Maugé – "It's always nice to win, but to win at Wembley and score the winner gives you a feeling I can't begin to explain. It has to be the most important goal I've ever scored."

Captain Heathcote – "Wembley is a special place and I'm sure it will be a day which sticks in everyone's memory for a long, long time."

Plymothian Evans – "It was fantastic, really enjoyable. I had a few nerves walking up the tunnel but once the game started, I was fine" – and his fellow Devonian Barlow – "You dream about playing and winning at Wembley but you never really think it's going to happen. It's brilliant."

However, even basking in the shallows of success, Warnock was not about to look for some laurels on which to rest. Having explored new waters by taking Argyle to Wembley for the first time, he revealed he wanted to guide them to the previously uncharted territory of the FA Premiership.

"I enjoyed my year at the top with Notts County and I'm still ambitious to manage in the Premiership," he said. "I believe it's not too late.

"People talk to me about the P-word when looking at Plymouth Argyle and I've never mentioned the word until today but let me tell them – we *do* have the potential to go all the way.

"I was told I lacked ambition when I came to Home Park – I was probably the first manager to win promotion to the First Division and end up in the Third – but we are not that far way from having a super side.

"We might need to bring in a couple more players but once we get the level of consistency we lacked at the start of the season, there's no reason why this club cannot climb higher."

The governor's forward planning was immediately, and harmoniously, backed by his right-hand man. "If this club is going to realise that potential, Wembley is the platform," said Mick Jones. "Let's go and do it."

As they spoke, you swore you could hear thousands of voices on coaches and cars clogging the M5 and A38 with green; on the Pilgrim Express trains passing through Taunton and Newton Abbot; 2,500 feet up Australia's Great Dividing Range; on a Type 23 frigate in the Caribbean; and in sitting-rooms across the West Country with radios tuned into Plymouth Sound and BBC Radio Devon roar their assent.

"Greeeeeen Armeeeeee!"

NW: I woke up at six o'clock on the morning of the final and couldn't get back to sleep. Once again I made sure that we all met at 10 o'clock. We went and put the kit out and a few players came with us. They took their cameras and took some shots of Wembley. Natalie and James came as well. Then we walked back to the hotel, which was good because all the fans were arriving by then and it was only 11 o'clock – unbelievable! It was going to be a tremendous afternoon.

Narino, the chef at the Hilton, has been in charge for the four times I have been there for the play-offs and he has been first class. I always have a fillet steak before the game at Wembley at lunchtime. I don't have any breakfast – just a fillet steak on its own – and it is always perfect.

I asked the players to meet me at 1.10 p.m. in their room with a video so we could just show the highlights of Darlington versus Hereford, first and second legs. Would you believe it, the scout who taped it for me had taped it on long play, so it was like watching Whacky Races going around, so we had a laugh and I said: "I don't want to talk about Darlington, anyhow. Let's get on with ourselves."

The wives arrived on time and we got one or two telegrams, then I told the players at one o'clock they could go and see their partners for 15 minutes and we would be setting off at 1.15 p.m. It took me about 10 minutes to sort the bill out, so we left at around 1.25 p.m., which was ideal really.

I know it sounds daft but we were watching the women's football beforehand and it was close. Darlington scored first against Plymouth, and then Plymouth equalised and

With lucky mascot Narino at the Wembley Hilton

they won on penalties in the end and I really wanted them to win. You know how superstitious I am – last year Huddersfield beat Plymouth women and I was ever so pleased and I thought it was a good sign. Our goalkeeper scored a decisive penalty. She doesn't know how chuffed I was.

Wembley was filling up by then so I went back down, got changed out of my blazer and into my kit to do the warm-up. I forgot all about taking the team-sheet in and they came knocking on the door about two minutes later for the team-sheet. I never even thought about it. I apologised when I got up there with Micky Heathcote.

I got organised for the warm-up and then got changed again, back into my blazer and walked out. I had a white rose in my lapel, but I snapped the white rose as I was walking up the tunnel and ended up with just a leaf. So I had to take that out of the lapel and then I held hands with Natalie walking up the tunnel.

I said to her then that I was ever so nervous and she said: "Do you know? I am. I feel a bit nervous this year." And I said it must run in the family.

I thought it was super. Looking around, I saw all the green and white flags, it was unbelievable. And said a little prayer. I think everybody prays at some stage, don't they?

I felt the players were right. I thought the preparation was good and I could see that their eyes looked bright, but after they had been presented I got them all together again in a circle and had a quick chat with them about the importance of the game. But, to be fair, when the referee blew the whistle I was just glad we didn't go behind in the first quarter of an hour because there were five or six of them who were just a little bit nervous. We were not ourselves at all.

It was brilliant sunshine and I had walked out in my blazer and slacks, but as I had done in the past I quickly changed in the disabled toilet situated in the tunnel and took my place on the bench. It was red-hot, and obviously I just had my shirt sleeves on.

Anyhow, we were so bad after 20 minutes I convinced myself that I had to put my jumper back on because we had done well with my jumper on previously. So I put my jumper back on over my shirt, even though it was red-hot and I was sweating cobs. However, I had convinced myself that things would change, and I must admit I felt happier after doing that.

I thought the turning point came after about 25 minutes. They had a great chance and shot wide. And I thought to myself then "I think that was their chance, I think we will win it now."

I was still glad when the half-time whistle went and I could have a chat with one or two lads. We changed one or two things but don't get me wrong, I was pleased – we had weathered the storm and I thought we were going to get stronger.

I told them that once again I thought we were the best side in the league, let alone just the play-offs, and it was the time they showed it as a team. No individuals, just show it as a team. We had got to grind them down.

I said to the lads that the next corner we got on the right wing, I wanted us to use the one we had done on set-pieces where Mark Patterson comes up. I said I wanted us to use that one just to vary it because the goalkeeper had done quite well from some of the corners. Little did I know that that corner-kick was going to win us the game and when it went in, you couldn't have got a prouder person than me.

To see your free-kicks go like that was tremendous and obviously to tell your players at half-time "This is what I want" and to see it come off is unbelievable.

I didn't really think Darlington were going to come back into it and when the whistle went, it was just tremendous. Obviously so many things go through your mind, you've got 10 months' hard work rolled into 90 minutes, it is very hard to describe. And fortunately for me, I have never tasted defeat at Wembley.

The euphoria is unbelievable. The crowd, I can't describe. I talked to some officials at Wembley itself and they said they have never heard anything like it. To stay behind like that, I don't know who thought about putting the song on, but Simply The Best was unbelievable and everybody joined in. I think one of the most exciting times was seeing all the fans singing Simply The Best.

I hope they've got it on video because it was so special. In fact I remember seeing Sam Rendell after the game. I had a laugh with his wife Gwen, because she had always wanted Semper Fidelis back and when they were singing Simply The Best, I said to Sam: "You are not going to sing to Semper Fidelis next year you know," and he smiled.

It was smashing to see Sam on the pitch – a lovely man, one of the best gentlemen. You can't praise him any more as a gentleman. He is top of the list – you couldn't really wish to meet a nicer bloke and I made sure at the end that he had his photograph taken with the cup.

At least Sam had seen his team play at Wembley.

I think everybody that came from Plymouth will remember the day for the rest of their lives. I found it quite incredible, really.

When Mick Jones came on the pitch after the game we just celebrated after we got the award. When he saw the cup he said to me: "Oh, let's run over there to them, look at that lot." It just wasn't like him at all. And I said: "Come on, you deserve it."

So we picked the cup up between us and ran towards the far side of the supporters and it was a great moment for us, but it just wasn't like Mick at all to finally let go of his emotions.

Yet I remember going down after all the interviews from television and radio had finished. By the time I got in, most of the lads were coming out. The bath at Wembley is about six foot deep. Mick Jones and myself went in there and I said "I don't give a damn if I stop in here an hour, mate." We had a long soak and then I had 10 minutes on my own in the bath, and everything went around in my head.

Those moments when you can get yourself together like that are very special as a manager. Obviously I was proud, the lads had done me well, but more so it meant so much to the supporters. I remember saying to the chairman on the pitch "What a fantastic support" and he was overwhelmed and said that he had never seen anything like it.

"Greeeeen Armeeeeee!"

One or two Press guys said about me being ambitious and did I want to manage in the Premier League? I said: "Yes, of course I do, and at this moment in time I have got nothing else on my mind except managing Plymouth, and trying to get them higher."

I must admit I felt very, very tired as I went into the Press conference. It was not like me at all really, but I think everything had just got to me a bit and I just felt emotionally drained.

I made up my mind that I wasn't going to have an alcoholic drink until I got onto the bus, and I took a couple of bottles of water up to meet Sharon and the kids.

We ended up leaving Wembley at about 6.45 p.m. and I knew the journey back would be good. All the lads were a different class on the bus. I telephoned the New Continental hotel and asked if we could pop in. All the wives wanted to go for a drink when we got back. Being in Plymouth, it would be midnight before we got back. They said we could go in for a drink. We only stopped for 10 minutes, because we were travelling to Scotland the next day after the Civic Reception.

I must admit, I wouldn't have minded going straight home and straight to bed. I felt that tired. I don't think anybody can realise what being a football manager is like. You are there, you get slated. If you are a supporter, you can shout at me, you can call me names, you can do what you want. I feel as if I have got the responsibility of so many thousands of people.

While I love the job, really I think you have got to be a certain type of person. You have got to have a broad back. Some of the letters I have had have been a disgrace really, but there again, I had quite a few letters from supporters saying "Don't listen to the minority, most of us are right behind you." And they went down well.

One guy who had a right humdinger in front of the dug-out had the cheek to write to me afterwards, having a go and saying that he thought he deserved some free tickets to watch a match. I wonder if he went to Wembley? No doubt he will be waiting until we have the next bad time to start again.

But that is what makes football so special and that is why managers, if you are going to stay at the level we are talking about, have got to be able to take it. Even though now and then, I react like I do. I think you have got to show that bit of passion, haven't you?

What pleased me more than anything today was that I have been in play-offs four times now and I have won every one because every time I have been in the play-offs we have had the best team on the day. Perhaps it's motivation.

Even today someone said to me what a lucky man I am. I don't think you get lucky four times but I tell you one thing, I wouldn't like to play against one of my sides.

Somebody said to me in the Press conference, you have always said that Scarborough was your biggest achievement, when you took them up from the non-league. And I said "Yes, and I don't think that will ever be beaten."

Anyhow, I sat down on the bus coming back with Mick Jones and we went through what had happened since we came to Plymouth to do what we had to do. When you saw the crowd at Wembley, this had possibly been my biggest achievement in such a short space of time, the space of 12 months.

What we did was incredible, so I think, at the end of the day, I would say that it had become the greatest achievement of my career, even surpassing Scarborough.

"TEN MONTHS, 90 MINUTES, 30 SECONDS"

NW: *I woke up on the Sunday morning after the final and looked out of the window. It was absolutely pouring down with rain and I thought to myself, "At least we had nice weather yesterday for the game."*

The journey home had been great. Obviously the lads were in high spirits. All the squad came back on the bus and all the vehicles went past, with scarves hanging from windows and horns hooting. I was shattered and remember having a little bit of a sleep at one stage. Then, about an hour before we pulled in, I turned off what you could call their "modern" music and just went to the back of the bus and said to them:

"Look lads, just a bit of quiet now. I would just like to say to all of you, a big thank you for the day. You have made me very, very proud today to be in charge of Plymouth Argyle and all you lads.

"We have had our disagreements over the 10 months, but you have all played a part one way or another. I am sure you will never forget it. I won't forget it and there are probably 50,000 or 60,000 people who will never forget it and at least 30,000 who have been watching us.

"You have worked hard all season, but you have stuck to your task. And now I want you all to have a good summer, and get ready. At least we will not be favourites next year.

"I think you all have room for improvement, but at this moment in time I just want to thank you all for the commitment and effort that you have put in over these last 10 months of the season."

And that was it, I went back down to the front of the bus.

When we got back to Plymouth we went to the New Continental for a drink, but within 10 minutes Natalie was sick so we went off home. We got home about 12.45 a.m. and then she was sick in the night and the following morning, so she had to stay at home with James while we went to the Civic Reception.

It was a marvellous occasion, an open-top bus from Home Park. I took my own video camera to capture the moments and took a few shots. It was good and the support outside the council chambers was very, very good.

The only thing about the weekend that saddened me was that one of our fans was taken to hospital and eventually died. Even an occasion like the reception, which was a super occasion for all the families, had to have a down-side to it.

There is one particular family in Plymouth who won't have good memories about us getting to Wembley and that saddens me. My condolences go out to the family of the fan.

It pleased me when I thought back to all the critical letters I received throughout the season. Some rude, some abusive, some downright vicious – there are some warped minds around, aren't there? It pleased me that those people would have gone to Wembley, praising the team. They know who I am talking about.

Because of the reception, I missed the start of our holiday with the kids. We were supposed to be going on the Saturday to Scotland, so we drove up, starting about 4.30 p.m. on the Sunday afternoon. At least we would have some time up there to get our thoughts together after all the euphoria and switch our minds off a bit.

We decided we had got to stop off overnight. Natalie was not too clever, so we decided to pull off at Kendal. By this time it was about 10.20 p.m. and we said we would go to the first hotel. We had to go right into Kendal and eventually we found a hotel which could let us have one room between us.

When we got there, there was a double-bed and a single-bed and we managed to get a put-up bed, but James just wasn't very comfortable.

We had a scotch and James had a lager, and he ended up sleeping in the bath with all his clothes on. Next morning I said: "After the first day of getting promotion to the Second Division – it's from Wembley and champagne to half a lager and sleeping in the bath. Nothing but success for the Warnocks!"

A final thought. As I prepared to leave the Wembley dressing-room, there was just me and this old boy in there. Terry. I knew him well. I'd seen him every time I'd been there. He'd probably been there since Wembley was built. He walked out and said: "Well, Neil, I will no doubt see you again," and just smiled. I said: "Four in six years is enough, isn't it?" And he said "Who can say in this game?" And the door closed.

I was left there looking around the Wembley dressing room, all the litter, rubbish and drinks spread around, the cup at one side of me, and just for that moment – it must have been only 30 seconds – I just closed my eyes. Everything you have read about in this book went through my mind in the space of those 30 seconds.

Ten months, 90 minutes, 30 seconds. What a season!

IAN BAIRD
Forward/midfielder
Date of birth: 1.4.64 (Rotherham)
Previous clubs: Southampton, Cardiff (loan), Southampton, Newcastle (l). Leeds, Portsmouth, Leeds, Middlesbrough, Hearts, Bristol City
League appearances (max 46): 24 (+3 as sub)
League goals: 5
Play-off appearances (max 3): 0
Play-off goals: 0
FA Cup appearances (max 3): 1 (+1)
FA Cup goals: 1
Coca-Cola Cup appearances (max 2): 0
Coca-Cola Cup goals: 0
Auto Windscreens Shield appearances (max 2): 0
Auto Windscreens Shield goals: 0
Total appearances (max 56): 25 (+4)
Total goals: 6

CHRIS BILLY
Midfielder/forward
Date of birth: 2.1.73 (Huddersfield)
Previous clubs: Huddersfield
League appearances: 19 (+10)
League goals: 4
Play-off appearances: 1
Play-off goals: 0
FA Cup appearances: 3
FA Cup goals: 0
Coca-Cola Cup appearances: 2
Coca-Cola Cup goals: 0
Auto Windscreens Shield appearances: 1
Auto Windscreens Shield goals: 0
Total appearances: 26 (+10)
Total goals: 4

WAYNE BURNETT
Midfielder
Date of birth: 4.9.71 (London)
Previous clubs: Leyton Orient, Blackburn
League appearances: 6
League goals: 0
Play-off appearances: 0
Play-off goals: 0
FA Cup appearances: 0
FA Cup goals: 0
Coca-Cola Cup appearances: 2
Coca-Cola Cup goals: 0
Auto Windscreens Shield appearances: 0
Auto Windscreens Shield goals: 0
Total appearances: 8
Total goals: 0

MARTIN BARLOW
Midfielder
Date of birth: 26.6.71 (Barnstaple)
Previous clubs: Trainee
League appearances: 25 (+3)
League goals: 5
Play-off appearances: 3
Play-off goals: 0
FA Cup appearances: 0
FA Cup goals: 0
Coca-Cola Cup appearances: 0
Coca-Cola Cup goals: 0
Auto Windscreens Shield appearances: 1
Auto Windscreens Shield goals: 0
Total appearances: 29 (+3)
Total goals: 5

KEVIN BLACKWELL
Goalkeeper
Date of birth: 21.12.58 (Luton)
Previous clubs: Boston, Barnet, Scarborough, Notts County, Torquay, Huddersfield
League appearances: 20
League goals: 0
Play-off appearances: 0
Play-off goals: 0
FA Cup appearances: 3
FA Cup goals: 0
Coca-Cola Cup appearances: 0
Coca-Cola Cup goals: 0
Auto Windscreens Shield appearances: 0
Auto Windscreens Shield goals: 0
Total appearances: 23
Total goals: 0

STEVE CHERRY
Goalkeeper
Date of birth: 5.8.60 (Nottingham)
Previous clubs: Derby, Port Vale (l), Walsall, Plymouth Argyle, Chesterfield (l), Notts County, Watford
League appearances: 16
League goals: 0
Play-off appearances: 3
Play-off goals: 0
FA Cup appearances: 0
FA Cup goals: 0
Coca-Cola Cup appearances: 0
Coca-Cola Cup goals: 0
Auto Windscreens Shield appearances: 0
Auto Windscreens Shield goals: 0
Total appearances: 19
Total goals: 0

GARY CLAYTON
Midfielder
Date of birth: 2.2.63 (Sheffield)
Previous clubs: Burton, Doncaster, Cambridge United, Peterborough (l), Huddersfield
League appearances: 32 (+4)
League goals: 2
Play-off appearances: 0
Play-off goals: 0
FA Cup appearances: 2
FA Cup goals: 0
Coca-Cola Cup appearances: 2
Coca-Cola Cup goals: 0
Auto Windscreens Shield appearances: 1
Auto Windscreens Shield goals: 0
Total appearances: 37 (+4)
Total goals: 2

CHRIS CURRAN
Defender
Date of birth: 17.9.71 (Birmingham)
Previous club: Torquay
League appearances: 6 (+2)
League goals: 0
Play-off appearances: 3
Play-off goals: 0
FA Cup appearances: 0
FA Cup goals: 0
Coca-Cola Cup appearances: 0
Coca-Cola Cup goals: 0
Auto Windscreens Shield appearances: 0
Auto Windscreens Shield goals: 0
Total appearances: 9 (+2)
Total goals: 0

JAMES DUNGEY
Goalkeeper
Date of birth: 7.2.78 (Plymouth)
Previous clubs: Trainee
League appearances: 0
League goals: 0
Play-off appearances: 0
Play-off goals: 0
FA Cup appearances: 0
FA Cup goals: 0
Coca-Cola Cup appearances: 0
Coca-Cola Cup goals: 0
Auto Windscreens Shield appearances: 1
Auto Windscreens Shield goals: 0
Total appearances: 1
Total goals: 0

CARLO CORAZZIN
Forward
Date of birth: 25.12.71 (Canada)
Previous clubs: Vancouver 86ers, Cambridge United
League appearances: 1 (+5)
League goals: 1
Play-off appearances: 0 (+1)
Play-off goals: 0
FA Cup appearances: 0
FA Cup goals: 0
Coca-Cola Cup appearances: 0
Coca-Cola Cup goals: 0
Auto Windscreens Shield appearances: 0
Auto Windscreens Shield goals: 0
Total appearances: 1 (+6)
Total goals: 1

SIMON DAWE
Midfielder
Date of birth: 16.3.77 (Plymouth)
Previous clubs: Trainee
League appearances: 0
League goals: 0
Play-off appearances: 0
Play-off goals: 0
FA Cup appearances: 0
FA Cup goals: 0
Coca-Cola Cup appearances: 0
Coca-Cola Cup goals: 0
Auto Windscreens Shield appearances: 0 (+1)
Auto Windscreens Shield goals: 0
Total appearances: 0 (+1)
Total goals: 0

MICHAEL EVANS
Forward
Date of birth: 1.1.73 (Plymouth)
Previous clubs: None, but had loan spell with Blackburn
League appearances: 41 (+4)
League goals: 12
Play-off appearances: 3
Play-off goals: 1
FA Cup appearances: 3
FA Cup goals: 0
Coca-Cola Cup appearances: 0 (+1)
Coca-Cola Cup goals: 0
Auto Windscreens Shield appearances: 2
Auto Windscreens Shield goals: 0
Total appearances: 49 (+5)
Total goals: 13

NICKY HAMMOND
Goalkeeper
Date of birth: 7.9.67 (Hornchurch)
Previous clubs: Arsenal, Bristol Rovers (l),
Peterborough (l), Aberdeen (l), Swindon
League appearances: 4
League goals: 0
Play-off appearances: 0
Play-off goals: 0
FA Cup appearances: 0
FA Cup goals: 0
Coca-Cola Cup appearances: 2
Coca-Cola Cup goals: 0
Auto Windscreens Shield appearances: 1
Auto Windscreens Shield goals: 0
Total appearances: 7
Total goals: 0

KEITH HILL
Defender
Date of birth: 17.5.69 (Bolton)
Previous club: Blackburn
League appearances: 21 (+2)
League goals: 0
Play-off appearances: 0
Play-off goals: 0
FA Cup appearances: 3
FA Cup goals: 0
Coca-Cola Cup appearances: 2
Coca-Cola Cup goals: 0
Auto Windscreens Shield appearances: 2
Auto Windscreens Shield goals: 0
Total appearances: 28 (+2)
Total goals: 0

CHRIS LEADBITTER
Midfielder
Date of birth: 17.10.67 (Middlesbrough)
Previous clubs: Grimsby, Hereford, Cam-
bridge United, Bournemouth
League appearances: 29 (+4)
League goals: 1
Play-off appearances: 3
Play-off goals: 1
FA Cup appearances: 3
FA Cup goals: 1
Coca-Cola Cup appearances: 0
Coca-Cola Cup goals: 0
Auto Windscreens Shield appearances: 1
(+1)
Auto Windscreens Shield goals: 0
Total appearances: 36 (+5)
Total goals: 3

MICK HEATHCOTE
Defender
Date of birth: 10.9.65 (Durham)
Previous clubs: Sunderland, Hailfax (l), York
(l), Shrewsbury, Cambridge United
League appearances: 44
League goals: 4
Play-off appearances: 3
Play-off goals: 0
FA Cup appearances: 3
FA Cup goals: 1
Coca-Cola Cup appearances: 2
Coca-Cola Cup goals: 1
Auto Windscreens Shield appearances: 1
Auto Windscreens Shield goals: 0
Total appearances: 53
Total goals: 6

DOUG HODGSON
Defender
Date of birth: 27.2.69 (Frankston, Australia)
Previous clubs: Heidelberg, Sheffield United
(who loaned him to Argyle)
League appearances: 3 (+2)
League goals: 0
Play-off appearances: 0
Play-off goals: 0
Cup appearances: 0
FA Cup goals: 0
Coca-Cola Cup appearances: 0
Coca-Cola Cup goals: 0
Auto Windscreens Shield appearances: 0
Auto Windscreens Shield goals: 0
Total appearances: 3 (+2)
Total goals: 0

ADRIAN LITTLEJOHN
Forward
Date of birth: 26.9.70 (Wolverhampton)
Previous clubs: West Brom, Walsall, Shef-
field United
League appearances: 40 (+2)
League goals: 17
Play-off appearances: 3
Play-off goals: 0
FA Cup appearances: 3
FA Cup goals: 1
Coca-Cola Cup appearances: 2
Coca-Cola Cup goals: 0
Auto Windscreens Shield appearances: 0
Auto Windscreens Shield goals: 0
Total appearances: 48 (+2)
Total goals: 18

RICHARD LOGAN
Defender/midfielder
Date of birth: 24.5.69 (Barnsley)
Previous clubs: Gainsborough, Huddersfield
League appearances: 25 (+5)
League goals: 4
Play-off appearances: 3
Play-off goals: 0
FA Cup appearances: 1 (+2)
FA Cup goals: 0
Coca-Cola Cup appearances: 0
Coca-Cola Cup goals: 0
Auto Windscreens Shield appearances: 1
Auto Windscreens Shield goals: 0
Total appearances: 30 (+7)
Total goals: 4

KEVIN MAGEE
Midfielder
Date of birth: 10.4.71 (Edinburgh)
Previous clubs: Armadale, Partick, Preston
League appearances: 0 (+5)
League goals: 0
Play-off appearances: 0
Play-off goals: 0
FA Cup appearances: 0 (+1)
FA Cup goals: 0
Coca-Cola Cup appearances: 0
Coca-Cola Cup goals: 0
Auto Windscreens Shield appearances: 1
Auto Windscreens Shield goals: 0
Total appearances: 1 (+6)
Total goals: 0

KEVIN NUGENT
Forward
Date of birth: 10.4.69 (Edmonton, London)
Previous clubs: Leyton Orient, Cork City
(l)
League appearances: 4 (+1)
League goals: 0
Play-off appearances: 0
Play-off goals: 0
FA Cup appearances: 0
FA Cup goals: 0
Coca-Cola Cup appearances: 2
Coca-Cola Cup goals: 0
Auto Windscreens Shield appearances: 1
Auto Windscreens Shield goals: 0
Total appearances: 7 (+1)
Total goals: 0

STEVE McCALL
Midfielder
Date of birth: 15.10.60 (Carlisle)
Previous clubs: Ipswich, Sheffield Wednesday, Carlisle (l)
League appearances: 2 (+2)
League goals: 0
Play-off appearances: 0
Play-off goals: 0
FA Cup appearances: 0
FA Cup goals: 0
Coca-Cola Cup appearances: 0
Coca-Cola Cup goals: 0
Auto Windscreens Shield appearances: 0
Auto Windscreens Shield goals: 0
Total appearances: 2 (+2)
Total goals: 0

RONNIE MAUGE
Midfielder
Date of birth: 10.3.69. (Islington)
Previous clubs: Charlton, Fulham, Bury, Manchester City (l)
League appearances: 39 (+1)
League goals: 7
Play-off appearances: 2 (+1)
Play-off goals: 1
FA Cup appearances: 3
FA Cup goals: 0
Coca-Cola Cup appearances: 2
Coca-Cola Cup goals: 0
Auto Windscreens Shield appearances: 1
Auto Windscreens Shield goals: 0
Total appearances: 47 (+2)
Total goals: 8

DANNY O'HAGAN
Forward
Date of birth: 24.4.76 (Padstow)
Previous clubs: Trainee
League appearances: 0 (+6)
League goals: 0
Play-off appearances: 0
Play-off goals: 0
FA Cup appearances: 0
FA Cup goals: 0
Coca-Cola Cup appearances: 0 (+1)
Coca-Cola Cup goals: 0
Auto Windscreens Shield appearances: 0
Auto Windscreens Shield goals: 0
Total appearances: 0 (+7)
Total goals: 0

SCOTT PARTRIDGE
Forward
Date of birth: 13.10.74 (Leicester)
Previous clubs: Bradford, Bristol City (who loaned him to Argyle), Torquay (l)
League appearances: 6 (+1)
League goals: 2
Play-off appearances: 0
Play-off goals: 0
FA Cup appearances: 0
FA Cup goals: 0
Coca-Cola Cup appearances: 0
Coca-Cola Cup goals: 0
Auto Windscreens Shield appearances: 0
Auto Windscreens Shield goals: 0
Total appearances: 6 (+1)
Total goals: 2

IAN PAYNE
Midfielder
Date of birth: 19.1.77 (Crawley)
Previous clubs: Trainee
League appearances: 0
League goals: 0
Play-off appearances: 0
Play-off goals: 0
FA Cup appearances: 0
FA Cup goals: 0
Coca-Cola Cup appearances: 0
Coca-Cola Cup goals: 0
Auto Windscreens Shield appearances: 0 (+1)
Auto Windscreens Shield goals: 0
Total appearances: 0 (+1)
Total goals: 0

DOMINIC RICHARDSON
Forward
Date of birth: 19.3.78 (Plymouth)
Previous clubs: Trainee
League appearances: 0
League goals: 0
Play-off appearances: 0
Play-off goals: 0
FA Cup appearances: 0
FA Cup goals: 0
Coca-Cola Cup appearances: 0
Coca-Cola Cup goals: 0
Auto Windscreens Shield appearances: 0 (+2)
Auto Windscreens Shield goals: 0
Total appearances: 0 (+2)
Total goals: 0

MARK PATTERSON
Defender
Date of birth: 13.9.68 (Leeds)
Previous clubs: Carlisle, Derby
League appearances: 42 (+1)
League goals: 0
Play-off appearances: 3
Play-off goals: 0
FA Cup appearances: 2
FA Cup goals: 0
Coca-Cola Cup appearances: 1
Coca-Cola Cup goals: 0
Auto Windscreens Shield appearances: 1
Auto Windscreens Shield goals: 0
Total appearances: 49 (+1)
Total goals: 0

ANDY PETTERSON
Goalkeeper
Date of birth: 26.9.69 (Fremantle, Australia)
Previous clubs: Luton, Swindon (l), Ipswich (l, twice), Charlton (who loaned him to Argyle), Bradford (l)
League appearances: 6
League goals: 0
Play-off appearances: 0
Play-off goals: 0
FA Cup appearances: 0
FA Cup goals: 0
Coca-Cola Cup appearances: 0
Coca-Cola Cup goals: 0
Auto Windscreens Shield appearances: 0
Auto Windscreens Shield goals: 0
Total appearances: 6
Total goals: 0

MICKY ROSS
Forward
Date of birth: 2.9.71 (Southampton)
Previous clubs: Portsmouth, Exeter
League appearances: 0
League goals: 0
Play-off appearances: 0
Play-off goals: 0
FA Cup appearances: 0
FA Cup goals: 0
Coca-Cola Cup appearances: 0
Coca-Cola Cup goals: 0
Auto Windscreens Shield appearances: 2
Auto Windscreens Shield goals: 0
Total appearances: 2
Total goals: 0

MARK SAUNDERS
Midfielder
Date of birth: 23.7.71 (Reading)
Previous club: Tiverton
League appearances: 4 (+5)
League goals: 1
Play-off appearances: 0
Play-off goals: 0
FA Cup appearances: 0 (+1)
FA Cup goals: 0
Coca-Cola Cup appearances: 0 (+1)
Coca-Cola Cup goals: 0
Auto Windscreens Shield appearances: 0
Auto Windscreens Shield goals: 0
Total appearances: 4 (+7)
Total goals: 1

CHRIS TWIDDY
Midfielder
Date of birth: 19.1.76 (Pontypridd)
Previous clubs: Trainee
League appearances: 1 (+1)
League goals: 0
Play-off appearances: 0
Play-off goals: 0
FA Cup appearances: 0 (+1)
FA Cup goals: 0
Coca-Cola Cup appearances: 1
Coca-Cola Cup goals: 0
Auto Windscreens Shield appearances: 1 (+1)
Auto Windscreens Shield goals: 0
Total appearances: 3 (+3)
Total goals: 0

PAUL WOTTON
Defender
Date of birth: 17.8.77 (Plymouth)
Previous clubs: Trainee
League appearances: 0 (+1)
League goals: 0
Play-off appearances: 0
Play-off goals: 0
FA Cup appearances: 0
FA Cup goals: 0
Coca-Cola Cup appearances: 0
Coca-Cola Cup goals: 0
Auto Windscreens Shield appearances: 2
Auto Windscreens Shield goals: 0
Total appearances: 2 (+1)
Total goals: 0

SAM SHILTON
Midfielder
Date of birth: 21.7.78 (Nottingham)
Previous clubs: Trainee
League appearances: 0 (+1)
League goals: 0
Play-off appearances: 0
Play-off goals: 0
FA Cup appearances: 0
FA Cup goals: 0
Coca-Cola Cup appearances: 0
Coca-Cola Cup goals: 0
Auto Windscreens Shield appearances: 0
Auto Windscreens Shield goals: 0
Total appearances: 0 (+1)
Total goals: 0

PAUL WILLIAMS
Defender
Date of birth: 11.9.69 (Leicester)
Previous clubs: Leicester, Stockport, Coventry, West Brom (l), Huddersfield (l)
League appearances: 46
League goals: 2
Play-off appearances: 3
Play-off goals: 1
FA Cup appearances: 3
FA Cup goals: 0
Coca-Cola Cup appearances: 2
Coca-Cola Cup goals: 0
Auto Windscreens Shield appearances: 1
Auto Windscreens Shield goals: 0
Total appearances: 55
Total goals: 3

	P	W	D	L	F	A	Pts
Preston	46	23	17	6	78	38	86
Gillingham	46	22	17	7	49	20	83
Bury	46	22	13	11	66	48	79
Plymouth A	46	22	12	12	68	49	78
Darlington	46	20	18	8	60	42	78
Hereford	46	20	14	12	65	47	74
Colchester	46	18	18	10	61	51	72
Chester	46	18	16	12	72	53	70
Barnet	46	18	16	12	65	45	70
Wigan	46	20	10	16	62	56	70
Northampton	46	18	13	15	51	44	67
Scunthorpe	46	15	15	16	67	61	60
Doncaster	46	16	11	19	49	60	59
Exeter	46	13	18	15	46	53	57
Rochdale	46	14	13	19	57	61	55
Cambridge U	46	14	12	20	61	71	54
Fulham	46	12	17	17	57	63	53
Lincoln	46	13	14	19	57	73	53
Mansfield	46	11	20	15	54	64	53
Hartlepool	46	12	13	21	47	67	49
Leyton O	46	12	11	23	44	63	47
Cardiff	46	11	12	23	41	64	45
Scarborough	46	8	16	22	39	69	40
Torquay	46	5	14	27	30	84	29

PLYMOUTH ARGYLE 1995/96

DATE	COMP	OPPOSITION	H/A	RESULT		SCORER(S)	POS
SAT AUG 12	EL	v Colchester United	(a)	L	1-2	Littlejohn	-
TUE AUG 15	CC1/1	v Birmingham City	(a)	L	0-1	-	-
SAT AUG 19	EL	v PRESTON NORTH END	(H)	L	0-2	-	24
TUE AUG 22	CC1/2	v BIRMINGHAM CITY	(H)	L	1-2	Heathcote	-
SAT AUG 26	EL	v Chester City	(a)	L	1-3	Williams	23
TUE AUG 29	EL	v HEREFORD UNITED	(H)	L	0-1	-	24
SAT SEP 2	EL	v Bury	(a)	W	5-0	Evans 2, Clayton, Billy, Littlejohn	24
SAT SEP 9	EL	v LEYTON ORIENT	(H)	D	1-1	Evans	23
TUE SEP 12	EL	v DONCASTER ROVERS	(H)	W	3-1	Billy, Littlejohn, Evans	17
SAT SEP 16	EL	v Barnet	(a)	W	2-1	Littlejohn, Evans	13
SAT SEP 23	EL	v Wigan Athletic	(a)	W	1-0	Littlejohn	10
TUE SEP 26	AWS	v PETERBOROUGH	(H)	L	0-3	-	-
SAT SEP 30	EL	v LINCOLN CITY	(H)	W	3-0	Littlejohn, Evans, og	5
SAT OCT 7	EL	v FULHAM	(H)	W	3-0	Baird 2, Littlejohn	4
SAT OCT 14	EL	v Mansfield Town	(a)	D	1-1	Heathcote	4
SAT OCT 21	EL	v TORQUAY UNITED	(H)	W	4-3	Littlejohn 3, Maugé	4
SAT OCT 28	EL	v Darlington	(a)	L	0-2	-	6
TUE OCT 31	EL	v Scarborough	(a)	D	2-2	Littlejohn, Leadbitter	6
SAT NOV 4	EL	v CARDIFF CITY	(H)	D	0-0	-	6
TUE NOV 7	AWS	v Northampton Town	(a)	L	0-1	-	-
SAT NOV 11	FAC1	v Slough Town	(a)	W	2-0	Heathcote, og	-
SAT NOV 18	EL	v Hartlepool United	(a)	D	2-2	Maugé, Evans	6
SAT NOV 25	EL	v ROCHDALE	(H)	W	2-0	Littlejohn, Evans	6
SUN DEC 3	FAC2	v Kingstonian	(a)	W	2-1	Littlejohn, Leadbitter	-
SAT DEC 9	EL	v WIGAN ATHLETIC	(H)	W	3-1	Littlejohn 2, Barlow	4
SAT DEC 16	EL	v Lincoln City	(a)	D	0-0	-	4
SAT DEC 23	EL	v CAMBRIDGE UNITED	(H)	W	1-0	Maugé	4
TUE DEC 26	EL	v Gillingham	(a)	L	0-1	-	4
MON JAN 1	EL	v EXETER CITY	(H)	D	2-2	Baird, Maugé	4
SAT JAN 6	FAC3	v COVENTRY CITY	(H)	L	1-3	Baird	-
SAT JAN 13	EL	v Preston North End	(a)	L	2-3	Heathcote, Saunders	5
SAT JAN 20	EL	v COLCHESTER UNITED	(H)	D	1-1	Baird	7
TUE JAN 23	EL	v SCUNTHORPE UNITED	(H)	L	1-3	Logan	7
TUE JAN 30	EL	v Northampton Town	(a)	L	0-1	-	7
SAT FEB 3	EL	v CHESTER CITY	(H)	W	4-2	Williams, Maugé, Partridge, Barlow	4
SAT FEB 10	EL	v Scunthorpe United	(a)	D	1-1	Evans	5
SAT FEB 17	EL	v Doncaster Rovers	(a)	D	0-0	-	5
TUE FEB 20	EL	v BURY	(H)	W	1-0	Heathcote	5
SAT FEB 24	EL	v BARNET	(H)	D	1-1	Partridge	5
TUE FEB 27	EL	v Leyton Orient	(a)	W	1-0	Logan	4
SAT MAR 2	EL	v GILLINGHAM	(H)	W	1-0	Barlow	4
SAT MAR 9	EL	v Cambridge United	(a)	W	3-2	Logan, Baird, Billy	3
SAT MAR 16	EL	v NORTHAMPTON TOWN	(H)	W	1-0	Evans	3
SAT MAR 23	EL	v Exeter City	(a)	D	1-1	Clayton	3
SAT MAR 30	EL	v Fulham	(a)	L	0-4	-	5
TUE APR 2	EL	v MANSFIELD TOWN	(H)	W	1-0	Corazzin	4
SAT APR 6	EL	v DARLINGTON	(H)	L	0-1	-	7
MON APR 8	EL	v Torquay United	(a)	W	2-0	Maugé, Littlejohn	5
SAT APR 13	EL	v SCARBOROUGH	(H)	W	5-1	Littlejohn 2, Barlow 2, Maugé	5
TUE APR 16	EL	v Hereford United	(a)	L	0-3	-	5
SAT APR 20	EL	v Cardiff City	(a)	W	1-0	Evans	4
SAT APR 27	EL	v Rochdale	(a)	W	1-0	Evans	5
SAT MAY 4	EL	v HARTLEPOOL UNITED	(H)	W	3-0	Billy, Heathcote, Logan	4

PLAY-OFFS

DATE	COMP	OPPOSITION	H/A	RESULT		SCORER(S)	POS
SUN MAY 12	1/2 1	v Colchester United	(a)	L	0-1	-	-
WED MAY 15	1/2 2	v COLCHESTER UNITED	(H)	W	3-1	Leadbitter, Evans, Williams	-
SAT MAY 25	F	v DARLINGTON	(N)	W	1-0	Maugé	-

Appearances (League: maximum 46): Williams 46, Heathcote 44, Patterson 42 (+ 1 sub), Evans 41 (4), Littlejohn 40 (2), Maugé 39 (1), Clayton 32 (4), Leadbitter 29 (4), Logan 25 (5), Barlow 25 (3), Baird 24 (3), Hill 21 (2), Blackwell 20, Billy 19 (10), Cherry 16, Curran 6 (2), Partridge 6 (1), Burnett 6, Petterson 6, Saunders 4 (5), Nugent 4 (1), Hammond 4, Hodgson 3 (2), McCall 2 (2), Corazzin 1 (5), Twiddy 1 (1), O'Hagan (6), Magee (5), Shilton (1), Wotton (1).

Appearances (Cups: maximum 7): Hill 7, Billy 6, Heathcote 6, Maugé 6, Williams 6, Evans 5 (1), Clayton 5, Littlejohn 5, Leadbitter 4 (1), Patterson 4, Blackwell 3, Hammond 3, Nugent 3, Logan 2 (2), Twiddy 2 (2), Wotton 2, Burnett 2, Ross 2, Baird 1 (1), Magee 1 (1), Barlow 1, Dungey 1, Richardson (2), Saunders (2), Dawe (1), O'Hagan (1), Payne (1).

Appearances (Play-offs: maximum 3): Barlow 3, Cherry 3, Curran 3, Evans 3, Heathcote 3, Leadbitter 3, Littlejohn 3, Logan 3, Patterson 3, Williams 3, Maugé 2 (1), Billy 1, Corazzin (1).

Appearances (Total: maximum 56): Williams 55, Heathcote 53, Evans 49 (5), Patterson 49 (1), Littlejohn 48 (2), Maugé 47 (2), Clayton 37 (4), Leadbitter 36 (5), Logan 30 (7), Barlow 29 (3), Hill 28 (2), Billy 26 (10), Baird 25 (4), Blackwell 23, Cherry 19, Curran 9 (2), Burnett 8, Hammond 7, Nugent 7 (1), Partridge 6 (1), Petterson 6, Saunders 4 (7), Twiddy 3 (3), Hodgson 3 (2), McCall 2 (2), Wotton 2 (1), Ross 2, Corazzin 1 (6), O'Hagan (7), Magee 1 (6), Dungey 1, Richardson (2), Shilton (1), Dawe (1), Payne (1).

Goals (League: 68): Littlejohn 18, Evans 12, Maugé 7, Baird 5, Barlow 5, Billy 4, Heathcote 4, Logan 4, Clayton 2, Partridge 2, Williams 2, Corazzin 1, Leadbitter 1, Saunders 1, own goal 1.

Goals (Cups: 6): Heathcote 2, Baird 1, Leadbitter 1, Littlejohn 1, own goal 1.

Goals (Play-offs: 4): Evans 1, Leadbitter 1, Maugé 1, Williams 1.

Goals (Total: 78): Littlejohn 18, Evans 13, Maugé 8, Baird 6, Heathcote 6, Barlow 5, Billy 4, Logan 4, Leadbitter 3, Williams 3, Clayton 2, Partridge 2, Corazzin 1, Saunders 1, own goals 2.

Final Position: 4th (Third Division). P: 46 W: 22 D: 12 L: 12 F: 68 A: 49 Pts: 78. Promoted via play-offs.

FA Cup: Third round.   **Coca-Cola Cup:** First round   **Auto Windscreens Shield:** Preliminary round.